# LOST IN
# MONGOLIA

# COLIN ANGUS

BROADWAY BOOKS || NEW YORK

# LOST IN
# MONGOLIA

RAFTING
THE WORLD'S LAST
UNCHALLENGED
RIVER

PRINTED IN THE UNITED STATES OF AMERICA

BROADWAY BOOKS and its logo, a letter B bisected on the diagonal,
are trademarks of Random House, Inc.

Visit our website at www.broadwaybooks.com

First edition published 2003

*Map illustration by Jeff Ward*

Library of Congress Cataloging-in-Publication Data

Angus, Colin.
    Lost in Mongolia : rafting the world's last unchallenged river / Colin Angus.
        p. cm.
    1. Angus, Colin—Journeys—Russia (Federation)—Yenisey River. 2. Angus,
Colin—Journeys—Mongolia. 3. Rafting (Sports)—Russia (Federation)—
Yenisey River. 4. Rafting (Sports)—Mongolia. 5. Yenisey River (Russia)—
Description and travel. 6. Mongolia—Description and travel. I. Title.

GV776.79.A45 2003
796.1'21'0957—dc21

                                                                    2003040438

ISBN 0-7679-1280-2

10 9 8 7 6 5 4 3 2 1

I would like to dedicate the book to
the men and women on the shores of the Yenisey
who helped us on our way.

# CONTENTS

MAP   viii

PROLOGUE   ix

TWO YEARS EARLIER . . .   xi

**PART ONE   GETTING THERE**
1   Why the Yenisey?   3
2   Welcome to China   13

**PART TWO   MONGOLIA**
3   Searching for the Source   25
4   Riding the Whitewater to
"Carcass Canyon"   45
5   Lost in Mongolia   71
6   An "Arresting" Time in Sühbaatar   103
7   Reunion Stories and Murderous
Ruffians   121

**PART THREE   SIBERIA**
8   Crossing the Border with Serious
Baggage   135
9   The Little Dory That Could   161
10   The Welcoming Arms of the Mafia   183
11   *Banyas* and Dam Fishing   202
12   Vodka and Old Salts   226
13   Above the Treeline and into the
Tundra   242

EPILOGUE   266

ACKNOWLEDGMENTS   271

Arctic Ocean

Kara Sea

TAYMYR
× end of journey
Karaul  Dudinka
● Norilsk
● Potopova

KHANTY-
MANSI

ARCTIC CIRCLE

EVENKI

Urals Federal
Region

Central Siberian Plateau

S i b e r i a

Yenisey R.

Ob River

RUSSIA

Siberian Federal Region

Yeniseysk ●
Lesosibirsk ●

Angara R.
Boguchany ●
Bratsk ●

Ust' Ilimsk

IRKUTSK

Bratsk Sea

Novosibirsk ●

BURYATA

Irkutsk ●

Lake Baikal

KAZAKHSTAN

TUVA  TUNKINSKIY

Tosontsengel ●

Carcass
Canyon

Sühbaatar

Ider River  Selenge R.

HENTIYN

Mt. Otgon Tenger ▲  Hangayn Mountains  Hutag ●  ★ Ulaanbaatar

HANGAYN
NURUU

MONGOLIA

Trans-Mongolia Railway

CHINA

0 Miles          200          400          600
0 Kilometers                              600

© 2003 Jeffrey L. Ward

Beijing ★

## Inset map

ROUTE OF THE
SOURCE-TO-SEA
YENISEY RIVER
EXPEDITION

Arctic Ocean

Karaul ●

Yenisey R.

RUSSIA

Angara R.

L. Baikal

0 Miles          400          800
0 Kilometers                    800

raft capsizes
× ● Hutag  Sühbaatar ●

KAZAKH.

Mt. Otgon Tenger ×  Selenge R.  ★ Ulaanbaatar

CHINA  MONGOLIA

The water roiled and bucked in large waves as the river was squeezed between the sheer walls. The air was a haze of cool mist, and a persistent roar filled my ears. I saw the raft teeter on a huge standing wave just inside the canyon as Ben struggled, pulling madly on the oars.

My kayak was incredibly maneuverable, but I had to be careful about some of the bigger rocks. I slid off a two-yard wave and down into a great recirculating hole. The gaping mouth of the vortex boiled and sucked at my tiny vessel, and I dug frantically to escape its grasp. My heart pounded from exertion. Where were Ben and the raft? I had lost him somewhere in the white fog of spray.

My lungs burned as the merciless river pushed me hard toward the canyon wall, threatening to pin the kayak to the jagged rocks. I struggled to get turned back downriver. A large hole appeared that was impossible to avoid—its swirling, circular current swallowed nearly the entire river. I dug hard with my paddle, hoping to generate enough speed to propel the kayak across the boil.

Dig! Dig! Dig! I screamed at myself. Pull! PULL!

I had barely made it to the middle of the hole when the rotating maelstrom pulled me backward and then under.

Everything went black.

I held my breath as the current battered and pulled at me, as if some malevolent force wanted to rip me from the kayak's cockpit and consume me. It pummeled my chest like a boxer. My lungs ached for oxygen as I spun around upside down. I was helpless, a plaything of the river god. The kayak did numerous cartwheels and then, as quickly as I had been pulled under, I was spat out downstream. I was wet, cold, out of breath, and chastened.

But I was alive.

*August 22, 1999*

"The Nile, the Amazon, the Yangtze, and then the Mississippi."

"So what's number five then?" I asked.

Ben looked up from the *National Geographic Atlas*. "The Yenisey River."

I'd never heard of the Yenisey, yet it was listed as the fifth-longest river in the world. According to the map, the Yenisey's headwaters were in the heart of central Asia and its mouth was 3,450 miles to the north, on the Arctic Ocean. Had anyone ever traveled its full length? Through what kind of landscape did it flow? My imagination conjured up scenes of a thunderous whitewater torrent on its way to the sea, dashing down the flanks of the Hangayn Mountains, roaring through steep-sided canyons, and cutting across expanses of frozen tundra peopled with nomads who lived in tepees.

"It looks like Camana, on the coast of Peru, would be the best place to start," Ben said.

We were in the Banff Public Library researching our upcoming expedition down the Amazon River. We were due to leave in two weeks, and it was no time to be daydreaming about other rivers.

Ben's face was tanned from the weeks we'd spent honing our whitewater rafting skills in the Rocky Mountains. Underneath the healthy glow, though, a world-weary tiredness had set in. His curly hair was slightly greasy and hung listlessly across his forehead and over his ears. Large, dark bags hung below his bloodshot eyes—the result of too much worry. I knew my own face looked about the same.

We were about to run one of the world's greatest rivers, and we were counting pennies and budgeting beyond belief.

I filed the Yenisey River in the back of my mind and devoted my attention to the maps of South America in front of me. Still, a seed had been planted.

*February 28, 2001*

More than a year later, after we'd run the Amazon, Terry Spence, the radio host at CFAX in Victoria, B.C., leaned closer to his microphone and said, "Tell me now, Colin, why is it that you want to travel a river—which nobody has ever heard of—that flows through remotest Mongolia and Siberia? Wasn't the Amazon enough for you? I mean, you guys were almost killed in South America. Haven't you heard of gardening or cricket?"

I laughed. What could I say?

It was true. We had successfully completed our voyage down the Amazon, facing death on numerous occasions. Many people believed that it was blind luck that had carried us across South America from the Pacific to the Atlantic Ocean. Maybe, but we accomplished what we had set out to do: We had traveled the length of one of the most famous rivers in the world. We had voyaged every inch of it, from its source in the remote mountains of Peru to the northeastern shoulder of Brazil, where it finally empties into the Atlantic Ocean.

In spite of the pain, the rot, the smell, the arguments, the gunshots, and the altitude sickness, I had never felt so alive or engaged. You cannot capture that feeling in a photograph or on videotape, or adequately convey it in words—much less experience it on one of those tourist bus excursion trips. It wasn't just the dramatic scenery and the fascinating people that had left their mark on me. It was the unique way in which, the more I shared time with the river—five months in total—the more I came to feel and respect its spirit and energy. That is what was tattooed on my soul.

For me the Amazon offered a view of the world that could never be re-created by a textbook or a documentary. The river ran past both the squalid and the sublime with indifference, offering to each a constant but ever-changing face. Old man river truly rolled along—a mile wide sometimes, swollen with the runoff of a continent. It was both creator and destroyer, depending on its mood. Its banks were testament to its generosity and its rage. It carried us through folded, rugged countryside, its currents sweeping us along like riders on the back of some giant, serpentine beast.

A river is the lifeblood of the land it flows through. Few parts of the earth are untouched by the sculpting force of water. Every organism is part of an intricately woven network of life that is nurtured by a watershed. The sap that rises in the trunk of a eucalyptus tree and the blood that pumps in the heart of an iguana are essentially the same fluid that permeates and flows across the landscape, that saturates the atmosphere and falls from the sky.

Rivers have always been key to the development of complex societies and the rise of civilizations. Irrigation, transportation, hydroelectric power, and food are a few of the gifts a river offers. That is why they fascinate me. Whether they are mythical rivers such as the Styx, historic rivers such as the Rubicon, or the mighty rivers of my homeland, such as the Fraser, I am compelled to learn all I can about them and experience them as fully as possible. From the moment it occurred to me that nothing was holding me back, I had to live and breathe the Amazon River, not just learn about it from books.

When I read Steinbeck's *Cannery Row* as a boy, I envied the idle lives of the indigent characters. Sitting on a dock, feet dangling in the water, tippling on a jug of wine—to my young mind it seemed the perfect lifestyle. That was before I felt the pull to explore and achieve. Whether this drive is conditioned or genetic, I have come to believe that in life you must strive to achieve—or your spirit will fade.

Our time on the Amazon provided me with the best of both worlds. I dangled my feet in the water, sipped the wine, and drank in scenery day after day while running a gamut that stretched from jagged, sky-scraping, snowcapped peaks to the world's largest expanse of lush tropical rain forest. At the same time, we remained focused on our goal—to become only the third team ever to run the length of the Amazon. The joy of completing that journey and the excitement of the accomplishment stoked my desire to run another river.

In some respects I was even more excited about our proposed five-month journey down the Yenisey River. Like the Amazon it would offer a raw, firsthand experience of varied geography and cultures. The big difference between the two rivers was the amount of information available. After exhaustive research on the Yenisey, we had been able to glean just a fraction of the knowledge we had gathered on the Amazon. Large sections of the river, especially the headwaters, were nothing more than a question mark in our minds. I felt our Yenisey expedition would be as close to true exploration as was possible in the modern world.

The excitement of venturing into unknown territory comes with a price. It would be much harder to make advance preparations since we could not anticipate all the situations we would be up against. The waterfalls and rapids could be so dangerous that it would be impossible for us to make it through alive. We were even unsure as to where we would be able to reprovision. Another big question was, how would we get home after reaching the end of the river? No matter how long we searched the Internet or pored over library books, there were a lot of unanswered questions.

What we did learn about the Yenisey was that it flows through a rugged, ever-changing landscape. From beginning to end it drops thirteen thousand feet and spans over 22 degrees of latitude—the equivalent of traveling from Southern California to Alaska. Many different ethnic groups live along its banks, some with roots established for thousands of years. We also found that the Yenisey region is heavily associated with death and despair. Spiritual leaders of the indigenous people were massacred during Stalin's era, and thousands of prisoners of war were transported along the Yenisey in ships to the death camps. Human bones were said to litter sections of the Yenisey's banks.

Instead of deterring me, the lack of information, the dangers and the hardships associated with our journey, only strengthened my resolve. Our descent of the Yenisey could be successful only with perfectly orchestrated teamwork, strategy, resolve, and a bit of luck. But I did feel it was possible. The goal was to get to the end of the river, and the journey would take place both physically and in our minds as we struggled to reach our destination. As well, I can never quite shake the notion that the more challenging the situations you put yourself in, the higher you set your goals, the more you will get out of life.

That's why I was willing again to risk life and limb to voyage down a river whose name and route would stump even *Jeopardy!* champions. And that's how I should have answered Spence's question. Instead, I was tongue-tied.

"We're always looking for excitement, and this is the longest river in the world that hasn't been run," I said. "I think it promises to be the adventure of a lifetime."

That wasn't too far from the truth either.

PART ONE

# GETTING THERE

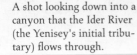

A shot looking down into a canyon that the Ider River (the Yenisey's initial tributary) flows through.

## WHY THE YENISEY?

*March 2000*

The successful conclusion of our Amazon expedition cemented our decision to run the Yenisey. Making my way down the Amazon, I realized I loved the excitement. I loved the sense of each day bringing new adventure. We had spent countless hours on languid Amazonian afternoons discussing and imagining what it would be like to descend the Yenisey River, traveling from the source of its most distant tributary in western Mongolia to its delta in the high Arctic. Our previous research had indicated that this was the last of the five greatest rivers that had never been run. In the mountaineering world, this would be the equivalent of finding out that Kilimanjaro had never been summited.

I call it "river running"—a horizontal version of mountain climbing, and every bit as dangerous. The challenges are different, but the hazards are just as life-threatening. Instead of avalanches, you have rock slides; instead of man-swallowing crevasses, seething rapids that rarely give up their dead; in place of high altitude and thin air, suffocating humidity, sweltering heat, freezing cold, and occasional gunfire.

Failure and death are constant companions in the world of river running. In every case, those who were first to descend the world's great rivers were bloodied. In the past, this could be attributed in part to inadequate equipment. Probably the main reason most of the longest and mightiest rivers have been navigated only recently is the advent of modern gear. Whitewater kayaks and rafts are essential to river running; without them, voyaging turbulent upper tributaries is impossible. Forty years ago, equipment crafted from space-age plastics and synthetic materials simply didn't exist.

The Nile wasn't run until 1972, when a team of kayakers finally made it through the treacherous headwaters. Both the Yangtze and the Amazon were first fully navigated only in 1986.

So river voyaging is an excellent antidote for anyone who complains there are no new adventures out there.

All major rivers are fed by a capillary-like network of tributaries. According to the unwritten laws of river running, to officially voyage the full length of a river, you must start from the source farthest from the sea. The first droplets forming the initial trickle must be followed initially by foot, then, when the flow is deep enough, by boat. You must travel downstream under your own power in kayak, dory, raft, or a similar vessel until you reach the ocean.

The Yenisey River's most distant source tributary begins in the rugged Hangayn Mountains of Mongolia and is called the Ider River. The Ider joins with the Mörön River, and later they are a primary component of the Selenge. After a journey across Mongolia and into Russia, the Selenge ultimately becomes the Yenisey proper, which flows into the Arctic Ocean.

Ben Kozel, my Australian mate on the Amazon voyage, was all for it. Siberia had intrigued him since childhood with its exotic, sprawling expanse of Russian wilderness. Combining it with another magical river journey appealed to his two greatest passions—adventure and geography. Scott, the South African member of our Amazon expedition, initially agreed to come along too, although he was less than enthusiastic. Our close calls in South America had shaken him, and for the time being he wanted to enjoy being back in civilization.

We had decided to begin our Yenisey expedition in April 2001. The river was frozen for two-thirds of the year, and we had a five-month window—from the end of April to the end of September—to travel the 3,450 miles. After the excitement of finishing the Amazon began to fade and Ben and Scott left Canada to return to their respective countries, I wondered if we could pull it off. Ben had to spend every penny he had on his plane ticket to Adelaide, in Australia, and I wasn't much better off myself—and April was only eleven months away.

Over the next few months, I hunkered down. By day I labored in construction to pay for groceries, and in my spare time I wrote a book on my Amazon adventure. By night I dreamed of Mongolia. Logistically the Yenisey would be much more intimidating than the Amazon. We would pass through countries renowned as bureaucratic nightmares, and, by our rough calculations, we needed close to $60,000 to make the expedition a reality.

In late fall I moved to Victoria, British Columbia, on the west coast, where the mild maritime climate would allow me to hone my whitewater skills during the winter. From my new location, I spent every minute of free time trying to market the Yenisey expedition to potential sponsors. We simply didn't have the cash to make it happen ourselves; if we couldn't get sponsors, the journey was already over. I spent long days in front of the computer creating proposals, sending e-mails, working on the expedition's website, and making telephone calls.

The usual reply was "Thanks for your inquiry, but we're not interested."

"Sponsorship" is one of those words that people tend to throw around casually, as though obtaining corporate backing were as easy as trick-or-treating. In reality, getting a company to part with its money is a very difficult task. I had previously—and fruitlessly—sought corporate support for a sailing trip I made across the Pacific and for the Amazon expedition. Now, as the departure date for our Yenisey journey loomed, I began to think we would have to postpone or cancel the expedition. Had I learned nothing from the past? Though I was growing more and more pessimistic by the day, I kept plugging away and hoping the gamble would pay off. Otherwise, half a year of my life had been wasted.

Still, the intimidating cost and the seeming impossibility of the Yenisey trip only whetted my desire. I pulled at my hair and tried to think of alternatives. There were none. No matter how hard we worked at our regular jobs, there was no way we could raise $60,000 in a few months. And banks aren't interested in lending money to crazy adventures. To add to the problem of our penury, Scott's scant enthusiasm seemed to dwindle by the day, and I felt sure he would back out.

*February 2001*

Scott officially bailed from the expedition. Both his parents had recently died and he was absolutely strapped financially. There was no way he could take the time off his job, he told us. Although I had suspected this was coming, it was still a major blow. On the Amazon, Scott had proved himself to be a strong, determined winger. He would follow through to the end, no matter what it took. Moreover, his easygoing nature made him an ideal team player.

In Australia, Ben said he had been in contact with Tim Cope, a twenty-two-year-old who had just returned from cycling across Europe and Asia. Tim had spent considerable time in Siberia and was able to give Ben great background about the people and the country, as well as detailed information on visas, officials, and what to expect in the cities.

Tim was intrigued by our plans, especially since he had crossed the Yenisey on his recumbent bicycle. He had looked down from the bridge, staring into the boiling, seething waters, and wondered what it would be like to travel via rowboat all the way to the Arctic. He had vowed one day to return and do exactly that. Ben's contacting him was incredible serendipity.

Tim and Ben got along extremely well and, given Tim's fluent Russian and his filmmaking skills, it seemed only natural for him to join us. Unfortunately, he was obliged to stay in Australia until June in order to complete his cycling documentary. He could meet us at Lake Baikal in Siberia, about a third of the way down the river.

There was no way Ben and I could complete the first, and most dangerous, leg of the expedition—through the remote, rugged Hangayn Mountains—by ourselves. We needed at least one more person to join us. I found that someone in Victoria, through the small production company that was developing a documentary about our Amazon adventure. They had hired Vancouverite Remy Quinter to do some scriptwriting for the film, and although I hadn't met Remy in person, we had corresponded via e-mail as he worked on his part of the script. One of his final e-mails casually mentioned that if we were ever looking for another team member, he'd be up for an expedition. He had studied Russian for three years in university, had filmmaking experience, and had done his own adventuring, including a cycling trip across New Zealand.

I invited Remy to visit me in Victoria.

"When do you want to meet?" he asked.

"How about I pick you up off the ferry that arrives at eight-thirty?"

I knew he'd have to wake up at 5:00 A.M. in Vancouver to catch the 7:00 A.M. departure from Tsawwassen. It was a good test of how much this journey meant to him.

"Sure," Remy said. "I'll be the guy wearing the green jacket."

I arrived at the ferry terminal in my decaying '87 Nissan truck and surveyed the handful of people milling around the entrance. A man with long, matted hair, his belongings wrapped in a blanket tied up with string, sat on a concrete rail. He wore a grimy green jacket. My heart sank as I pulled up in my truck. "Remy?" He shook his head and continued his conversation with the lamppost.

A clean-cut figure carrying a duffel bag appeared through the doors. About six feet tall, with short, dark, slightly receding hair and an athletic build, the green-jacketed man made his way toward me with a broad smile.

"Remy?" I inquired, extending my hand.

"That's right," he said, offering a firm hand in return.

We spent the day paddling kayaks in the placid postcard

waters of Victoria's inner harbor. Float planes landed and took off and brightly painted tour boats chugged to and fro while Remy and I discussed the Yenisey. At thirty-two, articulate and extremely ambitious, Remy seemed to have what it took to survive such a journey. And he was very enthusiastic. At the end of the day I shook his hand and welcomed him on board. In another week, Ben would arrive in Canada. We would all raft the nearby Cowichan River together as a way of getting to know each other.

Shortly before Ben arrived, I received two pieces of excellent news. Riot Kayaks of Montreal would supply us with two boats, and Aire, an American raft manufacturer, offered a 3.9-meter whitewater raft along with the oars and a rowing frame. We had purchased a raft from them previously for our Amazon journey and they had been impressed with the coverage that trip had generated for them. In Australia, Ben had tweaked the interest of Iridium satellite telephones; he proudly announced that they would provide two handsets, a solar panel, and unlimited airtime.

For the first time in months, it felt as though a dark cloud had lifted. Although the cat wasn't quite in the bag, things looked brighter. The Iridium phones especially would help to interest other sponsors. Now we would be able to file media updates and radio interviews from the field. The *Globe and Mail* agreed to print two full-page articles that I would write from the river. Things were finally happening.

*Saturday, March 10, 2001*

My truck insurance expired the day Ben arrived in Victoria. There was no point in wasting precious dollars continuing it, and we needed all the exercise we could get. I dug out two aged bicycles from the garage. Ben's would be the 1970s ten-speed, mine a decrepit mountain bike, the frame cracked under the seat post.

We frequently burst out laughing as we cycled madly around Victoria trying to keep up with the errands we'd set for ourselves. As we departed from polished radio studios or newspaper lobbies after giving interviews, we'd climb helmetless onto our bikes and ride away as quickly as we could before someone from inside could spot our mode of transport. Glancing at Ben as we sped down the streets, I couldn't help but think I'd slipped back into the seventies. The old-style bike, the long, curly hair, the jeans, the lack of a helmet—we looked like anything but hard-core adventures.

With three weeks to go, we had the team and most of the equipment. The research was completed and the budget finalized. The only thing lacking was cash. We each agreed to contribute $5,000. Although Ben was still penniless, he extended his credit card limit. Remy, combining his savings with what he could access on plastic, also put forward the allotted five grand. A payment from my publishing company for the Amazon book covered my share.

But $15,000 was not enough. Transportation costs alone, which included the shipping of our equipment, would nudge $10,000. Add to that visa costs, bureaucratic fees, accommodations, and so forth, and we'd be left with no money once the expedition started. Sponsors continued to offer equipment, but cash remained elusive.

To try raising some money, we would hold a presentation night in Victoria. The highlight was to be a screening of our Amazon documentary. The only problem was that the documentary wasn't finished. We decided Remy could do that while Ben and I promoted the event. If we had a good turnout, we stood to make a couple of thousand dollars.

Remy holed himself up in his dungeonlike basement suite and worked eighteen-hour days sculpting the footage. Ben and I plastered Victoria with posters advertising the event and hounded the media to promote it. It was the first presentation we'd ever organized ourselves and we felt extremely nervous. But the media were helpful. We were able to announce our screening on several radio stations, and the local daily newspaper, the *Times Colonist*, promised to print a large article.

### Friday, April 13

The David Lam Auditorium was packed, and our presentation was a huge success. It was a heartwarming experience to share our Amazon adventure with an audience from my hometown. At the same time, it gave us a nice little financial boost.

It wasn't enough, though. I would be leaving for China in four days. Ben would arrive three days after me and Remy four days after that (we had all purchased our tickets independently through different airlines). We decided to go ahead with the expedition and hope for a financial miracle while we were under way.

### Sunday, April 15

The phone rang late in the afternoon as I was in the midst of my final packing frenzy. It was Jonathan Waterman, a renowned mountaineer, expeditioner, and writer. He was a member of the Shipman/Tilman Committee, a board created by the W. L. Gore & Associates, Inc. (makers of Gore-Tex) to determine candidates for an annual grant.

"I just want to congratulate you, Colin. Your team is one of four we've chosen to give this year's grant to. You will be receiving about eleven thousand dollars."

I felt as if I were dreaming. All those sleepless nights, the stress, the anguish—gone. Relief washed through my body. It was the exact sum we needed to balance our budget. The expedition was going to happen.

I was flying out in two days. We had the gear and, finally, we had all the money.

An old man stands in the Gobi Desert.

# WELCOME TO CHINA

*Friday, April 20*

I arrived in Beijing on Thursday. Upon leaving the airport, I was immediately greeted by the unmistakable sights, sounds, and smells of China. Bicycles, rickshaws, pedestrians, and vehicles of all shapes and sizes choked the streets. Shining through the thick coal smoke and pollution, the bloodred sun added a surreal effect to the chaotic scene.

As I rode downtown on the bus, a ponytailed twenty-something California lawyer named Eric read out descriptions from *Lonely Planet* of the different hotels and hostels near the city center. During our final, frantic preparations for the expedition, I had done almost no research on China, so I listened intently. We disembarked at Tiananmen Square and began walking to the Xinhua Hotel, a place he said sounded clean yet reasonably priced.

The Xinhua proved to be very comfortable at 25 yuan (about $3) a night. Half the occupants were Westerners. The entrance was marble, the bathrooms clean, and the water hot. Out back was a restaurant-cum-bar that sold cheap Western and Asian food.

Later I ventured out into the packed markets, looking for a few last pieces of equipment. I met a pretty English-speaking Chinese woman, Kai, who agreed to accompany me so she could practice the English she had learned in university. She said she would help me find the best deal and engage in the necessary haggling.

Amid the throng of grasping hands and the cacophony of vendors, I found a durable backpack, fleece garments, hiking boots, and a camera battery for my Canon sports camera. Afterward, Kai invited me to her friend Lia's for Chinese tea.

I found myself seated in front of a table like no other I have ever seen. It was carved from a tree—a tree, I was told, that was three hundred years old. The tabletop wasn't in a single plane, but terraced, like hillside rice paddies. The rich, chestnut-colored wood was carved into a diorama of arched bridges, cobbled paths, and traditional Chinese homes. The numerous levels of this finely crafted piece of furniture sloped in a common direction, toward a drain at the tree's base.

Across from me, Kai and Lia sat on stools elaborately carved from smaller trees. Lia poured water from a steaming kettle into a small china bowl containing tea leaves. After letting the tea steep for a few minutes, she poured the translucent green brew into a delicate teapot adorned with red dragons. A small metal filter prevented the leaves from following.

Our three teacups waited on the highest part of the table. With a casual turn of the wrist, Lia sent tea splashing over the cups. She then flicked the cups onto their sides. Hot tea cascaded down the terraces and disappeared down the drain hole. She righted the now-warm cups and filled them once again.

Kai, who had been a spectator until this point, picked up one of the cups and handed it to me.

"*Ganbei*. Welcome to China."

*Saturday, April 21*

Ben was supposed to arrive at 3:15 P.M., and I went to meet him at the airport. At four he appeared through the customs gate, bedraggled and weighed down like an overloaded mule. His towering frame swayed under two twenty-nine-gallon dry bags plus a swollen backpack. His eyes scanned the roiling crowd. I ducked out of view behind a tall man and held my sign high: UGLY BASTARD.

Ben's bloodshot eyes spotted the sign and he staggered over, chuckling.

"Haven't you heard of airport trolley carts?" I asked, removing the lightest bag from Ben's shoulder.

"Thank God you're here," Ben said.

I was mildly surprised at this comment. Independent Ben was the type who normally couldn't care less if someone was waiting for him at the airport. With a sense of direction like a homing pigeon's, he could easily have found the Xinhua Hotel without my assistance.

"I've got no money, mate," he continued. "My card maxed

out yesterday in Canada. I had ten dollars left in my pocket, which I figured would be enough to get me to the Xinhua if you didn't make it to the airport, but then the bloody airport tax in Vancouver vacuumed the last dime out of me. If you weren't here, I would have had to walk to the Xinhua with these goddamned bags."

We threw the bright yellow and green bags into the gaping hold of a shiny new coach. The small, toothless driver prodded the bags inquisitively before charging the equivalent of $10 for both of us.

We'd been expecting this financial crisis. Ben had paid the expenses back in Canada while I was waiting for a check. It had arrived the day I left.

"So how much did it cost to ship the gear over?" I asked, as we settled into our seats.

Ben paused, momentarily distracted by a three-year-old Chinese girl in front who was peering over the seat back. Her hair sprouted straight up in a palm-tree ponytail. The girl giggled when Ben stuck a finger up his nose and crossed his eyes.

"Fourteen hundred bucks. It should arrive the day after tomorrow."

"Where do we pick it up?"

"They didn't know. The guy said we'd have to ask around over in the cargo part of the airport. Air Canada doesn't actually have its own cargo warehouse here, so it will be Air China looking after it," Ben said.

I felt a little nervous. Chinese officials are notorious for being harsh and unbending. I thought about how one of Steve Fossett's around-the-world balloon attempts had come to an end because the Chinese authorities wouldn't allow him to fly in their airspace. There was nothing we could do but cross our fingers.

The coach dropped us off in front of Tiananmen Square,

where we waited for the five-cent city bus. When it finally arrived, there didn't appear to be enough room for an anorexic ballerina. Half of China must have been on that bus! But somehow, after pushing and shoving and generally undoing the work of every Canadian and Australian ambassador who had ever visited China, we managed to cram our bags in, and the door closed, pinching my rear in the process.

"How the hell are we going to lug all our gear around?" Ben asked, once we were ensconced behind a thick wooden table at the back of the Xinhua. He looked much less stressed now that he had a large bottle of Chinese beer and a plate of rice and sweet-and-sour pork balls in front of him. We had been joined by Michelle, an attractive American who was teaching English in a small industrial Chinese city—a way of learning more about a country that fascinated her.

Ben continued, "Once we get the whitewater gear from the airport, there will be too much stuff for a taxi . . . even two taxis."

"We've got to get a truck somehow," I said. "I've learned how to count to ten in Mandarin, so I should have no problem negotiating prices on the phone."

Ben laughed.

"I guess once we get our stuff out of customs, we can just try flagging down a truck and wave some money at the driver," I added.

Ben nodded. There wasn't a whole lot more we could do. Even if we found someone who could translate and hire a truck for us, there was no telling how long clearing customs would take. We couldn't afford to pay a trucker to sit idle for a day.

While we were chatting with Michelle, an old Chinese man, his ancient face relatively unlined, entered with dozens of rice-paper paintings draped over his arm. He held out a piece of paper bearing a message in English: "My name is

Chan and I am 78 years old. I am a painter and I ask if you can please look at my work."

When I heard his fluent English, I wondered why Chan bothered with the explanatory card. He offered a scroll decorated with flowing Chinese characters. The black brushstrokes swept across the paper with a style and grace that only a steady, dedicated hand could produce. Chan passed his fingers across the beige paper.

"What does it mean?" Ben asked.

"Happiness is sex, drugs, and football," Chan said, with a forced smile.

"I see," said Ben. "What else do you have there?"

Chan showed us another dozen or so pictures—landscapes, animals, and more Chinese aphorisms. "You want buy?"

"We have no room," I said. "We are going down a river for five months and have no room to put any pictures."

Chan looked at Michelle.

"Not now. Maybe tomorrow," she said.

"Maybe tomorrow," Chan said, echoing. "Maybe tomorrow . . . maybe never?"

I gave him a couple of yuan. He smiled and moved on to the next table.

*Monday, April 23*

We had been led to believe that the food selection in Mongolia was limited to little more than rice and mutton. Rather than take a chance, we stocked up in China. Half a block from our hotel was an underground supermarket, hidden beneath the sidewalk, that sold nothing but strange preserved food. Sugared fruits, miniature sausages, smoked squid, dried seaweed, spices, fruit rolls, biscuits—all manner of dried and pickled fare lined the shelves. These products were perfect for our trip since they were packaged in durable, watertight plastic and were dirt cheap. The problem was determining what was edible.

Most of the items displayed were unrecognizable and we were unable to decipher the Chinese characters, so we embarked on a snack experiment, buying dozens of little packets for sampling. Back in our hotel room, Ben and I gorged on the food. Our palates were exposed to a whole new range of tastes, from delightfully delicious to positively putrid.

After deciding what we liked, we returned to the supermarket and purchased two shopping carts full of dehydrated foods and snacks, from milk powder to dried dog testicles (at least, that's what we called the sweet little balls of meat). We dragged the booty back to our room and added it to the growing pile of provisions and gear.

Our next job for the day was to apply for our Mongolian visas and book our tickets on the trans-Mongolian train. In the small ticket office we were told that our excess baggage must be weighed twenty-four hours prior to departure. The train would leave in three days. Next we dropped off our passports, photographs, and visa application forms at the Mongolian embassy, where we were told it would take a day to process the paperwork. We would be granted a thirty-day visa and would have to apply for an extension once we were in Mongolia.

*Tuesday, April 24*

We arrived at the embassy an hour early to pick up our passports, anxious to continue on to the airport and retrieve our gear. The woman in charge of issuing visas angrily told us to wait.

When the appointed hour of 3:00 P.M. rolled around, I approached the smug-looking cashier and paid 800 yuan for the two visas. I then went to the wicket to receive the passports. The icy-eyed woman behind the glass partition looked past me and beckoned to the customers behind. I stayed calm.

An hour passed and the woman continued to deal out passports to everyone save me. It had become obvious that she was deliberately ignoring me, possibly a punishment for arriving early. People came through the door, paid their money, and were beckoned ahead of me to pick up their documents. I could see our passports sitting on her desk, ready to go.

In frustration, I started asking Westerners who entered if they could assist me by not paying for their visas until I had been served. The woman, seeing the increasing congestion, sighed and finally passed over our passports.

We rushed off to the airport, only to find that our gear had been shipped to the Air China office downtown. And we were too late to make it there before closing.

*Wednesday, April 25*

I had learned from my days of sailing that customs is a nightmare at the best of times. But customs in Communist China is pure nastiness. Back in Canada, Remy had estimated the value of our goods on the waybill at almost $7,000. That large figure, I knew, would create havoc for us.

We arrived at the drab eight-story Air China cargo building at opening time—8:00 A.M. Our train was leaving the next day, and we needed to have our cargo weighed by noon. But no one spoke English. We were ushered from office to office in growing frustration. Finally we found a young woman who spoke halting English, and she was able to confirm that our gear had arrived.

After locating the waybill, she said, "Now you will have to see customs. We cannot release your cargo until you have customs clearance."

Luckily, the customs office was next door. Unluckily, we were dealing with Chinese customs. After eight hours of filling in forms, wandering from here to there, pleading and pulling our hair, we finally departed—empty-handed.

They would not release our equipment until we had paid thousands of dollars in import duty. It didn't matter that our gear would be in China for only two days—if we wanted to bring plastic boats into the Middle Kingdom, we had to pay the price.

Finally the stern customs officials relented and let us forward the equipment on to Mongolia with Air China. The price was exorbitant, but still cheaper than paying the duty. It's a good thing we weren't running the Yangtze River!

Remy had arrived from Canada and would stay in Beijing until the following Wednesday so he could obtain his Mongolian visa. For Ben and me, it was our last evening in Beijing, and we celebrated with a few beers in the hotel bar.

At 5:30 A.M. we said good-bye and headed off in an overloaded red taxi to the railway station. A long green-and-yellow train waited at the platform. Riding a growing sense of excitement, I mounted the metal stairs and surveyed the wooden interior. The train had an old, colonial feel to it. I was surprised at the luxury, considering the modest $40 ticket price. A richly patterned rug led down the corridor to our compartment. Inside, two friendly Mongolians sat on one of two large settees that were separated by a small wooden table. The settees doubled as beds, and above were two more beds. Linens lay neatly folded at the end of each settee.

We sat down and tried to introduce ourselves. A short while later, an attendant entered, offering tea. Ben held his pewter-and-glass cup up in a toast: "Next stop, Mongolia!"

The train lurched forward, and we began to inch toward the Great Wall and beyond.

PART TWO

# MONGOLIA

Remy, Ben, and Colin celebrating at the source of the Yenisey River.

# SEARCHING FOR THE SOURCE

*Friday, April 27*

During the night, the train stopped in a small station to change the wheel bogies. Before a train from China can enter Mongolia, the wheel assemblies have to be changed because the track gauge is different in each country. Every car is jacked up, the old wheel assembly is removed, and a new set is put in place.

Inside the train, we were jostled, shaken, and subjected to a hair-raising din. At the same time, customs and immigration officers were scurrying about—first the Chinese, then their Mongolian counterparts. Uniformed men and women demanded passports, checked bags, handed out forms, and continually barked, "Sit upright! Sit upright!"

Finally they left. I drifted off to sleep as the train entered Mongolia, somewhere in that sandy, desert darkness.

At about 7:00 A.M. I awoke and found we were gliding through the Gobi Desert. It was a forbidding, alien landscape. A howling wind scoured the flat, sandy countryside and whipped at the bloated livestock carcasses that lay everywhere in various states of decomposition.

How did people live in this land? Occasionally I saw a shepherd leading a flock of sheep or a herd of cows across the sand. Where was their fodder? I saw small knots of emaciated animals huddled together, the blowing sand swirling around their skinny silhouettes. But mostly I saw carcasses.

The dead were more abundant than the living—skeletons picked clean by scavengers and bleached white by the sun, half-eaten carcasses spilling their entrails onto the desert floor, and some so fresh it looked as if they were only sleeping. Mongolia had been suffering from a severe drought for several years, and the past winter had been so harsh that half the country's livestock had died from cold and starvation.

As I looked out at the devastation, I wondered what we would face as we traveled down the Yenisey. Although I was excited to be the first to voyage it, we would also be the first to face the hazards. How big were the rapids? And would the locals be so hungry they might take desperate measures?

When we arrived in Ulaanbaatar, the capital, we had three main chores to accomplish before Remy arrived. The gear had to be wrested from customs, our thirty-day visas had to be extended, and we had to get our equipment to Uliastay, the town closest to the starting point of our journey.

*Saturday, April 28*

Ulaanbaatar means "red hero." The city's name dates from the 1920s and the Communist revolution rather than from its illustrious past as a Mongol center, "the city of felt." Its architecture is similarly incongruous—concrete-block Soviet modern.

While it was a scruffy city, Ulaanbaatar proved to be more progressive than the *Lonely Planet* guidebook had led us to believe. All the technology of the Western world could be found there. Even the food was not too bad.

We were greeted at the train station by the owner of one of the city's guest houses, Nassan. Her knowledge of English was fairly good and the guest house rate was a reasonable $4 per night.

We quickly learned that hiring a Russian transport vehicle was the only way to get our gear to Uliastay. No buses make the 650-mile trip, and chartering a plane was out of the question.

I tried haggling with a group of truck drivers but soon found myself in a typical Third World situation. As people crowded around and jostled me, I felt someone trying to grab for my wallet. I swatted away the hand, but others grabbed at my video-camera case. I shouted for Ben and began bulling my way out of the crowd, trying to escape before things got out of hand.

Back in our room, I noticed that the bottom of my pocket and my backpack had been slashed with a razor. Although nothing had been lost, that clean incision so close to my privates made me shiver. "We'll go back to renegotiate with no valuables on hand," I told Ben.

I was pleased to learn that the Iridium satellite telephones got good reception in Mongolia. Outside of Ulaanbaatar, land phones are virtually nonexistent.

That night we talked to Remy in Beijing. He had booked his train reservation and would arrive on Thursday. His visa extension would be available on the following Monday, and we would then be ready to depart. Our expedition would begin about May 8, with the ascent of Otgon Tenger.

*Tuesday, May 1*

Deciding that discretion is the better part of valor, we let Nassan find a truck and driver to take us and the gear to Uliastay, a town about sixty miles from the source of the Yenisey. She struck a deal that would cost us $300.

Our gear had still not arrived via Air China and the office had no idea if and when it would arrive. That was a worry.

*Wednesday, May 2–Monday, May 7*

Between purchasing supplies, searching for maps, taking in the local sights, and dealing with officials, we practiced our Russian. But we were suffering from some kind of flu bug we'd picked up in China. It snowed throughout the week, and my flu was worsening by the time Remy arrived on May 3. Our gear also arrived safe and sound to our relief.

On Friday, during the three-block walk back from the bank, I lost my passport. I searched frantically, retracing every step, to no avail. Nassan and her husband, Inca, guided me through the bureaucracy. First we went to the police station and filed a report, and then to the Canadian consulate. But they were closed for the weekend, which was probably just as well.

We returned to the guest house, and I collapsed in bed,

consumed by fever. Shivering under my sleeping bag and a blanket, I worried about how warm I would be in the mountains. Would my thirty-dollar sleeping bag cope with those freezing Siberian winds?

On Monday morning I began taking antibiotics, and at 10:00 A.M. I trundled into the Canadian consulate.

"Basically, we need to get you a new passport before you leave Mongolia," Chris Johnson, the consular general, told me. "Normally when someone loses a passport, we issue an emergency document that is enough to get them home. That only takes a couple of days. You're going to Russia, though."

Chris said the word "Russia" slowly, as if to underscore the bureaucratic hell we were entering.

"The Russians won't accept any temporary documents. If you don't have a full-on passport, you'll be out on your ear."

It would take at least a month to get my new passport. I would have to start the expedition without it and return in four or five weeks' time. Looking at the map, I could see that the river met up with a railway line about seven hundred miles from its source. If we could cover the distance in a month, we could stop at that juncture. That way I could take the train back to Ulaanbaatar, pick up the new passport, and rejoin Ben and Remy.

There was nothing else I could do. By law I should not even have been leaving Ulaanbaatar—it is illegal to travel in Mongolia without a passport. However, if I waited until the replacement document arrived, I could kiss the expedition good-bye. We didn't have four weeks to spare, so I'd have to take the chance. From that point on, though, I would be haunted by the fear that any chance encounter with official-dom could bring a sudden end to my journey. Meanwhile, at the Canadian consulate, I filled in the myriad documents, handed over photographs and processing fees, and, nearly at closing time, coughed my thanks and went on my way.

*Tuesday, May 8*

Still feverish and crippled with flu, we had to organize a photo shoot. Our journey had attracted a lot of international media interest, and it was essential to keep the goat fed with photos and reports from the field.

Once under way, we planned to send verbal reports using one of the two Iridium satellite telephones we carried. Transmitting visuals was more problematic, so we wanted to provide the media with fresh images from Ulaanbaatar before we embarked. There was a river nearby that would make a perfect backdrop.

That morning, Ben and I returned to the truck stop to see if we could rent a Russian-built "Jeep"—a cross between a Land Rover and a real Jeep. This time we left our valuables behind.

A driver offered to take us for $20. We went back to the hotel, picked up Remy and the kayaks, and headed for the hills. The khaki vehicle handled the rutted, potholed terrain with ease. As we drove, I realized that the commercial demands of this trip were making me feel differently about it than I had about my previous adventures.

This journey was run much more like a business. In many respects, I had sold myself to make the trip a reality. On my sailing adventure and the Amazon expedition, I was exploring to satisfy my own curiosity. This time I was on a sponsored trip.

Companies had donated goods, services, or cash to make it happen, with the expectation that we would work with the media to get them as much promotion as possible. Rarely a day would go by without one of us spending some time on the satellite telephone doing interviews for media outlets around the globe. We were also photographing and filming the trip for both a future documentary and planned books.

With so much activity tied to the project, I found that its demands sometimes detracted from the experience. I consoled myself with the thought that I was making a living doing something I loved—I must be doing something right. Thirty was fast approaching, and I couldn't live on utility-grade chicken and potatoes forever.

About two hours outside of Ulaanbaatar, we reached a jade-green river and a group of Mongolian *gers,* the traditional transportable, tentlike homes favored by the country's nomadic herders. They would provide great local color. We dressed in our whitewater gear, feeling a bit silly as the locals gathered to gawk.

I'm sure the driver thought we were crazy, too. But we had work to do. We spent a few hours shooting video and stills from various angles and vantage points, then headed back to the city.

## Wednesday, May 9–Saturday, May 12

The antibiotics finally seemed to kick in and I felt a bit better, which was good, because we had started for the mountains. Our vehicle was a van on steroids. Imagine a gray VW bus body on top of a high-clearance four-wheel drive chassis and a set of huge, knobbly, truck-wrestling tires.

Our driver was a fifty-something, potbellied father of two named Shagga. He spoke no English, but his Russian was good, so he and Remy conversed fairly easily. Traveling from dawn until dusk, it took us four days to make our way to western Mongolia and the headwaters of the Yenisey River. I couldn't fathom how Shagga made any money from such trips. I figured the wear and tear on the truck would more than eat up any profits.

On the third day, for instance, while we were climbing a mountain pass, the rutted route was awash in spring runoff. Nearly a dozen trucks and a ragtag caravan of vehicles were either bogged down or held up by a transport trailer sunk up to its axles. Clawing away still-frozen ground by hand, emptying the load from one precariously balanced truck, braving death to jack up another teetering on a precipice—it took half a day for the motley collection of drivers and passengers to get that alpine traffic jam cleared.

For the last two days, there was no road, only a boulder-strewn, potholed track snaking across a vast, treeless steppe that stretched forever, for all we knew—a treacle-colored baize rolling between the monumental remains of long-dead volcanoes.

But we made it. Otgon Tenger loomed menacingly above our campsite, its jagged slopes covered in a tattered cloak of snow and ice. On a map it was clearly visible that the mountain range of which Otgon Tenger was a part marked the outermost perimeter of the Yenisey's watershed. Although the first trickles of the Yenisey begin a few hundred yards lower beneath the peak, we had decided beforehand we would climb to the mountain's summit. It seemed an appropriate sentinel to mark the beginning of our journey.

Shagga didn't want us to climb the mountain. Local Buddhists revered the jagged massif, he said. He was so sure we were going to die that he threatened to leave with all our gear if we didn't "promise to refrain from such foolishness." After we had scouted the terrain and planned our ascent, we lied to him. Remy told him we were just going to the base of the mountain to take a few photographs.

"You have made the right decision," Shagga said.

*Sunday, May 13*

We left at 6:00 A.M., hoping to ascend the thirteen-thousand-foot peak and return before sunset. It promised to be a long, hard day—but if we were gone for more than a day, Shagga would know we had lied and we'd risk being stranded with no ride and no gear.

At 3:00 P.M. we reached a broad, snow-covered shoulder just below the summit. We had long since consumed our meager rations, and we had a terrible time wading through the chest-deep snow without snowshoes. It was evident that the mountain was beating us. We backtracked and started up a second, steeper, but less snow-covered face. We made excruciatingly slow progress over the rocky scree.

By five o'clock Ben's blistered feet had given out. The effects of friction were especially severe on the back of his right foot. When he removed his boot, the silvery Achilles tendon could be seen within a scarlet sheath of hamburgerlike flesh.

"I've got to call it quits and head back down," he said, in obvious agony.

"I'll go with him," Remy said. "We'll set up a camp below for the night."

I decided to continue on alone.

Over the next two hours I forced myself to put one foot in front of the other one agonizing step at a time. I was exhausted and famished. I had consumed a chocolate bar and some other candy, sardines, and dried prunes. My body had burned through those calories a long time before, and now every muscle ached for more fuel.

I was on a treadmill. On and on and on I went. The climb was interminable, each step torture. Like an optical illusion, the peak seemed to beckon but never to draw nearer. I kept going.

The slope wasn't so steep that I required special equipment and, unlike the Andes, I did not have to battle altitude sickness as well as fatigue. This was first and foremost an endurance test.

Finally, at 7:00 P.M., I reached the summit.

I had dreamed about this moment for almost a year. In my mind, this peak was more than just a mountaintop. It was a jagged monument marking the most distant boundary of the Yenisey's watershed. Any precipitation that fell on the north side of this mountain flowed to the Arctic; on the south side, it drained toward the Gobi Desert and Mongolia's great salt lakes. I had tried to visualize this moment in front of my computer back in Canada. The true start of the expedition—and now I was there.

I was surrounded by shattered granite and cornices of snow. In the distance, heavy gray anvil-head clouds were piling up. The wind screeched across the peak like fingernails raking a chalkboard. I shivered—I was chilled to the bone. I had better get off the mountain before darkness or the weather trapped me. I snapped a few photos and scrambled downhill.

High on adrenaline, I was exhilarated. I flew down the flank of what only moments before had seemed my nemesis. I had conquered the mountain. My aches and pains were forgotten; my hunger had abated. I practically skipped down the steep, scree-covered slope.

I found Ben and Remy shivering in the tiny two-man tent. I curled up between them and fell asleep, contented.

*Monday, May 14*

Remy and Ben are not men who accept defeat. Each rose as if he were Sisyphus and, with no food in their grumbling bellies, they headed back toward the summit. I returned to base camp to alleviate Shagga's worries. I hoped he hadn't left, or worse, called the authorities.

I found Shagga overwrought, about to go for help. Much to his relief, I was able to make him understand that the photographs had taken longer than expected.

Later in the afternoon, a group of herders arrived at our camp in traditional Mongolian garb—long dun wool overcoat, orange sash around the waist, and leather boots with upturned toes. They exchanged greetings with Shagga and soon we were toasting each other with a quickly produced bottle of vodka.

After a few drinks, one of the herders challenged me to a bout of Mongolian wrestling, which is different from the Roman style featured in the Olympics. To win in Mongolia, you knock your opponent off his feet. If any part of your body other than your feet touches the ground, you lose.

I stood up to meet the challenge. The herder who had called me out was in a crouch, swaying back and forth on the balls of his feet, ready to pounce. His black eyes were fixed, calculating my every movement. He lunged forward, and I slipped to the side and dropped my 165 pounds onto his back, sending him sprawling.

The other herders cheered. One for me. The rest jumped up to have their turn. Half an hour later, I lay on the ground panting, wheezing, and coughing. I had been too hard on my body in the last few days, and now my flu symptoms were returning.

I spent the evening cooking: rice, beef sauce, and coleslaw. I knew Ben and Remy would be famished. They were when they returned about 11:00 P.M., exhausted and high on having made it to the summit.

Shagga leapt from his van and bear-hugged Remy. "I was so scared last night," he said. "All I could think about were the dangerous high mountains, the ice fields, the rocky rivers, and the wolves." He shook his head and a finger at Remy. "And you didn't tell me where you were going."

Remy smiled meekly. He and Ben were too exhausted to reply.

*Tuesday, May 15*

We rose early, facing another arduous day. Our approach up the Otgon Tenger massif had been from the south. The Yenisey began on the other side of that sinuous ridge. Rather than locate the source by going up to the summit again and descending on the other side, we took the van to find a point that provided better access to the northern face. We would then climb up again to locate the headwaters of the Yenisey.

The four-wheel drive lurched to life and we bumped along through a barren valley flanked with snowcapped peaks. The terrain was nearly identical to the rugged, barren Highlands of Scotland. The landscape was uniformly brown, with tufts of vivid green scrub grass poking through here and there like a punk's Day-Glo hairdo. The air was clean and thin.

Occasionally I heard a bird singing, and I could see large raptors—eagles and hawks—circling above, riding thermals as they scanned the valley floor for shrews, gophers, and marmots. Horses, sheep, yaks, and goats wandered freely in search of pasture. Twice the van was forced to ford streams so deep that water gushed through the door seals.

"Is Russian. Is good!" Shagga grunted, as he patted the dashboard.

As we neared the head of the valley at 9,000 feet, a knot of buildings came into view. The elaborate structures were architecturally out of place in this wild, remote country, where everyone lived in a *ger*. It looked like a holiday resort that had been hit by a neutron bomb. From far off, the buildings appeared magnificent and grand, but in fact they were old, decayed, and abandoned.

The large central building still had its copper roof and walls of stucco-covered stone. There was also a cluster of smaller structures and a child's playground with a wooden slide, a merry-go-round, and teeter-totters. The paint had worn off years ago and the weather had bleached the wood to a pallid gray. Any child's laughter had long since been replaced by the hammering of a loose door in the incessant wind. Around the buildings were stone statues of local wildlife: wolves, ibex, otters, yaks.

"Wow," said Remy, gazing around the ghostly scene. It looked like the location for the Jack Nicholson film *The Shining*. "Who went to all the work of building this? And why did they abandon it? There's not even a road up here. How would you get the materials in?"

Shagga told us the story. In the 1920s, when the Soviets had a strong presence in Mongolia, a high-ranking official had taken a liking to the local hot springs and built this retreat. "It was meant to be a place where burned-out politicians and generals could unwind," he said. "They built bathhouses and quarters of such decadence that even the most elite of society were happy in the middle of the Hangayn Mountains. They would fly them into the flat strip down the valley. But the Russians went home—or the money ran out—and it was abandoned. The water still flows, though. You'll be able to take a bath here."

I relished the thought of soaking my aching muscles in hot mineral waters. Our own Mongolian health spa.

We entered the nearest of the smaller buildings. Inside were three saunalike rooms, the walls paneled with wood that looked like mahogany. In the middle of each room sat a cast-iron tub. Steaming water gushed from a pipe, sluicing along the russet-stained bottom of the tub and out the drain. I put a metal stopper in the drain and waited for the tub to fill. Heaven.

Outside, as the sun set, the temperature quickly dropped to below zero. I sat and splashed happily, imagining what this resort would have been like in its glory. It was a great way to begin the trip.

This was as far as Shagga's battered gray van could go. From here to the Arctic Ocean, we would be under our own power.

*Wednesday, May 16*

Not wanting to go hungry this time, we packed a substantial amount of food for our ascent of the pass that led to the back side of Otgon Tenger and the Yenisey watershed. I made twenty-four flatbreads from flour, water, and salt. We also carried Mongolian salami, cheese, a pot of cooked rice, tomato sauce, candies, nuts, sardines, and dried beans.

With everything packed, we took a few minutes to say good-bye to Shagga. He would make the 250-mile drive back to Uliastay, drive around to the north side of the mountain, and deliver us our paddling gear. Our topographical map showed no roads, not even a track, on the other side of the pass, but the elevation looked fairly level. We kept our fingers crossed that Shagga and his amazing, truly all-terrain vehicle would be able to traverse the sixty miles or so overland from the nearest dirt track. We had little choice but to trust him, since we couldn't carry the raft and other materials up and over the mountain.

The area we were aiming for corresponded to the terminus of the blue vein on our maps that indicated the Ider River. Of course the Ider began higher than the map showed; it was simply too small to be marked. Now that we were in the region, we could see by looking at the folds of land roughly where the trickle would begin. We aimed for a col on the eastern ridge that descended from Otgon Tenger. On its north side would be the start of the Yenisey River.

At first we followed animal trails that led up the steep ridge. Patches of brown grass and shrubs clung precariously to the loose, rocky scree. We forded small streams—not part of the Yenisey system, but instead destined to disappear into the vast furnace of the Gobi Desert. As we gained altitude, patches of snow and small glaciers appeared—frozen tongues of white, as if the mountain were making faces at us.

We hiked for most of the day before we crested the ridge and beheld the vista, a narrow grayish-brown valley stretching into the distance.

"The first trickle of water we encounter on this side is the Yenisey!" Ben hooted.

We trudged down the slope of snow-dusted ice and rock, each step bringing us closer to the Yenisey's watershed. It really was all downhill from here.

We located the first drops of water in the late afternoon, weeping from the snow face. The icy tears combined into a more substantial trickle that gathered momentum and size as it began its run to the far-off sea. This swelling trickle was the beginning of the Ider River, the first capillary of the Yenisey system.

"This is it, boys!" Ben said. "We're soon going to travel along every inch of this river."

We took photographs as we splashed and drank the crystalline water. It was a mouthful of purity—cold, wet, and fresh, like drinking ice cream. It was hard to believe that downstream the river would become 135 million times larger than the flow that gurgled and murmured at our toes.

We continued downhill, watching the creek grow in size as

other rivulets joined it. Already it had eaten a deep channel into the mountainside, carving a small canyon below and helping create the valley that glimmered in the distance. Then, as dark, prune-colored clouds gathered on the far horizon, thick, heavy snow began falling. That dampened my exuberance. We were close to ten thousand feet and a storm was a serious threat. We quickened our pace as the wind shrieked and the snow thickened.

As we got lower, however, the snow and wind became less and less severe until the savage squall dissipated as quickly as it had enveloped us. We took advantage of the break in the weather to pitch the two-and-a-half-man tent. Ben nursed his foot, which was still causing him anguish. To avoid friction between the moving tendon and the bandage, he had broken the bowl off a plastic spoon, placed it over the wound, and bandaged it. Although it seemed to help, he remained in excruciating pain. Remy and I set up camp and made dinner. We devoured a pot of rice and sauce, then collapsed into sleep.

*Thursday, May 17*

It was another icy-cold alpine morning. We were greeted by a white sun glinting off the gray, hissing water of the Ider River, which was still merely a stream. The valley was eerily quiet, and the only animals we encountered were dead. The valley floor was littered with carcasses—more fatalities from Mongolia's hell-freezing winter. The decomposing horses, cows, and yaks emitted a grim aroma. We kept the tiny river to our left as we clambered over boulders, descended small bluffs, and squelched through marshy grassland. Frequently other small streams joining the Ider would block our path. Some we could leap across; others we were forced to wade through.

In midafternoon we encountered an encampment of four *gers*, and the bewildered herders waved us over. As we approached, they fettered a pack of rambunctious mongrels and, through sign language, invited us for a meal.

An older man with a shaved head and a kind smile led us to the nearest *ger*. He walked with a heavy limp, and it was obvious that his days of rounding up wild horses were over. We imagined that the rest of the men were out in the hills tending their stock. Aside from the old herder, it was women who surrounded us and peppered us with questions. Not understanding a word, we smiled and repeated the mantras "This is a lovely *ger* you have here" and "Such a beautiful country you live in."

It was our first chance to study the traditional home of the Mongolians. *Gers* (sometimes called yurts) are basically a variant of the tepee, composed of a felt covering supported by a framework of poles called *khana*. Each pole is shaped individually and supported by two central columns called *uni*. The result is a low, cylindrical abode with a shallow conical roof. The shape of these structures makes them ideal for Mongolia's harsh climate. Not only do the curved walls help deflect Mongolia's incessant winds, but they also reduce surface area, thereby minimizing loss of precious heat. The wooden door—the most substantial part of the home—always faces south, to take full advantage of the sun's warmth and light. The *ger* is an ideal home for a nomad; it can be disassembled or erected in a day and transported by oxcart to greener pastures.

Upon entering the austere, windowless structure, I was amazed at how colorful and homey the interior was. Richly patterned rugs covered the floor and portions of the walls. Two painted tea chests lay near the outside perimeter, and a collection of black-and-white family photographs was displayed on top of them. In the center, a metal woodstove, fueled with yak dung, cranked out the kilojoules; I immediately broke into a sweat. The old man, whose name we couldn't pronounce, gestured for us to sit on a narrow bed near the wall.

*Ger* dynamics seemed to follow the customs I'd read about. The west side of the tent, where we had been invited to sit, was the men's area, where the saddles, bridles, guns, and smoking pipes were stored. The women traditionally get the side toward the rising sun, and this section boasted children's toys, cooking utensils, sewing equipment, and decorations. Generally the men and women stayed on their respective sides, although crossing the invisible line did not seem to be strictly forbidden.

The back area of the *ger*, called the *khoimer*, is supposed to be the most important part of the home. Here are stored the most valuable possessions, usually inside beautifully carved or painted tea chests. This area also has spiritual significance; often some sort of Buddhist shrine has been erected.

This family seemed to be doing well by local standards, and the old man was pleased to get a chance to entertain us. He reached into a small wooden cabinet and withdrew an elaborate green bottle. My research had indicated that the two items most treasured by men in Mongolian society were pipes and snuff vessels. Judging by the ritualistic movements of the old man, I figured that this was one of the latter.

Our host, his hands trembling, handed Remy the finely crafted bottle, which was carved from jade, its top inlaid with silver. The stopper was also made from stone, and affixed to it was a miniature spoon for scooping out the contents. Remy withdrew the spoon from the vial heaped with the powdered tobacco and vacuumed it up his left nostril. Sniffling, he passed it on to me.

I was not really keen to snort the powder, especially with my runny, congested nose. But I remembered from the *Lonely Planet* guide that it is considered rude to decline gifts in a *ger*. I positioned the snuff spoon under my nose and took a big hoot. As the peppery sensation seared my nostril and my nose began to dribble profusely, the old man smiled.

One of the women added more yak dung to the fire. I was impressed by how well the dry chunks burned. There is virtually no agriculture in Mongolia, only herding. Still, I was amazed at how much their animals provided. Their clothes were made from wool and skins. The *gers* were shrouded with wool felt. The floors were covered with yak- and horse-skin rugs as well as more elaborate, woven wool mats. Yak meat is the staple food, and it is cooked on the scat of the very same beast.

When it is time to move to greener pastures, the families simply pack their *gers* into the back of a wooden oxcart and move on.

Despite the huge losses in livestock these people had suffered, they didn't seem to be faring too badly with food supplies. We were served a delicious dinner of beef strips, salty yak's-milk tea, dried yak cheese, and homemade bread. The flour for the bread was the only ingredient that hadn't been locally obtained. Our ever-smiling hosts invited us to stay the night, but we insisted that we had to move on. Shagga would be waiting for us farther down the valley.

As we made our way north, we passed a largish herd of chocolate- and ebony-colored yak. It was obvious which was the dominant male. The massive, shaggy bull aggressively shook its horns at us, much as a fighter might toss a shadow jab at an opponent during his warm-up. It eyed us menacingly as I unclipped the waist strap on my backpack in case I had to run.

After we had nervously passed the yaks, the clatter of hooves nearly gave me a heart attack. I spun around to face . . . not a raging bull, but four galloping horsemen. They reined in to a halt. I wouldn't say they were War, Destruction, Famine, and Plague, but they weren't the welcome wagon either. Each had one dead eye, all of them probably sharing a defective gene. Like characters from a creepy Edgar Allan Poe story, they gaped at us mutely with identical cyclopean glares. Then one muttered something and they wheeled, cantering away as briskly as they had arrived.

We continued walking until, as the sun was setting, we spotted the van.

Shagga greeted us warmly and professed great relief at our safe arrival. He told us how the van had been pushed sideways down the river by the current when he'd tried crossing the very flow we would soon ride. He patted his vehicle affectionately—it had made it through.

He had also brought with him a fresh loaf of bread, a can of sardines, condensed milk, and, most important, a bottle of vodka.

The valley was about three miles across, mainly steeply sloped grassland with patches of forest. The Ider was still a small river—we were only thirty miles from its source—but we would be able to launch the kayaks and the raft tomorrow. Ben, with his ailing foot, was especially ebullient over the prospect of the end of our hiking. And tonight there was vodka to drink!

Colin negotiating some whitewater.

## RIDING THE WHITEWATER
## TO "CARCASS CANYON"

*Friday, May 18*

After breakfast we said good-bye to Shagga. I felt an emptiness knot my stomach as, with a final chuckle of grinding gears and a cloud of dust, fatherly Shagga and the invincible van disappeared over the hills. Until now the vehicle had been our umbilical cord to civilization, the last link in a chain of transport that led back home. Now we were taking ourselves deeper into the wilderness in our plastic boats—boats that would go in only one direction.

Our gear was dirty and disorganized after a week of bouncing around in the back of the van. We inflated the big canary-yellow raft and assembled the aluminum rowing frame. The whitewater raft would be our beast of burden, carrying mounds of gear stored in five huge waterproof bags. The kayaks would be used for filming and scouting.

By 4:00 P.M. we were ready to launch. Remy and I sat in our kayaks in full armor: life jackets, dry suits, helmets, neoprene gloves, and booties. Ben was in the raft, finishing off the final adjustments on the oarlocks. All our equipment and food were stored in waterproof containers and lashed to the raft with heavy-duty cam straps. We were ready for the worst. The river flowed smoothly and fast where we were, but downstream I could hear the thunder of rapids. Since we were making the first recorded descent of the Yenisey, we had no idea what to expect. My heart was racing at the long-awaited prospect of my first paddle strokes on the upper Yenisey.

I pondered for a moment on the shore, trying to come up with a few profound words to mark this special moment.

"Hurry up, you slow-assed mother!" Ben yelled as he pushed the raft into the river.

"Y-E-E-H-A-A-A!" I screamed as I let my kayak tilt over the steep bank and down into the icy water. Remy followed suit.

We were on our way!

We soon encountered the first stretch of whitewater. Although it didn't contain any school bus—eating whirlpools, it was an invigorating introduction to the river. Ben charged through the waves and vortexes in the laden raft while Remy and I slowed our pace to maximize our enjoyment. It was refreshing being in the icy water again, dancing with the river. As the water splashed in my face, I realized that the months in front of the computer were paying off. After a short but exhilarating day on the river, we pitched camp for the night on a small island, immensely pleased with our accomplishment.

*Saturday, May 19*

We decided to take a day off to give our bodies a rest from the physical and mental exertion we'd put ourselves through—and to celebrate and savor the fact that we were finally voyaging the Yenisey River.

Breakfast was millet. We'd brought pounds and pounds of the fine, hard grain—in fact, millet was all we had for breakfast for the many weeks ahead of us. We had searched in vain for oatmeal in Ulaanbaatar. On our Amazon journey we had been perfectly content to eat porridge day after day; it is compact, nutritious, and easy to make. The young Mongolian shopkeeper had directed us to the millet (a staple used for bird feed back home) and said it was better than oats. In our naivete we had bought almost fifty pounds of the wretched seed.

We were learning that millet is about as good as boiled cardboard, and breakfast was fast becoming a dreaded time of day. Adding insult to injury, it takes an hour to soften the seeds into a palatable mush, so our precious fuel was being consumed at an alarming rate.

After finishing our gruel, each of us took advantage of the break to catch up on our reading, writing, and calls home.

One of the luxuries we had on the trip was the Iridium satellite telephones. It seemed surreal as we drifted through the Mongolian wilderness to be able to make phone calls to Manhattan or London or Sydney. The phones were especially useful for keeping our information up to date. During one call, Dan Audet, a pal in Victoria who was running the expedition's Internet site, told me that the lower Lena and Yenisey

were in flood. That winter Siberia had had its heaviest snow-
fall in a century. Now it was melting, and huge ice jams were
choking the rivers. Apparently the Russian army planned to
bomb some of the obstructing ice from airplanes in hopes of
triggering a breakup.

Where we were, there was no sign of flooding. The river
coursed through a wide, grassy plain, and I could see a handful of *gers* dotting the prairie and mounted horsemen tending to flocks and herds. Tall mountains rose in the distance,
blue and mauve sentinels watching over the valley.

We left our island camp and traveled about forty miles
downstream. There wasn't a tree in sight. On the horizon I
could see a line of rounded, sallow mountains. During the
day they changed color, as though they were an outcropping
of Australia's famous Ayers Rock. The sun painted them
gladiola red at one point during the day and purple at another, then burnished them to bronze in the evening. The
river meandered continuously in braids and oxbows as it
lazily crossed the plain. We were savoring the placid water
while it lasted.

The copper-colored river was now about 120 feet across and
running high from the snowmelt. It was impossible to see the
numerous shoals that lay inches beneath the surface of the
murky water. They became a nightmare for Ben in the raft;
he was constantly grounding the heavily laden vessel. The
countryside, in comparison, seemed a bucolic idyll, alive with
activity.

I saw chevrons of wild geese and strange swans whose
trumpeting call was no more than a squawk. Remy and I discussed how well we would be eating if we only possessed a
good slingshot. The corned beef was becoming a little monot-
onous, and we drooled at the thought of a fat goose sizzling

over the fire. There were also eider ducks, eagles, vultures, go-phers, and marmots. We passed small clutches of *gers* every seven or eight miles, and herdsmen could regularly be seen on the plain tending to their livestock.

The second most common domestic animal after the yak seemed to be the horse. The tough Mongolian horse is what enabled Genghis Khan to acquire his massive empire. Looking closely at them, it is immediately evident that they are much hardier than their North American counterparts. With no coddling whatsoever, these small, compact beasts must endure Mongolia's long, bitter winters and frequent droughts. We could see Mongolian equestrians racing though the countryside, their animals seemingly sustaining a per-petual gallop.

As well as being used as beasts of burden, the horses are also prized for the food they provide. Mare's milk is made into both cheese and an alcoholic drink. Horsemeat is a sta-ple, tasting very similar to beef. Allegedly Genghis Khan's men could travel indefinitely, living on the milk and blood of their horses if they had to (they would bleed their horses without killing them). All that was needed to support a co-hort of Mongolian warriors was grass.

The Mongols also had a telling technological edge: the best stirrups, and compound bows made of bone, sinew, and wood that could fire an arrow twice as far as a European longbow. Little wonder that at one time they ruled most of the known world—and would have added Europe to their conquests had the great khan not died when his hordes were within sight of Vienna.

It was about sixty degrees, just about perfect for paddling. In the distance, however, a sulfurous sky threatened. Closer in, near the mountains in the west, roiling clouds and black, purple, and blue thunderheads scrummed. Occasionally great shafts of sunlight lanced through the towering gloom.

As the volatile sky mocked our insignificant existence, Ben and I composed new lyrics to rock songs. We tried to outdo each other as we replaced the innuendos of AC/DC lyrics with our own twisted versions. Our only audience was the ducks, which quacked in protest.

Remy began analyzing the water quality for Stream-keepers, an international organization interested in monitoring the health of the Yenisey watershed. He checked its oxygen content, pH level, and clarity, plus the number of invertebrate life-forms. We'd do similar checks periodically during the trip, and the results would be posted for research. Drawing our own conclusions despite our limited knowledge, we figured that the river was fairly healthy. We'd have to wait for the expert diagnosis to see if we were right.

Near the end of the day, the sides of the valley crept in on the river until we were coursing through a broad canyon. I saw no herders or *gers*, but the banks were lined with tall, graceful larch trees and evergreens. The hillsides rose nine hundred feet above us.

We stopped for the evening and Remy began to make dinner. Ten minutes later, I heard a string of curses—the fuel line of the stove was blocked and the cable for cleaning it was stuck in the pipe. I left Remy trying to fix it and went to collect water from the river.

The water filter had stopped working, too! The $250 Katadyn water filter would not prime. I fiddled with the unit for half an hour before giving up. Remy said the last rites over the stove and I pronounced the water filter equally dead. Ben started a campfire. Luckily, there was plenty of firewood. Most of the land we had passed through bore nary a stick, so we were a little concerned about finding fuel downstream. I guessed we could burn yak dung if we had to.

*Tuesday, May 22*

We awoke to the sound of our tents flapping in the midst of a blizzard. The wind screamed down on us like a banshee. Snow whipped across the plain, settling in drifts that shifted and snaked. The two kayaks and the raft looked miserable as the snow piled up against them. We huddled in the tents like prison inmates, unable to continue in the face of such white fury. Outside were four inches of snow and a wind-driven wall of still-falling flakes. The dark river made a stark contrast to the chalk-white storm.

The blizzard abated later in the day and we set off, quickly encountering our first town of substantial size—Tosont-sengel, a hard-nosed lumber town of dirt roads, ramshackle buildings, and battered vehicles. We parked the raft near a decrepit yet still-functioning sawmill. Skeletal rusted cranes stretched skyward, awaiting the next load of lumber and the next sagging truck. I drew the short straw and was left guarding the boat while Ben and Remy scrounged for food.

Left by myself, I used the collapsible rod to cast a silver lure into the murky water. Within seconds I felt a bite and the reel screamed; in five minutes I had landed a five-pound rainbow trout. A few casts later, I caught another. We would eat well that night.

A growing crowd of locals began to gather, much like the crowd at the truck stop. They stared at me. I had read in my research for the trip that Mongolians despise fish and the rivers are an untouched resource. Apparently it was true. With every move I made, I could feel their eyes boring into me. They moved in. It could have been a scene from *Night of the Living Dead*. Children clambered over the gear; adults picked up and fiddled with anything they could.

I suppressed my raging anxiety and my strong Western

concerns about property ownership. I was in a different culture now and must accept their ways. These people were motivated by curiosity—or so I told myself.

After a couple of hours, Ben and Remy returned. Although the shops were spartan, they had found cooking oil, yeast, jam, condensed milk, and tins of corned beef. I headed into town with Ben to take a quick tour.

Returning to the boat, we found a flustered Remy amid a sea of brown faces. "The auxiliary first aid kit is gone," he said.

We searched everywhere. No luck—it had been pinched. Fortunately, most of the important first aid supplies were stored in a different container. From now on we would have to be more careful. It could have been the video camera or a satellite phone that was missing.

*Thursday, May 24*

"Hi, it's Colin, from Outer Mongolia," I said to Dan in Canada. I still thought it was amazing that I could dial up anyone I wanted from the middle of nowhere.

Dan told me that the Canadian news media were reporting entire villages washed away by the floods in Siberia. He thought we should change our plans to ensure that we had enough food to carry us along the northern stretch of the river. It sounded as if there would be little left by the time we got there.

We made our way slowly down the river for most of the day, all riding on the raft because of the molasses-like current. There was no point being cramped in the high-performance kayaks when there was no whitewater to contend with. The Big Bird raft certainly did its share of donkey work, carrying three men, five 130-pound dry bags, countless small dry bags, two large food crates, two kayaks, and some fifty pounds of firewood—about half a ton in total. We took turns on the oars to increase our speed. But the river was braided—splitting into numerous channels—and we frequently foundered in narrow, shallow passages.

The valley was about two miles wide, with rolling hills on either side. To the north were reddish-gray mountains cloaked in scrub brush. To the south I could see olive-colored pastures and Lincoln-green forests. If the weather had been nicer, I would have considered the view stunning. It was more difficult to appreciate when shivering from the cold under dull, dishwater skies.

Viewing this river after having done the Amazon was interesting. It gave me a perspective on how different rivers can be. Like the land the water flowed through, the upper Yenisey seemed cold, hard, and unforgiving. Even though the water was flat and easily navigable by small boat, we'd seen none of the locals venturing out in any sort of vessel. I could almost understand why they would shy away from the Ider. When you stood on the lonely riverbank, the swirling brown water seemed to accentuate the bleakness of the land, and the cold, buffeting winds seemed to originate from the river itself.

Even the *gers* we encountered were set well away from the banks. They nestled in the folds of the mountains, where they were sheltered from the winds. Their occupants made the long trip to the river every couple of days with oxcarts to fetch water in big urns. Aside from that, they stayed away from it—no fishing and no boating. Perhaps it would be different when we left the mountains.


*Friday, May 25*

The foul weather disappeared. Although frosty, it was sunny and windless. In spite of the cold, I went for a dip in the river. I had developed an itchy rash, probably from wearing the same clothes and not bathing for days. I was wearing my clothes even at night because my sleeping bag was of such poor quality. A scrub was called for, no matter how brisk.

We set off downriver and I sat on the back of the raft watching the Mongolian countryside drift by, feeling, for the first time on the journey, something like Huckleberry Finn. Remy pulled at the oars and Ben jotted in his journal beside me. It was a moment of transcendental contentment, one of those just-right stretches of time when everything comes together.

I think everyone yearns for that carefree-summer-afternoon feeling Twain evoked about the Mississippi. I know I love it. It is a feeling of being at one with the world, a feeling that there is no place you can imagine being except right here, right now. And you're happy. A moment like this is one of the reasons I go on these expeditions. I was happy.

The dirt track running along the bank beside us grew tired as the terrain got more rugged, eventually falling behind. A few more tributaries had thrown their lot in with the Ider, and the river had grown to a width of about two hundred feet. The mountains lining the valley were higher, boasting snowcapped peaks.

The rolling steppe was a unique landscape—the product of a millennium's grazing. It had an alien feel. I imagine that before man arrived, the valley was carpeted with forest. Now, nary a tree. We saw an occasional *ger* or log cabin, usually an eight-by-twenty-foot box featuring one or two shuttered windows and a sod roof.

A handful of herders spotted us, ran to the water's edge, and waved and yelled at us from the shore as we went past, gesturing like royalty. I imagine it was the first boat most of them had seen on the river—perhaps the first boat they'd seen anywhere.

The trout were making themselves scarce. Since the abundant catch in Tosontsengel we had dreamed up all sorts of recipes: trout stew, fish-head soup, trout stir-fry, trout sandwiches, trout salad, fried trout and fries. Unfortunately, we hadn't caught another fish.

By my rough estimate, in just over a week we had traveled about two hundred miles from the source. The 3,250 miles remaining seemed a little daunting, yet already we were falling into the rhythm of experienced explorers. We set up camp like a well-oiled machine. One of us started dinner while the other two pitched tents, unloaded gear, and did any other necessary chores. The cook was also responsible for turning our flour into flatbreads for the following day's lunch.

The day before, we had found the perfect implement to replace the stove—a rusty galvanized bucket I had spotted as it lay discarded on the shore. With a hole cut in the base for inserting firewood, it made a perfect stove. Pots could be set on top, and the fire was unaffected by the winds that plagued us. I actually preferred cooking on the bucket stove to the now-defunct MSR. It was simple, unbreakable, and put out much more heat. Now it took just a few minutes to boil a two-gallon pot of water.

We stopped beside a warm rocky bluff for a fine lunch of flatbread, sardines, and dried apricots. A dirty little boy with a bowl haircut materialized from among the boulders. As we ate, he sat half a yard away and simply stared, unblinking, wordless. Every few seconds he would make a slurping sound as he sucked back his saliva. We guessed it meant he was hungry, and offered him some apricots.

He hungrily gobbled them down.

Back on the river, Ben guided the raft as it slipped along through the spring-green valley. Then the mountain ranges converged and the river was forced through a narrow canyon. The stark rock formations reminded me of Ansel Adams's photographs of Yosemite and Monument Valley.

There was no vegetation. The river picked up speed and dry, jagged walls of slate-blue rock rose sharply above us. We pulled the raft up onto a small sandy island and called it a day.

*Saturday, May 26*

We awoke to find a cow wandering through our campsite, completely unafraid. When it grew bored with us, the beast proceeded to the river's edge and swam to the far shore. It reached the opposite bank, pulled itself up, turned, and fixed us with a stare.

*Moo*, the cow lowed, as though to say, Not bad, eh?

I had finally perfected the art of cooking millet. The fine yellow grain needed to be boiled vigorously for more than an hour, with the ratio of millet to water about eight to one. The result was the closest we'd ever get to real porridge. With a can of condensed milk and some prunes, it was actually digestible. That was good, because we had about thirty-five pounds still to go through.

About midday, we encountered a rickety wooden bridge wide enough to allow oxcarts to cross. Two men stood at the middle of the span watching us approach. Water sluiced past wooden piles driven into the riverbed. I guided the raft toward a slot just under ten feet wide, my concentration forcing me to ignore the men's yells above. Emerging on the other side of the piles, I looked up.

The men were dressed in blue felt coats with orange sashes, and they were gesturing to a little wooden shack attached to the far end of the bridge. They pointed at us and one brandished a fistful of bills in the air. I suddenly understood what they were communicating. It was a toll bridge, and they wanted us to pay for the privilege of going underneath!

I chortled and kept rowing as their shouts faded into the distance. Considering it was the first boat they had probably seen on the river, they sure were quick to try capitalizing on it.

The river ran through arid, sun-baked canyons and narrow, parched valleys, but we encountered none of the rapids we had feared. Whenever I thought this must be one of the remotest places on the planet, another *ger* or decrepit log cabin would appear.

Father on, the river ran between sheer cliffs that rose perpendicular to the water's edge. Later, when the canyon opened up again, we spotted a two-humped Bactrian camel, but it ran off before we could snap a shutter.

When we called it a day, it was my turn to cook, and I made pit bread with a stew of dehydrated squid that we had brought from Beijing. To make the bread, I carved a pit in the sandy loam with a paddle and built a fire in the bottom of the hole, placing rocks amid the burning wood to absorb the heat. The bread dough was made from flour, salt, yeast, sunflower seeds, and aniseeds. After kneading the dough and letting it rise, I placed it in our large cooking pot. The pot was then placed on top of the embers and rocks, and I built another fire on top, letting it burn vigorously for about ten minutes. I then buried everything with the dirt excavated earlier. An hour later, I dug up the now golden-brown treasure loaf.

We feasted, if I do say so myself.

*Sunday, May 27*

As the days passed by, I could feel my mind-set slowly adapting to expedition mode. The cycles of the days, the serenity of the river, and the solitude of just three men in a wild land had culminated in an incredible sense of well-being.

It always takes a while to get used to this lifestyle. At first the mind and body balk at the bad hygiene, the physical hardships, and the rootlessness. Eventually, though, the body gets used to the changes; the luxuries of home are forgotten, and a nomadic sense of home is established. I understood why the Mongolian gypsies seemed so satisfied with their simple, wandering life and professed to want no more. I no longer felt as though I didn't have a home. The land had become my abode, and wherever there was land, I was at home.

We called the section of river valley we were traveling through "the Land of the Horses." The animals were ubiquitous, and because of the heat, they liked to lounge belly-deep in the cold, dark-blue river.

The severity of navigable whitewater is measured on a scale of one to five, with Class V being the most severe. Class I describes small, standing waves and would be quite safe if you fell into the river. Class V, on the other hand, is extremely dangerous, and any small mistakes or an involuntary dunking can lead to fatal consequences. Class III is invigorating but not dangerous for a well-trained and experienced rafter. As we continued down the valley, Ben nimbly guided the raft through some Class III rapids and a maze of semisubmerged boulders. We hadn't yet encountered whitewater measuring greater than Class III—so far, the river had been a cakewalk. At least the splashy whitewater offered a brief respite from the relative monotony of ocher landscape and gently rolling river.

Just before lunch we approached another, smaller set of rapids.

"Let's do some filming here," Remy said. "We could use the head cam and get some shots of the raft coming through the rapids."

We pulled the raft into shore. While Remy and I began to assemble the equipment for the shoot, Ben picked up a satellite phone and called his mother. He had done the same thing the day before, deciding to make a phone call just before the nastiest task of the day—breaking camp and loading the boat. Remy and I ignored him and unloaded the kayaks. We carried the gear downstream, readied the cameras, and prepared for the shoot. When everything was set, Ben racked the phone.

"Could you make a bit more effort to schedule calls during free periods?" I sniffed. "That was quite a bit of work."

Ben glared at me, offended at the implication that he wasn't carrying his load.

We ate lunch in silence and pushed off again, without clearing the air.

Ahhh, the glory of being the first to run a river! There will always be some sort of excitement to take your mind off petty arguments. About 4:00 P.M. we rounded a sharp corner in the valley and entered a tight abyss. The pastureland, the people, and the *gers* were all left behind, and we were embraced by a fairy-tale land of pristine wilderness. Sheer cliffs walled in both sides of the canyon entrance; the only way in was by boat. A female moose stood by the riverside drinking her fill. As we slipped through the canyon of sandy beaches, towering cliffs, and virgin forests, a new sound began to reach my ears—the thundering roar of monstrous rapids.

We stopped the boats on the rocky bank so we could scout what was ahead from shore—a feat in itself. The bank we were following soon became a pink granite cliff bordering the swift-moving water. I followed Ben and Remy in bare feet as we climbed along the base of the cliff, clinging to tiny, slippery holds. At one stage I almost slipped into the hissing green water. The roar we heard coming from around the corner could mean death to a swimmer—or perhaps just a few nasty bruises.

At last we were able to see the source of the intimidating rumble: an unbroken chain of rapids—Class IV and worse. It would be runnable with our raft and kayaks, but by no means easy. The rapids continued around another corner and out of sight. We had no idea what to expect beyond that point, and no way to find out.

By the time we got back to the boats, it was 8:00 P.M., so we decided to set up camp and leave the excitement for tomorrow. Our jubilation at encountering this jewel of a canyon seemed to have pulled us together as a group. We talked excitedly through dinner about the water we'd be running the next day. Sitting around a blazing campfire, we laughed off the lunchtime squabble and celebrated. We would be the first people ever to ride these rapids, the first to descend "Carcass Canyon" (we had named the place after a rotting yak that lay bloated and covered in maggots at the entrance).

*Monday, May 28*

Remy and I would go in the kayaks while Ben rode the raft through the rapids. After breakfast we sat for a moment at the edge of the current. At this point I always feel a kind of centering in the pit of my stomach, a calm before the storm. We gave each other a nod and Ben pulled on the oars, plunging into the welcoming foam at the start of the rapids.

I followed behind the raft and was immediately reminded of the power of river hydraulics. Conflicting currents played tug-of-war, like crazed river gods fighting to eat the plastic-coated human. I flailed desperately with the paddle, trying to keep upright and at the same time attempting to maneuver the boat to the least dangerous parts of the river. A sharp bend in the river siphoned most of the water straight into an undercut cliff, possibly a fatal hazard. I powered with all my might toward the right side of the river and away from the cliff, where the water was pushing me. A huge rapid, essentially a horizontal whirlpool, lay directly in my path, and I had no choice but to go straight into it. Immediately everything went black as the powerful undercurrents dragged my buoyant vessel and me deep under the surface of the river. After holding my breath for what seemed an eternity, I burst back into the air. I paddled hard and pulled the boat free of the whirlpool's grasp and into the calmer water below.

After I emerged from the vortex, Remy came along behind me. "I thought you were a goner," he said.

I grinned. "Just working on my aquatic gymnastics."

The bend in the river appeared and we moved quickly through hissing waters toward it. Fortunately, it hid no killer chute or precipitously steep falls. Ben stood in the raft in the calmer current and tossed me a casual wave. We continued downriver, navigating some smaller, less challenging rapids before calling it a day at about three, utterly exhausted. We set up camp in a tiny meadow beside the river. There was a strip of virgin beach, and behind us a stand of trees clung tenaciously to pockets of soil on the steep slope. Across the muddy river, maroon cliffs rose about 350 feet into a cerulean sky.

It was my turn to cook, so I quickly foraged from our great outdoor vegetable garden. I made coleslaw using our cabbage along with wild onions, which I also added to our potatoes. I found plenty of rhubarb and mint, too. The mint went in a thermos with hot water and sugar to make a very pleasant tea. I stewed the rhubarb for dessert. It was nice having something sweet again, as we had run out of chocolate bars.

I was suffering from a strange pain in my hip. There was no bruise or cut, not even a mark, and most of the time it didn't hurt. I could walk, poke my hip, press it, and massage it, and feel nothing—completely normal. But when something accidentally bumped against it from a certain angle, I would feel one of the most excruciating pains of my life. It felt as though someone were jabbing a knife in and twisting. It would last only about ten seconds, and then everything would be fine again. I reckoned it was just a rebellious nerve.

I took three still cameras, the video camera, and a satellite telephone up the side of the canyon to take some photos, carrying the equipment in a rubberized fabric dry bag. When I was about two-thirds of the way to the top, the bag brushed gently against my hip. I screamed and my arms shot out spasmodically. The dry bag sailed through the air, landing among the rocks about ten feet away. When the pain subsided, I opened the dry bag, expecting the worst. Thankfully, nothing was broken. (Over the ensuing months, the sporadic pain subsided, and I never did find out what had caused it. Probably something to do with sitting in the cramped kayak.)

The rocky ground I was clambering over was fairly dry, and there was an amazing splendor of plants. Peppermint, dill, and sage bloomed among the rocks and fissures in the cliff face, as well as onions and mint. Bluebells, lilacs, and a colorful palette of other flowers carpeted the ground, along with some striking, pungent plants that I didn't recognize.

Once atop the peak, I was awestruck by the panorama. I snapped roll after roll of film. I had seen nothing to compare with this vista—the brown snake of the river slithering between mountains, monumental rock formations that resembled giant shards of glass—it was unbelievable.

I had a feeling that "Carcass Canyon" was a unique landscape within Mongolia. In all my research I had seen no photographs of Mongolian scenery that even vaguely resembled what we were experiencing. We were probably the first Westerners to lay eyes on it.

That is the beauty of running a river, especially when you are the first. You could look your whole life for a place like this and never find it. You could study maps, seek the best advice from local guides, and still it would remain elusive.

Running a river takes you at random through the country-side. You find these spots not because you're looking for them, but simply because you have decided to travel every inch of the water's course.

*Tuesday, May 29*

The next rapids we ran were technically challenging, and we bumped merrily along, shooting lots of pictures and record-ing lots of video. At one point I duct-taped the camera to my helmet to film the raft and the other kayak running some teddy-bear rapids.

It was a great day.

Looking at our map, we estimated that we would arrive at the confluence of the Mörön River the next afternoon. From there on, we would be on the river known as the Selenge. A few years earlier, a couple of Australians had run the Mörön and Selenge rivers to the Russian border. We would no longer be the first Westerners to lay eyes on the landscape.

Although the latest rapids hadn't been too treacherous, during peak flow they would probably be murderous. A col-lection of driftwood about seven feet above the waterline gave an idea of how deep the river could get. It had probably peaked about four to six weeks before, when the snowmelt off the Hangayn Mountains was at its heaviest. Most of the surrounding mountains were now bare.

*Wednesday, May 30*

I made rhubarb rice pudding for breakfast. It was a meal fit for kings—and a whole lot better than millet. Afterward, Remy and Ben cooked more rhubarb to eat once we were on the river. We carried the tasty sweet-and-sour preserve in three jars we'd emptied of mayonnaise and sauerkraut and washed out.

Many bizarre multilegged creatures were ambling around our campsite: dung beetles, large hairy spiders, centipedes, a variety of ants. Ben and I sat transfixed for ten minutes watching the efforts of an ant lion. The larva of this insect digs a conical pit in the sand and buries itself at the bottom. Unsuspecting ants tumble over the edge of the pit and can't climb back up on the unstable sand. The foraging ants seemed fairly clued in, staying away from the hole in the ground. Finally, with a bit of help on our part, a black ant went tumbling into the pit. Like a monster from a sci-fi movie, a huge set of pincers reared from the sand and dragged the struggling ant under and out of sight.

At about 11:00 A.M., the canyon widened into a red-rock valley that opened up into a landscape of steppe and distant mountains. One thing that remained constant was the number of carcasses strewn along the riverbank and in the river. Cows, horses, camels—the death toll was sickening. In the midday heat of seventy-seven degrees, the stench at times was unbearable. We found a clean stretch of river and pulled in to eat a lunch of flatbread and pâté.

"We should be at the confluence with the Mörön soon," I said to Ben. "I'm looking forward to the Selenge."

"That would be a good name for a book," he said.

"What's that?"

"The Selenge, the Ider, and the Mörön." Ben laughed. "I just have to figure out who's the moron, you or Remy."

He laughed again, heartily. On an expedition, little things often seem incredibly amusing—often only to yourself. I ate my lunch.

All of us rode the raft because the river seemed to be on

Valium. The rowing seat was about a third of the way from the stern. One of us sat behind the rower and one sat on a kayak strapped across the front of the raft. With all the gear it was a tight squeeze, but we managed to get comfortable.

For several miles we frequently saw camels ambling along the riverside. Their two humps reminded me of the stylized camels of my childhood. Like a cowboy from the Wild West, a young boy trailed a herd of horses along the riverside. He drove them at a canter, easily outpacing us.

We reached the confluence of the Mörön at 6:30 P.M. We could hear the river before seeing it—the Mörön was in flood. Swollen with snow and glacial melt, it had spilled over its banks, inundating the low-lying forests on either side. The flood was bulldozing its way east. As the two rivers churned together at the confluence, the Ider threw its volume into the effort, and we found ourselves barreling down a torrent clotted with gray silt and debris. It seemed like we were finally catching up to the floodwaters that Dan had repeatedly warned us about on the sat phone.

The mountains where the Mörön River originated must have had much more snow than the Hangayn peaks, thus the huge difference in water levels between the two rivers. Looking at the map, I saw that the Mörön began near the Russian border, in the Hovsgol Mountains, an area that had endured the same heavy snowfalls as Siberia.

The new river—the Selenge—was born in a tumult. We moved at twice the speed we had been used to, fairly rocketing along. When we spotted a nice piece of high ground well above the surging floodwaters, we steered the raft to shore and secured it.

Stinging nettles were everywhere, so I harvested some and cooked them in boiling water. As a child I read a book that mentioned nettles were edible—after being cooked. I imagine that, sautéed with onions, spices, salt, and an Oxo cube, nettles might be divine. Alone, they left a lot to be desired. But our supplies were down to rice and millet and a few cans of meat—not much until we could reach Sühbaatar—so every bit extra helped. I handed a couple of the nettle leaves to Ben to sample.

"Not bad," he said. "What did you spice them with? I feel a nice, warm, burning sensation spreading through my stomach."

"Just salt."

"I think you might want to boil them a little more," Ben said nervously.

We lay down to sleep on the high bank. I could hear the fast-running river several feet below us.

*Thursday, May 31, 2001*

We had camped on one of the few high banks, but we awoke nearly at water level. The Selenge River had risen through the night, and dirty, clotted water the color of caramel clawed at the bank a foot or so from our tent. The river had been flooding the day before, but we had not expected it to rise so quickly—or so violently. Logs, trees, bloated carcasses of unidentifiable ungulates, flotsam, jetsam, and great clods of earth surged by in the churning current.

Our piece of high ground was fast disappearing. We packed our gear quickly, sloppily cinching down the bags in high hopes that we were in for a good, speedy day's rafting.

The flooding river was not a great concern. The broad valley ahead was a flat and gently sloping steppe. There were no rapids or waterfalls to fear—just roiling, surging water. Our self-bailing whitewater raft was built to surf these conditions with élan, and for an hour or so we did. It was a wild experience as the raft careened down the waterway. Staying in the main river channel, however, proved impossible. The powerful current muscled us into a flooded forest, propelling us past thick branches, logjams, and a maze of alder, birch, and smaller, shrublike plants whose limbs scratched and whipped us. The more substantial boughs stabbed at the raft, and downed trees threatened to overturn it. If someone got sucked into any of those hazards, he would be flattened by the current and drown.

At the oars, I pulled this way and that as Ben and Remy called out warnings and advice. Trying to maneuver the half-ton vessel through the obstacles proved futile as we sluiced along at six knots or more. The river was overpowering; I could only attempt to keep the raft upright for the duration of the ride. As the forest grew thicker, disaster seemed inevitable.

A tree limb struck Remy on the chest and bunted him into the water. He grabbed the perimeter rope as he fell and managed to haul himself back into the safety of the raft. "I'm okay," he spluttered.

The raft was being pummeled from every side as it raced through the trees like an out-of-control bumper car. My heart pounded and my lungs burned from exertion. I pulled with all my might on the oars, desperately trying to slow us down, frantically trying to buy time. It was no use.

The raft slammed into a huge bough and came to a shuddering halt. Tons of water pressed on the upstream side. The bough creaked but refused to surrender to the force of the river and the raft. Each of us immediately understood what was about to happen, and we leapt onto the downstream pontoon. Our combined 550 pounds might as well have been guano—too little, too late.

Water breached the upstream pontoon, and in a matter of

seconds, the river had swarmed over the float. Although the raft was built to take the weight of eight men and their gear, the river simply swallowed it. We scrambled onto the very bough that had caused our misery, just as the pontoon on which we were standing shot skyward and the raft turned turtle.

The river continued to bull the now upside-down raft, pushing it farther under the overhanging limbs, grinding and scraping its bottom on the branches, until the perimeter line snagged. Snapping taut, the line jerked the upturned raft and spun it around in the current. There it sat in calmer water, at the end of its tether.

The kayaks were submerged, as they had been lashed atop the raft. But the gear underneath wasn't as securely tied in place as it should have been. The last thing we had anticipated was capsizing, and nobody had double-checked the cam straps. With the boat held stationary and the current clawing at the bags, items were working loose one by one. Paddles, bags, life jackets, and other material popped to the surface and were washed away. All our equipment, all our food, all our money! We jumped in to save what we could, pitching the items we could snare onto a nearby strip of marshy grass that was still above the waterline.

Remy corraled the dry bag that contained our passports and money. Ben grabbed a food bag. I snatched at pots, pans, potatoes, bags of rice, a flashlight, a spatula, and other bits and pieces of our expedition, tossing what I could toward the grass, and scrambled for more. Many of the items I pitched landed back in the river and were swept away, but Ben was more accurate. I managed to save a twenty-gallon food container and wrestled it ashore.

Remy sat there dejectedly. "The film bag is gone," he announced.

"Are you sure?" I asked, glancing downstream.

"It went down at the same time I was snatching the passport bag," he said. "There was no way I could bring in two bags at once. It's gone."

I had a sinking feeling in my stomach. All the documentary footage and half the photographs were in that bag. Without the footage, we had no documentary. I felt sick.

We had encountered Monet skies at sunset, plains and valleys littered with dead livestock, towering cliffs and staggering chasms, undulating scrubland thick with wild horses, and people living as their ancestors had centuries ago, when they ruled the known world from the Middle Kingdom to Europe. All the planning, all the work, all those experiences were now diminished immeasurably. If the documentary footage was lost, our sponsors would be disappointed—big-time.

My mind replayed the scenes as vividly as video. I couldn't accept that our only record of those memories was gone. "We need to right the raft and get one of the kayaks loose," I told Ben. "I'm going after the bag."

"Let's get the raft upright, then," he replied.

He slipped back into the water just upstream and let the current carry him down toward the tree that had flipped us. It was a dangerous maneuver. If he missed the tree or was unable to grab an overhanging branch and pull himself up out of the water, the current would propel him downstream through a fatal tangle of branches and logs.

Ben made it and hauled himself up onto the bottom of the raft. He scuttled across to the port side, where the throw bag was secured. The bag contained a hundred-foot length of coiled rope with a weighted end. Ben tied the free end of the rope to a D-ring on the starboard side of the raft and then tossed the bag to me. I straightened the synthetic line and secured it to a sturdy birch tree.

The current was too strong, and Ben could do little to free the raft. The perimeter line was looped around a tree branch and drawn taut by the pressure of the current on the raft. The constant friction had gnawed a one-inch trough in the bough. We could cut either the line or the branch. Ben took out his Leatherman multitool, extracted a tiny serrated blade, and began sawing through the wood. The raft snapped free and Remy and I, who had been holding the line slackly, were yanked forward. We staggered, regained our footing, and found ourselves in a tug-of-war with the current. It lasted for only a moment before we pulled the raft into the calmer eddies near our marshy refuge and quickly righted it.

In total, about thirty minutes had passed since we had capsized. The film bag was waterproof. Unless it had become snagged in the flooded undergrowth, it was bobbing its way toward the Arctic Ocean, and every minute that passed made its recovery less probable. We freed the kayaks as quickly as we could, and I grabbed a paddle and slipped on a spray skirt. I briefly pondered putting on my life jacket, but decided it would only increase my chances of becoming ensnared if I was swept into a sieve.

"I'm off, guys."

"Good luck," Ben said as he pushed the kayak into the current. His voice was dead and flat. Like me, he was feeling pessimistic.

In hindsight, I suppose we should have discussed how we would meet up again, but at the time it didn't seem too important. Every second was precious; I had to begin pursuing that bag as quickly as possible. Anyway, it seemed pretty obvious to me that I would simply stop farther downstream and wait for the other two to catch up in a few hours. At the moment, my only concern was to bring our documentary back from a watery demise.

As Remy and Ben began straightening the raft and sorting out what was left of the gear, I set off alone.

**5**

Ox skull and ox cart over-looking the Ider River.

## LOST IN MONGOLIA

*Thursday, May 31*

It was exactly 1:23 P.M. on my Timex. I hoped that by keeping track of the time I could calculate how far downstream the bag would have traveled. I was wearing nothing but a pair of khaki pants—no shirt, no shoes, no socks, no underwear.

Within minutes I realized that a grid-style search was out of the question. The kayak, like the raft, was grabbed by the current and hurled along at breakneck speed. I could only ride the flood, with not a chance of poking around the inundated trees and bushes. Being dragged through the forest at such speed was surreal.

The Riot "Big Gun" Kayak I was paddling was designed to navigate the biggest whitewater, and this would be the ultimate test. It had greater buoyancy than regular boats, which kept it stable as whirlpools and boils grabbed at its hull. Its curved rocker allowed me to maneuver with lightning speed through the forest. There was no better boat for such conditions.

I weaved between the trees like a character on a speeder in *Star Wars*. As I sped along, I became more and more convinced the bag was lost forever. It could be anywhere, and it was green—perfect camouflage. The floodwaters had made the river more than one and a half miles wide now, maybe more; it was impossible to determine for sure because I was in the middle of a forest. The river extended as far as I could make out through the bushes on either side.

Logjams, piles of debris, and tree-branch sieves, each a potential killer, lurked everywhere. Dodging the obstacles, ducking overhanging branches, and staying upright while moving at several knots was wilder than any video game I'd ever played—crazier even than most of the whitewater I had run.

It was obvious that if the bag was in the forest, chances of spotting it were slim. The seven mile per hour current ripped me downstream uncontrollably; there wasn't a hope in hell of finding a dark green bag in this fluid maze of trees and logs. I decided that the only chance of finding it was to paddle downstream as hard as I could and get ahead of it. Then, if I could find a section of river with higher banks, I could wait on the shore and watch the entire flow until the bag of film came drifting by. Unless it had become snagged somewhere in the woods, I didn't see why this plan wouldn't work.

Regardless, it would also be an ideal place to wait for Remy and Ben. Like the film bag, they wouldn't be able to slip by unnoticed. I calculated that the bag had been drifting freely for half an hour. It could be up to five miles down-stream, so I would have to paddle hard for about two hours to be certain of getting ahead of it.

Getting through the forest was easier said than done. Branches clawed at my naked torso, and the warren of over-hanging boughs and flood flotsam was treacherous. Hurtling toward one branch, I purposely capsized the kayak to avoid being decapitated. Once clear of the offending limb, I righted my boat with a sweep of the paddle.

Eventually I emerged from the woods. The river had one defined bank, but still spilled across the valley floor on the other side. It was ripping along at about seven or eight miles per hour. Finally, two and a half hours after setting off, I reached a low canyon. One side was fractured roseate rock that rose up 160 feet from the water's edge. The other shore, about 750 feet across, was a seven-foot dirt bank—the edge of a rolling steppe that undulated toward a line of old, rounded mountains shimmering mauve and blue in the dis-tance.

Just beyond the pink cliff I guided my kayak onto a sandy strip of riverbank. Little vegetation could survive in the dry soil other than a stand of larch and alder trees. This would be a good spot to watch for the film bag—I was surely ahead of it now—and to wait for Ben and Remy. I sat under a rather pitiful alder and began my vigil.

I wasn't worried. The guys would reorganize the raft, jury-rig another paddle, and come downriver. It might be a few hours, maybe a day in the worst-case scenario. Just a lit-tle discomfort to endure until they arrived. There was no way I could return upstream. It would be impossible to go against the current, and even more impossible to find the boys in the flooded forest—that tiny island of high ground was protected by a maze of thick woods awash in surging currents. I had no option but to sit there and wait. It was 4:00 P.M.

I stared at the river. Whole trees, logs, branches, bloated cows, a dead dog. But no green bag, no bright yellow raft, no Ben and Remy. I was certain that to leave the river's edge for even a moment was to invite disaster—the raft would pass on by and the boys would miss me. Or worse, that's when the film bag would ghost by. But staring at the rushing water was hypnotic.

As the sun began to set at 10:00 P.M., a feeling of gloom settled over me. I wondered where Ben and Remy were and what were they eating. My stomach growled its displeasure at having had nothing since breakfast.

At that altitude, nearly seven thousand feet above sea level, the temperatures were still dropping close to zero at night. Without a shirt, shoes, a sleeping bag, or a blanket, I did not relish my prospects. I checked my pockets: a lighter and a kicked-up multitool like a Swiss Army knife, with needle-nose pliers, screwdrivers, a file, a fish scaler, a leather punch, and a knife.

In the dying violet light, I began collecting firewood in preparation for the frigid night. I was already shivering. There wasn't much to burn, just some small, rotten branches, nothing that would burn for any length of time. But it was all I had—and better than nothing. I built a small pyramid of wood shavings.

Taking out the lighter, I thought about how it had been submerged several times in the last day. This triggered a momentary reverie. Seven years before, I had been aboard my twenty-seven-foot sailboat crossing the infamous Tasman Sea between Australia and New Zealand. For five days huge waves and sixty mile per hour winds had pounded my leaky vessel incessantly. By the time the storm abated, the cabin was a soggy mess. During the blow, I had eaten every bit of food that didn't require cooking. Craving a hot meal, I pulled out a carton of waterproof matches to light the burner and prepare a pot of rice. The first match fizzled. So did the next—and the next, and the next. The damp sea air had killed them. I ate the rice, pasta, onions, potatoes, and dried beans raw. Ever since, I've made a point of using lighters instead of matches. So, in this remote swath of wilderness near the Russian–Mongolian border, where few Westerners had ever ventured, with nothing to fall back on—here was the moment of truth.

The lighter hissed to life on the first flick. The yellow flame licked the shavings aflame and soon I had a crackling little fire, but the cold breeze from the mountains blew shivers down my spine. Even with the fire, I couldn't get totally warm.

I dragged my kayak as close to the fire as I could without melting its plastic shell. Then I pulled on the neoprene spray skirt and climbed inside. I huddled in the kayak for about an hour, growing more and more uncomfortable and cold. When I got up and tossed another stick or two on the fire, the inside of the kayak began to warm up. I realized that by removing the foot brace I could probably get my entire body inside the boat under the spray skirt. I climbed out again, quickly undid the screws with my multitool, lifted out the foot brace, and wriggled back inside. It was a tight fit, but I could pull the spray skirt closed over my head and trap all my body heat inside.

I lay in the darkness of the sealed kayak for about five minutes before claustrophobia and my need for oxygen left me gasping. I pushed my face out past the rubber skirt and gulped fresh air. Then I lay with only my face exposed, my body cramped and unable to move an inch in any direction. After an hour or so, the discomfort forced me out to stretch. The fire was dead and it would be too difficult to light another in the pitch black. No amount of calisthenics could warm me up, so I climbed back into the kayak. It, too, was now icy cold.

My teeth chattered, my muscles knotted and cramped, and my toes were in danger of frostbite. My legs fell asleep because of the constricted circulation and my back screamed in agony. I got up again, opened the multitool, and hacked away at the rude lump of plastic protruding from the seat that was torturing me relentlessly. It took forty-five minutes to chisel off the nub—a testament to the ruggedness of Riot Kayaks. The offending plastic polyp removed, I could finally lie in the kayak without feeling as though someone were sticking a stiletto into my kidneys.

*Friday, June 1*

The night had seemed endless, and no one could have welcomed the first gray heralds of dawn more than I. Around me, color was seeping back into the land, and the trees and steppe emerged from the shadows. Frost crystals blanketed everything. As light spilled across the valley, my own breath appeared as great white clouds of vapor. My toes didn't hurt anymore—they were numb.

By 9:00 A.M. a pink sun had lifted over the mountains, warming the air enough so that I could get out of the kayak. As my aches and pains dissipated and I stopped shivering, hunger and thirst began to torment me. I was reluctant to drink the river water because of the hundreds of decaying carcasses I'd seen. I had once been warned that some of the most dangerous pathogens are found in water contaminated by decomposing flesh. We had always filtered and boiled our water. But even though I had a fire, there was no way I could boil water without a container, and the last thing I needed was a major intestinal ailment.

I decided that the best strategy for the moment was to wait. As for food, I couldn't do any foraging, since I couldn't take my eyes off the river for more than a few seconds at a time. The river was so wide that Ben and Remy could easily pass and not see my tiny kayak pulled up on the shore. As for the film bag, I had abandoned all hope of seeing it again.

I estimated the site of the capsize to be about twenty or thirty miles upriver. Most likely Ben and Remy had taken longer to get organized than I had first guessed, and they had probably ended up having to camp there for the night. Surely they would have struck camp by early morning, though, knowing I had no emergency blanket, no clothes, and no supplies. They would make an effort to get downriver as soon as possible. I just had to be patient.

Meanwhile, I had to deal with that blowtorch of a sun. The day before, I had paddled under a similar acetylene sky, and my shoulders and face were now burned an angry red. Pulling the dense flotation foam off the foot brace, I began carving it with my multitool. It took about thirty minutes to shave and whittle the three-inch-thick dark gray foam into a crude but functional hat. The brim extended perhaps four inches in front of my face. It looked ridiculous, but it was fairly comfortable, and the shade over my singed eyes was a godsend.

I pulled out the two blue flotation bags stuffed into the stern, deflated them, and used their inflation cords to tie them together and create a pair of rudimentary shoulder pads. They needed frequent readjusting and did little to shade my stomach, but at least my shoulders were covered.

The hours crawled by, my stomach moaned, my throat grew parched, and my tongue thickened. The thirst was excruciating. Finally I could bear it no longer and I succumbed. I lay on the bank and took long, slurping gulps from the river. The water tasted so good! Once I had started, there was no point in being shy. I drank until my belly was swollen and my thirst was finally slaked.

I lit another fire and continued my vigil of watching for Ben and Remy. The rushing water was mesmerizing. I turned away from it and my gaze fell on the iridescent embers of the fire, which were equally bewitching. I awoke with a pool of drool on my chest, my head against the kayak, the fire dead and cold. The sun was still high in the sky. My watch said 2:00 P.M.

I frantically scanned up and down the river. Nothing. Had they passed? Would they have seen me? Jesus, that was the question. *Would they have seen me?* Probably not.

I sat down again. This was definitely not good. Surely they would have covered the twenty or thirty miles if they had begun paddling that morning. The river was rushing along; the raft would have made good time. They must have passed without seeing me. Then again . . .

My mind replayed the arguments over and over. How long should I wait? Hours? Days? Surely they had passed. But perhaps they had dawdled; perhaps they had got hung up on another snag.

The muddy water rushed on.

I was alone and starving in the wilderness without any real survival tools. Worse, even if I found help, I was in a Third World country with no money and no identification. After three years of drought, Mongolia had suffered a winter so severe that half the livestock had died. For a country whose main occupation is herding, that was a catastrophe. Starvation stalked the countryside. I was alone in an alien, in-hospitable land without even a shirt on my back. Where was that big yellow raft?

Four o'clock came and went. I amused myself playing with the ants, spiders, and beetles that marched industriously across the beach. Six o'clock—dinnertime—and little had changed except the angle of the flame in the sky and the sharpness of my hunger pains. I rekindled the fire, stood my kayak on its nose as a more obvious marker, and did a quick forage. I walked along the riverbank but found nothing—just scrubby trees and sandy soil. I ventured deeper into the woods. Away from the river, the soil became richer and the undergrowth thicker. After about twenty minutes, I returned to the riverside with a large bouquet of nettles and rhubarb.

I crumpled the nettles into a tight ball and soaked them in the river. Then I placed the soggy heap in the embers of the fire and covered them with hot rocks. I skewered the blushing stalks of rhubarb as if they were gourmet foot-long hot dogs and broiled them over the flames. They turned into a hot, sour mush that only a starving man would relish. The nettles could have passed for smoked spinach.

I took a long draw of murky river water and leaned back against my kayak. This was living. But my stomach groaned, far from content. I stared balefully at the dark roils and swirls of the river. I was tormented by the thought of another freezing night squeezed into my kayak.

A white birch murmured in the evening breeze. I recalled that a childhood friend's father had tapped his birch trees and boiled the sap down into syrup that was fabulous on pancakes. I slashed the tree's bark with my knife. Sap oozed out of the gash and I licked at it hungrily. It was bittersweet, but not bad. I sucked sap for nearly an hour while keeping my eyes on the river.

When I was finished, the fire was out and the heat of the day nearly gone. Still no Remy or Ben. Where were they? Had they died? Was I really alone in the middle of nowhere? I could wait no longer. I was becoming more and more convinced that they had passed me while I slept. There was also a chance that the flow of water in front of me wasn't the entire river. So far, the Selenge had been a convoluted labyrinth of braided channels. Behind the low, grassy hills, perhaps another branch of the river flowed and Ben and Remy had drifted down that, completely oblivious to me on the other side of the valley. I slipped my kayak into the water in the slim hope of finding my friends camped downstream. Anything was better than sitting there hungry, doing absolutely nothing.

The river was flowing deep and fast. On either side now was rolling, treeless steppe—perfect pasture. Within half an hour I spotted two *gers* set well back from the river's edge. As I drew closer, I could see two men silhouetted in the twilight as they filled large urns with river water. Nearby a bored ox stood harnessed to a wooden cart.

My arrival startled the two men and they jumped back. Immediately they began speaking rapidly to each other in Mongolian.

"*Sambano!*" I yelled (one of the few words of Mongolian I knew, *sambano* means "hello").

The men fell silent and stared. I'd forgotten to take off my foam hat, and the limp flotation bags hung loosely about my neck. I looked ridiculous.

"*Sambano,*" replied the younger man tentatively. He was perhaps twenty years old.

I smiled at them and slowly they smiled back. Then they erupted with dozens of questions—I think. It was incomprehensible.

"I don't speak Mongolian," I said in broken Russian.

They looked confused and rattled on.

The taller, slightly older man pointed to my kayak, said something to his partner, and the two of them burst into hysterical laughter. I had no idea what was going on. How could I tell them that I was in trouble, that our raft had flipped, and that I'd spent the last two days alone and hungry?

The men were peeing themselves over the kayak and my outfit. I gestured for them to try it out. The taller man looked at it suspiciously. He tapped it on the side and marveled at how light the paddle was. Then he cautiously slipped inside. I handed him the paddle and his pal pushed the kayak into the river. He had made barely two strokes before the kayak capsized.

The Mongolian by my side exploded in laughter and clapped me on the back, as if to say, "Good on ya! Serves the bugger right."

As his friend spluttered to shore, he was laughing too. He pulled himself out of the river and, from their animated conversation, I figured he was daring his friend to give the kayak a try. Not a chance.

Their shenanigans ended, the taller man introduced himself as Tengel; his younger friend was Batbayer. They loaded the last two urns of water onto the cart and beckoned me to follow them. I was exhilarated—surely they would at least shelter me for the night. I could deal with the hunger as long as I didn't have to spend the night in the kayak again; it was a torture chamber.

I followed the men into the nearest *ger* through the three-foot-high wooden door. An oil lantern cast a dim twilight inside the windowless home. About seven people of various ages sprawled on the floor. An attractive woman of about thirty-five, her long hair in a ponytail, bustled around the woodstove. The smell of some kind of simmering stew wafted through the air, making my stomach growl.

Tengel announced something to the crowd and all eyes turned to me. Smiles and questions were directed my way until Tengel held up his hand and spoke. I imagine he was saying something like, "He's mentally retarded and doesn't know how to speak," because everyone burst out laughing.

The woman at the stove handed me a bowl of jaundiced lumps and gestured for me to sit down on a yak skin. I had no idea what was in the bowl, but it looked more substantial than warmed-over nettles and birch sap. It was real food. I had not eaten proper food for more than thirty-six hours, and I was exhausted. I popped one of the chunks into my mouth and bit down hard. It was a jawbreaker—I almost broke a tooth.

As I sucked on the lump I began to detect a cheesy taste, and realized it must be dried yak's cheese. Everyone watched me. Fortunately, it was bloody good. And more food was coming! A girl of about twelve cut a flat sheet of dough into thin strips and tossed them into a large, sizzling wok. As the noodles cooked, she added chunks of meat. A few moments later, a chipped brown ceramic bowl of the steaming mixture was placed in front of me. It was great; the meat was tender and tasty, but a little different from anything I had tasted before.

"*Moo?*" I said to Batbayer, pointing at my plate with one hand and using the other to indicate horns on my head.

"*Neigh!*" he whinnied, shaking his head like a horse.

Everyone laughed. I did too, and continued with the meal. Afterward, sated for the first time in days, I could barely keep my eyes open. The rest of the family began slipping off to sleep and the other guests left for the night. Tengel handed me a warm skin, and within minutes I had fallen asleep.


*Saturday, June 2*

I awoke with a start. Inside, the *ger* was pitch black. I looked at the luminous face of my Timex—8:00 A.M. Damn, I'd overslept!

I bounced up and bolted outside. I scanned upstream and downstream—nothing. The men had left, save the old grandfather. The women and children stood in the doorway and outside the *ger*, watching me. The ponytailed woman beckoned for me to come back. Inside the *ger*, she offered me breakfast—a cold version of supper. As I ate, she reached into a small wooden chest and withdrew a pen and a piece of thick yellow parchmentlike paper. The woman offered me the pen and gestured for me to draw.

I sketched pictographs of my experiences. I drew a cartoon raft with the kayaks lashed on top of it. I drew three stick men inside the raft. I indicated a flipping motion with arrows and drew an upturned raft. I drew a river around the raft and Ben and Remy standing on the banks waving at me as I departed in a kayak.

The woman scrutinized the drawing and nodded sympathetically.

Throughout the morning I took shifts with the children on the bank, waiting for a yellow mirage to appear on the shimmering horizon. At midday the men came back on horseback. We gathered in the *ger* and the old man plucked tobacco from a leather pouch and rolled cigarettes with yellowed newspaper cut into rectangles. He offered the first dart to me, and soon we all were puffing away while the women prepared another round of horse meat and pasta.

After lunch, Tengel pointed suggestively to the ponytailed woman (whom I assumed was his wife) and to me. He made exaggerated thrusts with his pelvis while pointing back and forth between us. I laughed nervously. He repeated the crude gesture.

The woman smiled, settled herself on a hide, and beckoned to me suggestively. Tengel pointed to the baby snoring nearby, to my blue eyes, and to his wife, and again thrust vigorously with his hips. If they wanted a blue-eyed baby in exchange for their hospitality, I supposed I could oblige, I thought. I took a tentative step toward the woman. The dozen or so spectators—Tengel, his friends, the other women, the children—jostled for the best possible view. Nobody was going to leave. I was expected to do it with a studio audience!

I sat back down, my face flushed.

Everyone appeared to be disappointed. Tengel's wife rose sulkily and returned to washing dishes. I went back to the riverside, leaving the men smirking.

Watching the river was difficult. It strained my eyes, and my mind drifted with boredom. A few of the men wandered down and offered to relieve me, but they quickly tired of it too, going back to their horses or flocks. At about 1:30 P.M., the thunder of hooves from an arriving horseman brought everyone outside. The rider dismounted and spoke seriously to Tengel, his eyes flashing in my direction with every other word.

Tengel motioned me inside the *ger*. He took out the pictograph and pointed to the stick men, Ben and Remy. He indicated that the man had seen two men in a boat, and the horseman nodded mutely. Relief washed over me. They were downriver—all I had to do was catch up.

I hugged Tengel. Everybody was grinning. I hugged all of them. As I was about to push off, Tengel handed me a small silver pocketknife. He wanted to trade it for my multitool— a souvenir of the crazy man who had come down the river. I made the swap.

I pulled the plastic flotation bags over my head and covered my shoulders. Tengel laughed and shook his head, pulled off his T-shirt, and handed it to me. I thanked him. With a wave, I was down the bank and back in the river.

Within minutes the *gers* were far behind, and I was alone with the self-satisfied feeling that my ordeal was nearly over. My stomach was full, Ben and Remy were downstream, and I would soon be joining them. I dug into the water with long, hard strokes. They would pitch camp a few hours before sunset and I would be able to spot the tents on the riverbank. I paddled harder.

What must Ben and Remy be thinking? I had not seen

them in over two days. I prayed that they hadn't called home and spread word of my disappearance. My mother, who always assumes the worst, would be frantic. Weekly reports of our progress were being published and broadcast around the globe. It was the first time I had considered the broader repercussions of my predicament. I hoped Remy and Ben had handled our separation cautiously.

Every bend in the river played with my emotions. I was sure I would see the raft humping along up ahead. But dinnertime came and went—my stomach marked its passing with protest growls—and still no sight of them. Perhaps I had misunderstood the horseman, or perhaps he had been mistaken. Doubts dogged me like the Furies. They must be downstream, I reasoned, short of having had a catastrophe. Perhaps I had misunderstood how far downstream the herder had spotted the raft.

It grew too dark to continue without fear of passing them in the night. Dejectedly I pulled my boat up a slick clay bank, lit a fire of driftwood, and shivered listlessly in my kayak. As the temperature dropped, I lay uncomfortably counting the hours through the frigid night. At least Tengel's T-shirt provided a bit of extra warmth.

*Sunday, June 3*

I rose and foraged for food. There was no rhubarb, but I did find small onions growing among the nettles. I gathered a large bundle and brought them to the fire to roast. They were remarkably satisfying, caramelized sweet by the flames—far superior to hot nettles. I threw some onions in the kayak for later and left immediately. I hoped to catch Ben and Remy before they struck camp that morning.

We had decided while we were still in Canada that if we

got separated we would meet in the next major settlement. I remembered from the map that the next village on the river was Hutag, which I reckoned was about twenty miles away. If I didn't catch the raft before Hutag, the chase would end there, I was sure of it.

I paddled with purpose but conserved my energy. It was very hot, perhaps eighty degrees, and I took long drafts from the river. But I was growing more and more fatigued. I stopped paddling late in the afternoon, too weak and exhausted to move my arms. I let the current carry me, correcting my course occasionally with a few feeble strokes. My only goal was to reach Hutag. I drifted along quietly in the afternoon heat, my eyelids drooping. Twice the kayak started to roll as I drifted off to sleep, waking me with a start.

By about three, an urgent shout from the shore roused me completely. Was it Ben and Remy? I could make out three men on the riverbank waving and yelling. They didn't look like my friends, but they were still a long way off. I paddled toward shore.

For a moment I was disappointed when I saw that all three were Mongolian. Then I saw, nestled in the grass at their feet, our film bag. The men saw the look on my face, pointed at the bag, and guffawed.

I ran the kayak up on shore and climbed the bank to join them. Thank goodness, they were honest. We engaged in an incredible game of charades—I mimed what I'd been through and they pantomimed how they had found the bag. One of the men held up his fishing stick with some line wrapped around it and feigned a cast. He put a hand above his eyes as if seeing something out in the river. Then he indicated the bag and pointed to an eddy about 150 feet away, near a pile of boulders. He made swimming motions, pointing to the eddy and then to the bag.

I opened the SeaLine dry bag, amazed that, after three

days in the river, everything was still dry: spent film canisters and cassettes, thirty rolls of unused Kodak film, a paddling jacket, a pair of pogies (neoprene hand warmers that loop over the paddle), the video camera carrying bag, a supply of paper and pens, and even a creased copy of the *Vancouver Sun* announcing our departure from home two months before.

I was elated. Hutag was a few hours downstream, and soon I would be reunited with Ben and Remy. We'd be on our merry way once again. What a happy ending!

I offered the men pens as a token of my appreciation. The man nearest me shook his head and instead pointed to the newspaper. I handed it to him and the men excitedly began tearing it into small rectangles. The quietest member of the trio pulled out a pouch of tobacco and they began rolling cigarettes. Then they sat engaged in what appeared to be competitive smoking, watching with interest as I emptied the bag, which was too big to fit inside my tiny boat, and redistributed the various items inside and on top of the kayak, using cinch straps. It took little time, and I had soon bade them good-bye and was under way, heading for Hutag.

At about five, I saw wooden buildings and the smokestack of a sawmill three miles away. Drawing nearer, I couldn't help but think it resembled a town from a cowboy movie. Ramshackle plank buildings scattered the sloping hillside, and a few of the more important structures flaunted unpainted wooden false fronts that looked as if they were about to fall off. Horses tied to hitching posts waited patiently along the sides of the dirt main street. Kids were playing along the river's gravel edge, splashing in the water to cool off from the afternoon's heat. They waved and were soon swimming beside me, trying to climb up on the kayak as I slowly steered to shore. I spoke to the oldest-looking boy, a lad of about fourteen with a shaved head. "Two men,"

I said, pointing at myself and holding two fingers in the air. "You see?"

The dark-skinned adolescent stared mutely. He didn't understand. If anything, he looked scared. I drew a boat in the mud with two stick figures beside it. "You see?" I said again. He shook his head slowly. I wasn't sure if that meant he hadn't seen them or he didn't understand. The other kids stared blankly at me too. Surely Ben and Remy were around?

I undid the straps securing the precious film bag, shouldered it, and started toward the village, which was about two hundred yards from the river. My bare feet squelched through the mud, and sometimes I sank as far as my calves. I emerged on the far side of the marshy ground sporting crisp copper socks of mud.

A steep hill sloped upward to the town. I followed a trail to the top, where it met a mahogany dirt road that ran between two rows of weathered clapboard shacks. It was hotter away from the river, perhaps eighty-five degrees. Supposedly one thousand people lived in Hutag, but not one was to be seen. Exhausted, I trudged down the dusty track into the village. A heat headache boomed in the back of my head.

I passed a couple of horses idling at hitching posts. I could hear a domestic dispute somewhere, a man screaming at someone. As I came to the town's only crossroads, an old woman appeared, pulling a small cart bearing an empty water urn.

"*Sambano,*" I said, trying to sound cheerful.

She stared stonily at me. Then her gaze fell back to the dark dust and she continued her trek toward the river.

"*Sambano?*" I repeated at the departing figure. I could have been talking to the wind. The slatternly houses returned my gaze blankly. What to do? A gentle breeze provided a moment's respite from the heat, a horse whinnied, and I turned to see a horseman.

"*Sambano,*" I said.

The gray-haired man looked at me with hard jade eyes, and for a moment I thought he was going to give me the same treatment as the old woman. "*Sambano,*" he replied, stopping the horse to speak with me.

Using gestures and by drawing in the sand, I conveyed to him that I was looking for two men who had come down the river.

He shook his head: "*Ooguee.*"

I pointed again at the figures in the dust and looked pleadingly at him as if he had misunderstood.

He shook his head again. "*Ooguee.*"

I was alone. Devastated, I slumped down against the dry bag. The horseman left me there.

I fell asleep, and it was dark when I awoke. I found my way back to the kayak. The children had long since gone. I was hungry and homeless in Mongolia.

I thought about knocking on a door and asking for charity, but given the reception I'd received already that day, I wasn't ready for more rejection. I slid into the kayak for another night of uncomfortable slumber. Tonight, at least, the paddling jacket and the neoprene pogies would keep me and my feet warm. It meant I could sit upright, and that was more comfortable than being squished underneath the spray skirt. I also emptied the valuable cassettes from the dry bag into the stern of the kayak and slipped the twenty-five-gallon synthetic sack over my upper torso like a giant condom. I looked completely ridiculous, but I was warm and dry.

## Monday, June 4

I stared at the river for a long time, lost in thought. I was flummoxed. What should I do? Were Ben and Remy still upstream? Were they downstream? Were they dead? Or were they headed overland, having abandoned the expedition? Should I wait there or push on to Sühbaatar, the closest city downriver? Five days later, were my rafting partners still sitting where we had flipped? The distance from there to where I was now could be covered by raft in one long day.

Nothing made sense to me. Ben and Remy were intelligent fellows. They couldn't still be upstream, could they? No, there was no way they could fail to understand the importance of heading downstream as soon as possible to catch up with me. They knew I would be unable to return upstream; they knew I had no food, clothes, or money. Unless something dire had happened, they should be here. Perhaps they *had* carried on to Sühbaatar, about two hundred miles downriver.

If I'd had the luxury of food supplies, I could have waited patiently by the riverbank for a week. If my colleagues still hadn't arrived, then I would simply carry on downstream, full of energy. But without food, every day left me weaker. What should I do—sit and slowly starve? Assuming the odds were fifty-fifty that they were upstream or downstream, it made more sense to continue on down. Even if I didn't find my friends in Sühbaatar, I had a better chance of finding help there. As well, actually moving—feeling that I was making progress—would do wonders for my languishing psyche. The hungry idleness and boredom were torture.

I was addled, and I needed food. I picked up the film bag and staggered back to the village. Perhaps I could trade some Kodak film for something to eat. It took a bit of searching, but I found a store, a clapboard building devoid of paint, with a large, gaping door. I went in and smiled at the adolescent girl behind the counter. I've seen warmer cold fronts. Still, I went about my shopping.

The wooden shelves groaned with cans of corned beef,

biscuits, sardines, onions, ketchup, rice, pasta, and other staples—a cornucopia for a hungry man. I wanted it all. I pointed to a bag of sweet, biscuitlike flatbreads, two inches wide, half an inch thick, and six inches long. I held up two fingers; I reckoned the biscuits were the cheapest food that didn't require cooking. She placed two bags on the counter—twenty biscuits in total—and indicated on a piece of paper that the price was 2,000 togrogs (about $2).

I put a five-roll pack of 35-millimeter film on the counter and gestured "trade" by moving my finger back and forth. The girl shook her head and bolted out the back entrance. I stood stunned. What was that about? Should I leave? Did I look that disheveled and scary?

A moment or two later, a middle-aged woman entered the store and fixed me with a stern eye while the girl stood in her shadow. The woman took her place behind the counter, keeping me nailed to the floor with her gaze. She poked a finger at the piece of paper bearing the price of the biscuits, drumming on it to emphasize the price.

I pointed at the film. She shook her head. I opened up the dry bag and put two more film canisters on the table. The woman could have been a star poker player—not a flutter of her eyelids, nothing. I was desperate. The thought of eating nettles again for dinner instead of these sweet carbohydrates made me want to scream.

The woman waved her arm as if to dismiss me. I shook my head and refused to leave. "I'm starving, madam," I began in English. "Starving. Do you know how much this bread would mean to me? How much I crave even a morsel of food? Do you understand what a stupid predicament I am in because my friends aren't where they should be? Do you realize what an uncompromisingly cold bitch you are?"

She swept the film canisters off the counter into the pocket of her apron and shoved the bread at me. I grabbed it with

the speed of a pickpocket and was out the door like a ga-
zelle, grinning obsequiously and muttering my profoundest
thanks. I sauntered back to the kayak like a man who has just
won the lottery, my new lease on life clutched to my chest.

I sat on my kayak and considered my choices. If I rationed
the flatbreads strictly, the two bags would last three days. I
shuddered at the prospect of waiting in vain hope that Ben
and Remy would appear from upstream. Surviving in this
hard-bitten town would be painful, and I didn't think I could
do it. There was only one realistic alternative: to continue
downstream. If I paddled almost nonstop, I could get to
Sühbaatar in perhaps three or four days. It would be hard,
but I liked that idea better than just sitting there. Without resources, without language skills, and with nothing to do,
Hutag would be a hellhole for me. And what would I do when
the biscuits ran out?

I could no longer delude myself into thinking that I just
had to wait long enough and my saviors would come. In
Sühbaatar I had a better chance of finding help. Near the border, where the Trans-Mongolian Railway crosses into Russia,
Sühbaatar was home to roughly sixty thousand people.

My mind made up, I opened the first bag of biscuits and
withdrew two sticks. I nibbled at the first biscuit as if it were
the finest food—caviar or foie gras. Fabulous! The sweet,
crumbly bread coated the inside of my mouth; it was a tran-
scendent moment. I savored every swallow. When I had finished, I pushed off, leaving Hutag in my wake, a pretty
sight—to look back on.

The river was flat and the glacial surge had subsided. A
huge, empty distance stretched ahead of me; I could not fool
myself that a happy reunion was just around the next bend.
I had an enormous distance to cover with only a lunch box's
worth of food. And, at the end of it all, I might still find myself alone and destitute. I took long, slow strokes.

Patches of larch forest could be seen in the distance on the north slopes of hills to the south. As the hours passed, the forests became less intimidated by the river and ventured closer. At 2:00 P.M. I opened my spray skirt, reached into the kayak, and extracted two more precious breads, eating them slowly while drifting on the river, not daring to waste a moment on shore when I could be moving.

Coniferous thicket now cloaked the riverbanks, and somehow this comforted me. For me, forest always adds a touch of mystery to the landscape—so much might be hidden within. Open prairie seems empty to me, a stark reflection of how alone we are.

*Cuckoo, cuckoo.* The sound came sharply from the forest shadows. *Cuckoo, cuckoo.* I'd never heard a real cuckoo before, and it sounded just like a clock. Since the calls were repeated at fairly regular intervals, my bored mind began to wonder if that was why cuckoos had become such an integral part of the clock industry. After finishing my breads, curiosity got the better of me, and I started timing the cuckoo calls on my watch—forty-five seconds, ninety seconds, seventy seconds, eighty-eight seconds—there was no pattern. I was disappointed in the birds.

As I journeyed downstream, the land grew more rugged. In place of the weathered, ancient hills I had come through were fractured mountains faceted with granite cliffs. I entered a low, serpentine canyon, dreading the thought of running whitewater in my exhausted state. But, around a bend, the river straightened its run and threw itself down a steep incline.

I've never been on a river that flowed down such an extreme slope without rapids. There wasn't any kind of turbulence. The river simply picked up speed and calmly headed downhill. The incline lasted for at least three miles—as far as I could see before the next bend took it from sight. I imagined the river frozen solid and then someone gently placing a marble on it. The little glass orb would pick up speed, bouncing and clattering over tiny frozen ripples, on and on for a seeming infinity.

I had been in my kayak for 90 of the past 110 hours. Pressure sores were developing on my buttocks, and my twisted spine yearned for a horizontal Sealy Posturepedic. Even my toes and legs were becoming blistered from the unvarying contact between skin and plastic. I tried numerous positions to relieve the pain. I undid the spray skirt and pulled my knees up to my chest, but because the boat became too unstable I spent all my energy avoiding a capsize. I pulled both my legs out of the boat and draped them over the front deck. This was good for a few minutes—until my bum started to ache. I gave up searching for a new position and simply endured the pain.

About 8:00 P.M. I spotted wild roses growing at the base of a cliff. I had heard that rose hips were edible and high in vitamin C, so I paddled over and beached the boat. I grimaced as I got out of the kayak and forced my knotted muscles to do new tasks. Numerous wasps and flies buzzed around me as I climbed the loose scree to the rosebushes. It was still early in the season and there were no hips—just a blush of flowers and buds. I didn't know if they had any nutritional value, but I ate them nonetheless. The dark green buds were bland, slightly bitter, and fibrous. The pink and salmon flowers, on the other hand, were quite palatable—slightly sweet and not nearly as fibrous.

I wandered from plant to plant, eating the biggest and fattest flowers. There was also some rhubarb growing among the rosebushes, and I used Tengel's pocketknife to harvest the stalks, carefully cutting off the poisonous leaves. As I walked back to the boat, a pigeon-sized bird startled me as it flew out from under my feet. Its nest must be nearby, I figured, and began searching. On the rock face I found a nest of mud, sticks, and straw the size of a cereal bowl. Inside were three speckled eggs a little bigger than quail eggs.

Normally I'm a conservationist, but at that moment I was starving. I picked up an egg and cracked its thin shell by squeezing my fingernails together. I pulled off the top and inside was a mess of ruby veins and milky fluid. I closed my eyes and emptied the contents into my mouth. The warm, rich egg slipped down my throat. Delicious! I briefly thought about rationing the other two but decided they were too fragile for the journey. I slurped them down too, hoping it wasn't an endangered species.

Back at the kayak, I nibbled on a stale biscuit. Then I stowed the rhubarb and pushed into the river again.


When the last iridescent streaks of day had been wrung from the sky, I headed toward the riverbank to retire for the night. Then, a few feet from shore, I began to ponder the futility of "camping" through the relatively short period of darkness. I could spend a sleepless night sitting in my kayak on the shore, or I could be out on the river. Even if I didn't paddle at all, I would at least gain some progress from the current. The daytime warmth was dissipating rapidly, so I put on my watertight paddling jacket, covered my fingers with the neoprene pogies, and headed back into the river.

I still couldn't believe my luck in having found the film bag. Without that precious bag, I would have no biscuits and no warm paddling jacket. I had been able to find that tiny, camouflaged sack, yet two men and a bright yellow raft had disappeared off the face of the planet.

A veil of darkness obscured my view of the river below, and I shivered nervously. The river was full of lethal dangers that in the light of day could easily be avoided. Night was different. I shuddered at the thought of how easy it would be to get swept into a semisubmerged tree, its branches raking the inky water like the tines of a fork. A logjam or a set of rapids could quietly swallow me up and the world wouldn't notice. Even I wouldn't be fully aware of what was happening as my life was stolen from me. There would be a thump in the blackness and next thing I would be underwater, a blind man fighting a losing battle with the current. Perhaps a few days later, a herder would come to the river's edge in sunny daylight with his water urns. He would find my body tangled in a mess of fallen trees—a white corpse undulating in the current, its limp hands waving to the fish.

I tried to suppress these morbid thoughts and turned my mind to friends at home and happy scenes from my past. A dusting of stars hung above, but they shed little light and the moon had not risen. I could see the blinking navigation lights of a jet telegraphing its way across the sky. I imagined the passengers nibbling on their meals, sipping wine, and watching a bad in-flight movie. Civilization was right there—so close it seemed I could reach out and touch it.

A long, lingering growl from my abdomen ended my reverie. But more worrisome than my discontented stomach was a rumble in the distance. Unable to see, I had no idea what was disturbing the river. The ominous sound became a dull roar and passed harmlessly to my left. Still I couldn't determine its source.

In the black fog I found myself in, I couldn't even tell where the riverbanks were. Occasionally I bumped into a rock or a gravel shoal. Sometimes I drifted too close to shore and could feel the scraping of the bottom. Thankfully, those were the worst hazards I encountered.

Eventually the moon rose and I could see moderately well. But the temperature on the river was close to freezing. I paddled vigorously to stay warm—harder than I had during the day. Still, I was chilled; my teeth chattered within minutes if

I stopped for a rest. It became a routine: paddle till exhaustion stopped me and then rest until my teeth were chattering.

## Tuesday, June 5

The garnet gash on the horizon that signaled the sun's return was a joyous moment. I promised myself that once it warmed up, I would find a comfortable spot ashore and sleep. By about nine the day had warmed to a bearable temperature, and I made for a picturesque grassy bank on a little island. At last I could sleep relatively comfortably!

I enjoyed two biscuits for breakfast and lay down on the beach feeling that I might make it after all. An exhausted, sleepy feeling enveloped me, and I wriggled my body to create the perfect hollow in the warm sand. All night long, as I'd voyaged through that terrifying darkness, I had kept myself sane by envisioning this moment—blissful sleep and rest for my aching muscles.

Not two minutes after I lay my head down, clouds of blackflies and mosquitoes began their attack, rising from the river's edge and swarming me. The nights were no longer dropping below freezing, and the bug season had well and truly begun. For half an hour I tried to outwit my tormentors. I wrapped my head in Tengel's T-shirt, enclosed my torso in the paddling jacket, and covered my feet with the spray skirt. It was no use. The stinging, bloodsucking clouds made their way through the cracks and gaps, making my life a misery. It was agonizing. I was so tired and sleepy, the sand was so soft and flat, and the air temperature was a perfect seventy degrees.

"LEAVE ME ALONE!" I screamed at the insects. I was close to having a nervous breakdown. If only I could get some decent sleep.

The number of blackflies was only increasing, and now I

was inhaling them with every breath. They were flying into my eyes and ears, and I realized I had no choice but to climb back into my kayak and escape to the center of the river—replacing one form of torture with another.

On the river I tried to sit upright while my head did the sleep-jerk over and over again. It was five days now since I had last seen my friends, and I'd hit rock bottom. The lack of sleep and sustenance was grinding me down; I didn't know how much longer I could survive. My emaciated body was in constant pain from living in my yellow sardine can.

But the worst part was not knowing when or if it would ever end. For all I knew, Remy and Ben might be back in Canada. Maybe there was more damage to the raft than I had been aware of and they couldn't continue. After waiting for me for a couple of days, they might have hiked out to the nearest road and escaped from this godforsaken land. Who knew? Strangely, I now found it hard to visualize reuniting with them. Somehow it seemed that my present way of life was meant to continue for eternity. The river would never change, I'd continue finding just enough food to keep me alive, and Sühbaatar and the rest of my life in Canada would remain a figment of my imagination—along with my two friends.

Nervously I began to wonder if I was going nuts. Maybe Sühbaatar didn't exist at all, maybe I had somehow dreamed it up in my food-deprived state of desperation. Maybe civilization didn't even exist. Perhaps the only real things in this world were the river and the goddamned kayak. Somehow the world of automobiles, skyscrapers, and fancy restaurants seemed just a wild and crazy vision—a dream.

I had to focus. Just keep going. "Stay on the river and focus," I said out loud. "One day you will lie in a bed again. One day you really will sit in a restaurant and order a mouthwatering dish."

All day I paddled like a zombie, my mind blank, my eyes staring downstream. If I had to urinate, I did so in a cup-shaped piece of plastic cut from the kayak seat and tossed the pee overboard. I rinsed the same scoop and used it to drink water from the river, no longer caring whether it was safe. I munched on rhubarb stalks and paddled without a break.

I could see dark clouds building on the horizon, tall, murderous-looking thunderheads. A wind picked up, teasing the river into a heavy chop. Soon I was facing waves that fought me to a veritable standstill. But when the thirty-mile-an-hour, dust-laden winds had all but arrested my progress, I began paddling hysterically. Instead of waiting on the shore for the storm to subside, I became enraged, and my anger allowed me to draw energy from my deepest reserves. My paddle tore violently through the water, ripping and spraying—almost to no avail. On some of the more exposed parts of the river, I would barely cover five hundred yards over the course of an hour.

Now would have been the time to stop and sleep. The wind would keep the insects at bay, and I could conserve my precious energy. But the rational part of my brain was no longer in control. Instead, the primitive depths of my cerebellum had taken control. I was going to Sühbaatar—and nothing would stop me. The storm was merely an adversary that needed to be defeated.

"DAMN YOU, STORM!" My screams were lost in the gale. "YOU CAN'T STOP ME!"

I was a veritable Lear on the Selenge, howling at the cosmos.

In the midst of the mounting tempest, a man appeared on the riverbank. It was an odd, mystical scene, like something you might see in a Chinese rice-paper painting: a sage with a long, wispy beard falling to his chest, calmly surveying nature's gargantuan fury. I was startled to see anyone, let alone someone meditating in the midst of the growing storm and the raging river.

I pulled the kayak ashore and caught his attention. "You see boat?" I asked, tapping the side of my kayak.

The wizened old man stared at me—I must have been quite a picture. The wind howled around us. I scratched a picture of a boat in the dirt. The old man nodded vigorously and made a motion as though pulling on imaginary oars.

I nodded excitedly.

He pointed at me and held up two fingers. "Two men," I cried gleefully. He nodded. Hallelujah!

The old man pointed to a shaft of sunlight lancing through the clouds. He arced his arm from one horizon to the other, indicating the solar transit, and held up two fingers. "Two days!" I said, overjoyed. "Two days? They come by two days ago?"

He smiled at my enthusiasm. Two days ago!

If I understood the old man's gestures correctly, Ben and Remy must really have been moving. The old man motioned to me again. He pretended to be asleep. What did that mean?

Heavy rain began to fall and the wind continued. Hmmm. I still wasn't sure what the sleeping gesture meant—maybe he wanted to know where I was sleeping? Who knew? I thanked the old man for his information and returned to the kayak. Assuming that I hadn't misunderstood, I probably wouldn't catch up to Ben and Remy before Sühbaatar. I wondered how far it was to my destination. Without a map for reference, I had absolutely no idea how far I had traveled. I guessed I had another couple of days to go, maybe three. I could have asked the old man, but I had learned from experience that asking for distances from river folk tends to result in less than reliable answers. In most cases, it leads to disappointment.

The rain lashed down in torrents as I paddled back into the current and into an even darker night, my world little more than pain, paddling, and cold. I no longer knew whether I was tired from lack of sleep or because I was in the early stages of hypothermia. My teeth had been chattering and I had been shivering for hours.

Black, black, black—not the slightest glimmer of light stimulated my retinas. My eyes could have been torn from their sockets, and I wouldn't have noticed the difference. Still, I couldn't bring myself to stop. What would I do? Sit in the mud, a sopping, shivering, pathetic mess? My paddling was without direction, since I had no way to orient myself. Over the hours I must have paddled toward every point of the compass—upriver, downriver, and across the river. I paddled only to keep warm. Periodically, in that sea of ink, the bottom of my boat would hit mud. I would simply turn around and head in the opposite direction.

About midnight the wind began to ease, but the rain continued more heavily than ever. My teeth had been chattering nonstop for four hours; I was beginning to feel like I had lockjaw. Muscles all over my body were cramping spasmodically, and I began to fear that I might involuntarily capsize and be unable to extricate myself from my kayak. *Just keep paddling . . . just keep paddling,* I told myself.

At two in the morning I could just make out the faint glow of the rising moon through the clouds. I could now use the moonlight to orient myself. The river was supposed to be flowing east, so I paddled straight for the barely perceivable glow. My collisions with the muddy riverbank became less frequent.

There was something odd about the moonlight, something unnatural. Two hours of paddling later, the angle of the light hadn't changed. It looked almost like the glow of a city . . . could it be? I tried not to get excited; I didn't want to set myself up for crushing disappointment. It had to be the moon. But then again . . .

Back in Hutag, when I had initially calculated how long it

would take to get to Sühbaatar, I had factored in a break of six hours a day, and I had instead been moving almost constantly. The current had been galloping along too, perhaps faster than my conservative estimate of four miles an hour. Still, if the light ahead really was my destination, I must have been going like hell.

By four-thirty I was certain. Sühbaatar was mine!

I gobbled four biscuits and drove my paddle through the water, fueled by euphoria. A short time later, as the first timid light of dawn penetrated the glum skies, I reached the outskirts of a concrete city. Sühbaatar was still asleep, and the rain was falling in sheets. Unsure what to do, I pushed my kayak onto a lonely bank, pulled the dry bag over my head to protect me from the rain, and shivered off into unconsciousness.

Shot of the Ider River with raft as a speck.

## AN "ARRESTING" TIME IN SÜHBAATAR

*Wednesday, June 6*

I stirred into motion again at 8:00 A.M. and paddled the mile or so into Sühbaatar through torrential rain. I was a yak's spit from the Russian border, as the guidebooks like to say. The city offered a cold, hard face in the gray rain. I prayed that Ben and Remy were waiting for me.

I dragged the kayak up a muddy bank near the brick train station. People stared as I passed. Who wouldn't? I was bearded, grubby, soggy, shivering, and shoeless, and peering at the world through eyes turned into glowing embers by sleep deprivation. God, I hoped the boys were at a local hotel with money, clean clothes, and food.

I stumbled up to the railway station hotel. The plump woman behind the desk lowered her teacup and eyed me as if I were a touch of indigestion.

"My friends. Two men. Here?" I held up two fingers, knowing my simple English would not be understood.

She stared mutely.

I decided to try a different approach.

"Room for one," I said, pointing at myself.

"Passport," she demanded coldly, holding out a creased hand.

"No have passport. No have money. Will have later. Please, room for one."

She kept her hand out. Very cold, and getting colder. The look in her eyes would freeze rivers. Withered, I turned tail.

Too bushed to search for Remy and Ben, I walked into the train station, put my kayak on the floor, and took a seat. Relax for three hours, I thought. Dry off, warm up; the rain will have abated and I can begin the hunt. I peeled off my dry-dry top, which I'd been wearing nonstop for the past four days. Unlike a regular rain jacket, that garment allows absolutely no air circulation to take place. Awash in my own putrid smell, I fell into a deep sleep, surrounded by women in smart gray skirts and high heels and well-dressed Mongolian men in Western shirt-and-slacks combos under imitation-Chinese ski jackets.

"Passport!"

My ears rang as I was rudely awakened by a nudge in the ribs from a uniformed policeman.

"My passport no here," I said. "Friends have passport."

"Passport!" he repeated.

Another policeman materialized from the shadows and stood menacingly nearby. I held my hands up in the air in the

universal language of surrender: "No passport! *Ooguee* passport! *Nyet* passport!"

They understood. The officer indicated for me to follow.
They put my kayak into a storage room and led me into a
dimly lit office furnished with a plastic laminate desk and
four steel-and-plastic chairs. The first police officer pointed to
a seat and I flopped down. He said something to his partner,
who departed, shutting the door.

The first policeman settled behind the desk and we sat
silently across from one another for about ten minutes. A
woman of about twenty, dressed in camouflage fatigues,
walked in. She spoke with the policeman and then turned and
addressed me. "Hello, sir," she said.

They were the first words of English I'd heard in a long time.
I was staggered. "Hello, how are you doing?" I stammered.

She smiled. "Not bad, thank you. Lieutenant Chentio
want know why you here. Why no passport?"

Over the next hour, using broken English, diagrams, and
maps they supplied, I explained how I had arrived in the farthest reaches of central Asia with nothing more than the tattered clothes on my back, an odd-looking canoe, a sack full of
film, and a wild story.

They learned all about my expedition and about the flip,
and that it had been almost a week since I had last seen my
friends and begun living off the land. The police officer was
clearly much more sympathetic after the translator finished
relaying my harrowing account.

"Follow me," he beckoned.

The officer and the interpreter led me out of the train station to the local army headquarters, a block away. Men and
women in camouflage doing drills filled the parade ground. I
was led to an office decorated with maps and photographs.
Bookcases crammed with paperwork stood on either side of a
cracked window.

"Sit down," the woman said, nodding to a padded seat near the door.

Two men entered. One barked at a soldier outside the door. The grunt disappeared, returning almost instantly with a tray of thickly buttered black bread and a thermos of tea. Ecstasy! I couldn't believe my luck.

Over the following hours, the senior officers sat talking about me in Mongolian. Phone calls were made to Ulaanbaatar, the head immigration office was contacted, and even Nassan was telephoned at her guest house. Every so often, the translator asked me a question and relayed the answer, and one of the men would talk into the telephone or fall into an animated, but to me incomprehensible, discussion.

One thing was evident—Ben and Remy weren't in town.

The men arrived at some sort of agreement. "We will finish this later," the translator said, and motioned for me to follow her out of the office. "For now Lieutenant Bolor will look after you."

She led me into the next office, where a potbellied man of about twenty-five slouched in an easy chair, his feet on the desk, snoring. The smell of alcohol was pervasive.

"Bolor!" the translator said sharply.

He opened his bloodshot eyes and stared at us, rubbed the veined orbs, and said something to me in Russian.

"He is not Russian. He is Canadian," the woman said in English.

"Hey, man, how's it going?" he responded, offering a hand. "I don't get to use my English too often."

I couldn't believe it. It was the best English I'd heard spoken in Mongolia.

"Are you hungry, my friend? Come on, let's get this man some decent food." He yelled to the soldier standing guard at the door.

"How do you drink in Canada?" Bolor asked.

"Beer, whiskey, rum—all sorts," I answered.

"Yes, but *how* do you drink?" Bolor repeated. "I'm talking about your hard drinks. Do you add water, ice, soda? Do you sip it? Do you use big glasses or shot glasses?"

Bolor rose, pulled a key out of a small drawer in the desk, and unlocked a large metal cabinet. The top half contained dozens of handguns, the lower a rack of rifles standing at attention.

"Are they Russian?" I asked.

"Of course they are Russian," Bolor replied. "Do you think we buy our guns from China?" He turned from what he was looking for in the cabinet. "And the Americans," he added, rolling his eyes, "they charge too damn much!"

He laughed and reached for something behind the long guns. Then he produced a bottle of vodka. "Now I will show you how we drink. This is our little secret, though."

He closed the cabinet just as the guard returned with a big bowl of stew, Russian bread, and another thermos of tea.

"Eat, eat, my friend. And what size of feet do you have?" Bolor said, looking at my bare feet.

"Ten."

"No, no. European."

"About forty-two, I think."

"You need boots." Again he barked at the sentry in Mongolian. "Now let us drink," Bolor said, passing me a mug of vodka.

I downed it in one draft. "How come you speak such good English? Have you lived abroad?"

He clapped a meaty hand on my shoulder and laughed. "We Mongolians can't afford to go on holidays abroad. I can barely afford the staples such as vodka. No, my friend, I just had a very good teacher from San Antonio, Texas, who taught at our military school."

"So why is your English better than everyone else's?"

Bolor shrugged. "Some people are good at riding horses. I am good at learning languages. I speak Russian too. Have some more vodka."

He refilled my mug as I tucked into the meal. It was the first warm food I'd had in a long time, and I began to feel better and better.

Two hours later, a decision had been made as to what would be done with the bizarre Canadian. I would be billeted in a hotel, and when Ben and Remy arrived, I would pay the bill. I would receive army rations three times a day and would not be allowed to travel anywhere without the army's permission, since I didn't have a passport—not that I could have or would want to in my penniless state. I was overjoyed. What a fabulous solution!

It kept getting better. Two female officers in short skirts led me to the hotel. It was the same one I had tried to book into that morning, and I smiled smugly at the woman behind the desk while the officers told her I would be staying there—whether she liked it or not.

"Room forty-two," Officer Batjargal said, handing me the key. "Follow us."

The room was spare: two small single beds covered with wool blankets. There was no other furniture.

"The toilet is down the hall," Batjargal said. "You can clean up there. We bring food later."

With that, the officers left.

I lay down on the bed. It was fabulous, but my fetid smell drove me to the washroom. It was almost as rank as I was. In one corner was a toilet, the basket beside it overflowing with crumpled pieces of newspaper covered in feces. There were two basins with no mirror. I could coax water out of only one tap—it was icy cold—but I did my best, giving my filthy, greasy body a frigid, soapless scrub. I returned to my room damp and smelling worse than ever, but I couldn't have cared less. I collapsed on the bed and slept the sleep of the dead.

An incessant banging on my door woke me about 7:00 P.M. A young male soldier of about eighteen wearing khaki fatigues stood there smiling, holding a large jar of steaming food. I dove into the stew of beef, pasta, and potatoes. He watched, fascinated, as if my eating habits were better than television.

He politely declined when I offered a piece of bread. When I finished he collected the jar and spoon, reached into his pocket, and handed me some chocolates. With a wink, he left.

### Thursday, June 7

My primary goal, now that I had a secure base, was to let the rest of the world know I was alive. After breakfast, I headed into town. The railway station was the hub of economic activity. Trains rolled out laden with logs and lumber destined for China. Others, hauling copper ore, chugged in the other direction—across the frontier into Russia for processing. Lieutenant Bolor had told me there were too many Russians working in Mongolia's copper industry. "We have the copper, and they take the money."

Most of the housing I saw consisted of squat five- and six-story concrete apartment blocks. It looked like a ghetto. I made my way to the post office and the public telephones. A man at a desk near the entrance beckoned.

"Telephone? I like use," I said in English.

He handed me a form and a pen. The Mongolian script was only a graphic design to me; I could not read what it said. On a calculator the man indicated the number 1,000—1,000 togrogs, or about $1.

"I make collect call, no free?" I babbled in pidgin English. I felt as though I were in a Monty Python sketch, as if pidgin English were more understandable than regular conversational speech.

He tapped firmly on the calculator. I offered a roll of Kodak film from my pocket. "Trade film for phone call?" I said, twirling my fingers in the only true Esperanto—charades.

He shook his head. I left.

It had been more than a week since I had last seen Ben and Remy. They must be puzzling over my fate—heck, I had left them wearing only a pair of pants. They probably weren't even sure whether I had a multitool. I was certainly baffled about them. Where were they? Were they all right? Surely, with all the gear, food, and money, they were okay. Maybe the boat was damaged.

But they also had two satellite telephones. Even if one had conked out, the other should be working. I was sure everyone back home had heard about my disappearance. My mother would have been frantic when she heard I was missing with no food, gear, or money.

A woman in a gray skirt and blouse approached, hurrying awkwardly along in her high heels with the look of someone late for work.

"Internet?" I asked her, my hands miming typing on a keyboard.

She pointed to the north, barely breaking her stride. I crossed my fingers and lit out in the direction she had indicated. After a few blocks, I stopped a Mongolian man and went through the same mime. He looked at me as if I were mad.

I continued. The next person pointed west. I indicated my thanks and headed that way. I stopped a third; she pointed more southeasterly, almost back the way I'd come. I walked in that direction. A block or so later, I asked another, sure I was going to spend the day going around in circles. But this person seemed much more assured. He nodded and indicated a block that way and around a corner. I found it within minutes—at the local library.

"Internet?" I asked the librarian.

She nodded and quickly seated me at the computer. I didn't mention that I was penniless—and togrog-less.

Half an hour later the deed was done. I sent messages to my mother, my sister, and Dan saying that I was alive and well. I asked each of them to relay that to Remy's pager, along with the news that I was in Sühbaatar. I knew Remy regularly used a satellite phone to check for messages on his pager. Soon everyone would know I was fine.

The librarian handed me a slip of paper: a bill for 2,700 togrogs. I smiled at her. I didn't care what happened now. The messages couldn't be yanked back from cyberspace—they were gone. I handed her three rolls of Kodak film. "Trade," I said warmly, my free hand doing the talking. She shook her head, obviously irritated. I sat back down in my chair and shrugged. "No money," I said. "Just film."

We played tennis for half an hour. She would point to the bill and I would shrug. Back and forth we went.

"Only film. I pay you when friends arrive. The film is much more valuable, so I make sure to pay later." Finally realizing that I was adamant and had nothing better to offer, she put the film in a drawer. I pointed to the calendar: "I pay in three days."

The librarian nodded incredulously and went back to her work.

I returned to my room to find Officer Batjargal and another woman waiting. "We think maybe you sick of army food," Batjargal said. "We bring you some different food."

Her friend, Ihagvaa, was dressed in civilian clothes. She handed me a plastic bag containing a container of Chinese food and a bottle of mango soda. I felt guilty. Soldiers don't make a lot of money in Mongolia, and here they were spending their meager earnings on treats for me.

"Thank you. You shouldn't have," I said gratefully.

"It is nothing," Batjargal said, smiling. "You spend many days on the river with no food. You must be hungry."

We chatted for ten minutes and then they went back to work. The Chinese food was divine. An hour later, another knock on the door. The soldier who had delivered my breakfast stood with a tray of army rations.

"Thank you very much, sir," I said, though my words were incomprehensible to him. "I'm going to get fat living here."

I ate another meal.

A few hours later, another rap at the door. A soldier of about twenty stood there, shifting awkwardly. "Hello, my name Ulzikutag. I see you yesterday over at base," he said, extending his hand. "I hear about your problem and think you might be hungry."

Ulzikutag handed me a plastic bag containing sweetbread. I invited him to sit down.

"I am very interested in Canada. Number two in world, isn't it?" he asked.

I nodded.

"Ontario. Quebec. Celine Dion. Toronto. Vancouver. And the hockey player . . . the one with the big bent nose . . . aaah . . . Wayne Gretzky! Yes, he is the Great One, isn't he? In Mongolia, we play a bit of hockey—not much, though."

"Wrestling is the sport of Mongolia," I said, able to speak from firsthand experience.

He nodded.

"I must go back to work now. I will visit again tomorrow if it is okay," Ulz said.

"Of course."

I was sitting munching the sweetbread when there was another knock at the door. It was the army dinner ration—a jar of turnips, potatoes, and mutton.

Later, Lieutenants Bolor and Chentio arrived. "We thought you might be a little hungry with just the army gruel, so we brought you a little more," Bolor said, handing me a packet of cookies and two beers. "Sleep well, and see you tomorrow."

I was overwhelmed by the generosity of the soldiers. As Bolor turned to leave, Chentio said something to him in Mongolian.

"Oh yeah, Chentio wants you to have these," Bolor said, passing me 3,000 togrogs. "Now you can buy yourself some toiletries and a few coffees."

I was speechless. They grinned and were gone. Mongolians—the most generous people in the world.

With my new bar of soap, I spent an hour scrubbing my putrid clothes in the sink before calling it a day.

*Friday, June 8*

I had discovered the worst razor in the world: "Big," made in Korea. It tore out every hair on my face and shredded my skin. More pleasantly, I brushed my teeth for the first time in nine days. I was also able to lather and wash my entire body; not quite a shower, but I sure felt cleaner and smelled a whole lot nicer. Putting on my dry and crispy-clean clothes, I felt human again.

After breakfast, Bolor arrived. "I received a call from the Canadian consulate in Ulaanbaatar," he said. "You must come down to the base now. You will meet the commander."

The room, with its cathedral-like, fourteen-foot ceiling, trembled with authority. A large older man, whom I assumed to be the colonel, sat in a thronelike chair behind a heavy, solid oak desk. Expensive rugs draped the walls. Two board-room tables created an aisle leading up to the desk. He motioned me to sit down behind one table. Lieutenant Bolor was told to sit at the other.

Six or seven officers entered; each saluted the colonel and took a seat near Bolor. Three women—I imagined there to translate—sat at my table. We sat in silence, apparently waiting for someone else.

The colonel looked at his watch and spoke. The ponytailed woman beside me translated. "You realize you no arrested?" she asked.

"Of course not. You guys have been treating me well. You help me."

"The colonel is concerned. He said the Canadian consulate call this morning. A Canadian journalist phoned and asked about you. He say you are arrested at Russian border."

Oh, God. What kind of rumors were circulating back home? I imagined the newspaper headlines: "Canadian Rafter Faces Siberian Firing Squad." Back on Vancouver Island, my mother must have been catatonic with worry.

"We just want to make it clear," she said. "You must stay here because you have no identification, but you no under arrest."

I nodded.

The colonel asked another question. The girl paused, unable to think of the English equivalent. Bolor tried to help from across the room. "He says—"

The colonel barked. Bolor lowered his head to look at the table.

"We are also worried about your friends," the ponytailed woman added. "If the water is strong, if they go over the Russian border by accident . . ." She paused as she tried to convey the gravity of their situation. "Maybe shoot."

The fenced-off border region between Russia and Mongolia is a no-go zone. The guards stationed in the many lookout towers along the razor-wire line have orders to fire at anyone foolish enough to wander without authorization into no-man's land. I didn't know how much danger Ben and Remy might be facing. I had traveled the same stretch of water, and the feeble current of the Selenge wasn't likely to overpower the raft and push them beyond the Orhon River into Russia. Ben and Remy had a good map and would know that they must hang a right to reach Sühbaatar.

Nonetheless, the army seemed fairly concerned about this danger. "Is there any way we can warn your friends?"

"Perhaps. If I can contact my mother, I can leave a message for her to pass on if they call her. I can give her Bolor's number. They phone Bolor."

The colonel's cell phone rang, to the tune of a trashy Western pop song. It was the Canadian consulate on the line, so he handed the phone to me. Arianaa, a consulate employee, had heard from my mother, who had received my e-mail and imagined the worst—her half-starved son trapped in a distant hinterland without a penny to his name, cast as the lead in a Mongolian remake of *Midnight Express*. She had phoned the Canadian High Commission and asked if they could help me. They, in turn, had contacted Arianaa, who tracked me down through the Sühbaatar police department—not, however, before a Canadian reporter had called and asked about my "arrest."

"Everything is fine," I assured Arianaa. "The army is feeding me well, I am sleeping in a hotel, and it is just a matter of waiting until Ben and Remy arrive.

"Oh yeah," I finished, "could you do your best to dispel any rumors that the army is brutalizing me?"

I handed the phone back to the colonel. The meeting was over. Officer Batjargal and her friend Ihagvaa joined me as I left the base. "Are you hungry?" she asked in slow English. "You like join us for lunch?"

We went to a small restaurant near the market and I was treated to bean noodles, vegetables, beef, and a cup of coffee. The women told me they were taking an English course at the library, and it wasn't often they got to practice with a real English-speaker. I felt a bit better about my mooching, since they were getting something out of it.

"You play chess?" Ihagvaa asked.

"Sure. Not very well, but I play. You play?"

She smiled like a hustler. "Yes, I will play you later."

I returned to my room, still a bit worried and gloomy about Ben and Remy. Traveling at a reasonable speed, it shouldn't have taken them more than five or six days for the raft to get here. Were they sitting at the point of capsize waiting for me? Did they think I was going to come crashing out of the bushes with a big silly grin on my face ten days later? I was beginning to feel dark about them. But at least I wasn't starving anymore.

At 8:00 P.M. Lieutenant Bolor arrived in a crisp white shirt with epaulettes—his uniform when performing immigration duties on the train. "Colin, I want you to have dinner at my house and meet the wife and kids. I asked my wife to make a special Mongolian dinner for you."

"I'd love that."

We went to his cozy duplex on the east side of the city. His wife, a slim, pretty woman, was watching a Russian game show on TV.

"My wife studied medicine in Russia," Bolor said. "Now she thinks she's Russian. We get three clear Mongolian stations, but she always has to watch this." He gestured at a snowy, interference-plagued screen. I could make out a gray-haired man asking questions of an enthusiastic audience. When someone gave the right answer—I presume that's what was going on—he clamped a traditional Russian fur hat with earflaps on his or her head. If I hadn't known better, I would have sworn it was a U.S.-produced satire.

Bolor's three-year-old son came running up to me with a friendly smile, until he saw my eyes. The blue freaked him out and he ran away, screaming.

Dinner was steamed dumplings, vegetables, and beef stew accompanied by honey tea. However, as I lay on the couch with a full belly, I had difficulty enjoying the evening. I was too worried about Ben and Remy.

*Saturday, June 9*

At 11:00 A.M. I found myself in a tidy one-bedroom apartment belonging to a friend of Bolor's, an immigration officer. There were five of us sitting in a circle on the living room floor—a policeman, a customs officer, Bolor's friend, Bolor, and me. In the middle stood a bottle of vodka. I had been roused from the hotel, brought to the apartment, and told, "It is Saturday, the day of merriment."

The immigration officer had just moved in. There was no furniture other than mats on a pale blue carpet. Curtains and a curtain rod lay near the window waiting to be installed. The walls were covered with paper roses on a pale pink background.

"Drink, drink," the immigration officer said, handing me a mug. He spoke no English save the words *hello* and *drink!*—the latter always an exclamation admonishing one for abstemiousness.

We had been throwing back vodka for a few hours when Bolor received a call that sobered him up. "I must go to the Russian border," he said, hanging up. "There is a small problem. A wolf hunter got shot in the leg while riding his horse over the border." As he was about to leave, he added, "Hey, would you like to see Russia, Colin? Come with me."

Always game, especially when mildly intoxicated, I traipsed after him to his military vehicle. The border was about a half hour away and open only to Russians and Mongolians. To keep immigration procedures simple, Western tourists could only cross the border on the train.

The border was defined by two identical, parallel walls running like rail lines across the countryside, decorated with tinsel-like loops of barbed razor wire. Watchtowers were manned by well-armed soldiers perched atop the walls every thirty yards or so. However, the first thing that caught my attention was a large cathedral on the Russian side.

Cars, trucks, and throngs of pedestrians moved slowly through the checkpoint. Soldiers on each side examined documents and scrutinized each person who crossed.

I watched the traffic for half an hour under a blazing sun while waiting for Bolor to finish his business. A beautiful Caucasian girl with piercing blue eyes came and sat beside Bolor's driver and me. I assumed she was Russian until she started chatting to the driver in fluent Mongolian, which left me unsure.

Bolor returned. The wounded hunter was already en route to a hospital. We returned to the city and I went back to the hotel. About eleven-thirty, just as I turned off the fluorescent light, there was a knock at the door.

"Hello?" I asked, as I climbed out of bed, pulling on my pants.

No reply. Was it Ben or Remy pulling a prank?

I opened the door and found a smiling Officer Batjargal and Ihagvaa. Batjargal was in uniform: short skirt, white-collared shirt with epaulettes, and a cap. Ihagvaa was wearing camouflage pants and a jacket. I could smell vodka.

"I hope we no wake you," Batjargal said. "We just wonder if you like us to take you on tour of the city?"

"Now?" I asked. Suddenly disco and vodka seemed like an exciting prospect, given my recent lifestyle.

"No, tomorrow about ten or eleven."

"Sure," I said, mildly disappointed.

"All right, see you tomorrow," she said.

They giggled and were gone.

*Sunday, June 10*

From my hotel window I could see a small boat on the river. It was too far away for me to make out whether it was the raft. I jumped into my new boots. A thunderstorm broke almost as soon as I emerged from the hotel, drenching me to the bone as I jogged to the riverside.

The shadowy boat got closer to land, and I could see someone hauling on long oars. Yes! It must be them! Relief poured over me. The lads were all right, I'd have money again, and we could begin our next stage into Russia. Ben and Remy were so overdue I was sure the army was beginning to think they were imaginary. Then the deluge let up and I could see the craft more clearly—a fisherman in a steel boat.

I returned to the hotel disappointed and dried off.

Batjargal and Ihagvaa arrived as scheduled and took me to the local museum. We were encouraged to touch the many hands-on exhibits, including a human skeleton dug up from somewhere, probably the local graveyard. I finally figured out why I'd seen so few animals on my journey: Mongolia's wildlife had been stuffed and moved to the Sühbaatar museum. Bears, wolves, moose, elk, foxes, and condors posed menacingly throughout the corridors and chambers. I suspect that the taxidermist had had a bit too much vodka while he worked, though, as some of the disheveled specimens looked as though he had done little more than yank out their insides and stuff their hides with crumpled copies of the *Sühbaatar Herald*.

We went for lunch to the army canteen just as another thunderstorm broke, carpet-bombing the city with hail the size of Volkswagen Beetles.

While we were eating, Bolor arrived at the mess hall, looking serious. "The commander wants us to stand and watch out for your friends at the junction of the Orhon and Selenge rivers. He wants you to be there too."

The women, his friend the immigration officer, a soldier called Naraa, and I piled into an army jeep. "I will just get a bit of food from the store," Bolor said. "We may be there for a while."

Expecting him to return with rice and corned beef, I laughed when I peered into the bag. It contained three bottles of vodka, cigarettes, and a couple of packets of candy.

The trip to the confluence took us past a series of long-abandoned factories. I saw huge, disintegrating conveyor belts, rusted loading cranes, giant culverts, and crumbling brick buildings. It was sad. So much manpower and so many resources had gone into those megaliths, and now they were mere relics of the former Soviet empire. In the museum I had noticed in the display text that the output for textiles and wheat had dropped steadily since 1990.

We were soon in the countryside, and we quickly found a spot from which to monitor the river. A local fisherman came by and gave us a five-pound fish, so we set about preparing a delightful picnic. Naraa and I ate the roe while the others gagged. We roasted the fillets on a fire, and the fish was fabulous with the vodka.

At dusk there was still no sign of the raft, so we headed back to town. As we approached the city, I looked at the concrete apartment blocks that were a legacy of the Soviets. They might seem ugly and faceless to Western eyes, but I could understand why the Mongolians had no complaint. Their *gers* were similarly faceless and drab on the outside; it was inside that you found the character and traditions handed down from the days of the great khans.

"See you tomorrow," Bolor said as he dropped me at the hotel. "Let's hope we see your friends too!"

**7**

View of the Ider River.

## REUNION STORIES AND MURDEROUS RUFFIANS

*Monday, June 11*

We sat on the beach at the confluence of the Orhon and Selenge rivers, again keeping watch for the raft. Naraa, Bolor, and I went swimming to escape the mosquitoes. It was another sweltering day. About 5:00 P.M. Naraa left to take a walk, but soon came sprinting back. He gestured for us to follow. Judging by his mischievous smile, I expected to be led to a couple having sex in the bushes. Instead, he took us to two fishermen packing dynamite into pop bottles.

Until thirty years ago, I was told, these rivers teemed with fish. But Russian influence and hard times had overridden the Mongolians' traditional disdain for seafood. Over the past couple of days, I had noticed that the few fishermen we passed had scant catches. These particular fishermen figured dynamite would be a quicker and surer way of harvesting a catch. A wrinkled old man with a cigarette dangling from his mouth poured the powdery explosive into a Coke bottle. He passed it to his younger assistant, who tamped it with a blunt stick. The assistant put a lid on the bottle and inserted a fuse enclosed in a thin copper pipe through a hole in the lid.

The fishermen drifted downstream in a ten-foot steel rowboat. We followed, walking on the railway track that ran parallel to the river. They got ahead of us, and by the time we caught up, they had already tossed their homemade depth charges overboard and were searching for dead or stunned fish. They found none, and came to shore dejected.

They told Bolor we could have a ride back to the confluence in their truck, which was parked on the other side of the tracks. We were happy to accept, and soon the large flatbed, loaded with the boat, was bouncing across the rough terrain.

An old woman and a young boy leading a goat waved for our truck to stop. The woman spoke to Bolor while the boy picked up the goat and handed it to me. The black-and-white animal bleated as I hauled it onto the back of the flatbed. The boy leapt up nimbly and slapped the goat on the rump.

Bolor said, "She says your friends have arrived! They reached the confluence and have begun rowing up the Orhon River. Let's head into town to meet them!"

As we rumbled along the dirt road toward town, I couldn't help but feel a twinge of doubt. Too many times my hopes had been raised in vain. I hoped the old lady was right. Two hours later at eleven, in fading twilight, we spotted the scruffy, sunburned duo rowing up the river. It had been twelve days since I'd last seen them. "Ahoy, mates!" I yelled from the shore.

"Is that Colin?" I heard Ben's voice carry across the water. He was pulling on a pair of homemade wooden oars. As the boat drew closer, I could see that the two of them were grinning like fools.

"And at last, after eleven days, the team is reunited!" Remy said.

We slapped each other on the backs and smiled from ear to ear. I couldn't wait to find out what had happened to them. With the help of Bolor, Naraa, four kids, and a taxi, we stored our gear in the railway station and in my hotel room. Once the local helpers had left, Ben, Remy, and I sank onto the beds to swap tales.

After I had departed in my kayak, Ben and Remy began the lengthy job of salvaging the remaining gear and the raft. On their tiny, swampy island, the first task was to determine what gear had been washed away. They emptied out the dry bags and began going through a mental checklist of what was absent. The two camera tripods, two kayak paddles, two oars, an oarlock, a jacket, and some clothes had been washed down the river. They began the task of drying out the gear and rigging up a means of propelling the raft with just the one oar and kayak paddle remaining. Eventually they rigged a system where the single oar was affixed to the stern so that it could propel the boat with a sculling motion. One person would sit up front with the kayak paddle to assist with the more difficult maneuvering.

"After we sorted all that out," Remy explained, "I did my laundry for the first time in weeks, and Ben went over the raft with a fine-tooth comb, looking for leaks. We kept fires going at night in case you were trying to make your way back to us."

I was flabbergasted. For the past eleven days I had wondered, why the holdup? What tragedy had prevented the guys from moving downstream as soon as possible? Hearing the answer made me angry. "Did you guys really think I would be able to paddle back upstream against that current? Even if I could have, did you think there was a chance I'd have found that postage-stamp patch you were on, amid thousands of acres of flooded forest?"

Remy hung his head. "Well, we thought there was a chance. You could have carried your boat upstream overland and then launched above us."

"Hmm . . . so you guys figured I would hike twenty-five miles in my bare feet with a forty-five-pound boat on my back, no food, and only the slimmest chance of finding you, rather than sitting on the riverbank farther downstream?"

"We thought it was a possibility," Ben said. But on the video they shot at the time of the flip, Ben told the camera, "We reckon what Colin would have done is continue downstream to a spot where he can see the entire river. He will then wait there until we come down." Even though they had understood the situation, they had spent three days looking for pinhole leaks in the raft and doing their laundry. Meanwhile, I was downstream, starving and freezing to death.

For a moment or two I really wanted to have it out with them, but then my anger vanished. What the hell—the ordeal was over, and we were all alive and ready to continue on the next leg of the journey. To bear a grudge would only make the next stage more difficult. "Forget it," I said. "Keep going with the story. I want to know everything. Tell me every detail."

Remy continued, "We thought about leaving on the second day, but we were worried we might miss you if you were trying to get back to us. We were also absolutely exhausted from the effort of keeping the fire going through the night. So we decided to stay another evening. We intended to leave at the crack of dawn on the third day, but by the time we took down camp, repacked all our gear, and made a few phone calls, it was noon. And we wanted to make sure the gear was secured properly if the raft flipped again.

"When we finally got back on the river, the floodwaters had abated a bit, but we still found it extremely difficult to maneuver through the forest, especially with our new rowing system. We took turns powering from the back with the single oar and steering from the front with the kayak paddle. We made it out of the forest without any further mishaps, but we were really beginning to worry about you. Every time we rounded a bend, we were paranoid that we'd find a capsized kayak.

"When we finally reached some *gers* on the riverbank, we knew something was going on by the way all the people were running to the river's edge. When we drew closer, someone yelled, 'Colin!' We thought our search was over. We expected you to emerge from a *ger* with a grin on your face. Instead, one of the men showed us the pictures you'd drawn to tell them your story. We gathered that you had stayed in the *ger* for one night, and that it hadn't been that long ago. We felt sure we'd be reuniting with you soon. And we knew you'd had at least a little bit of food, because one of the men, with a big grin on his face, gave us a pantomime of you arriving skinny and going away fat.

"Once we knew you were okay, we relaxed a bit. We were sure we'd find you in Hutag. As we got better at handling the sculling oar, the days took on a regular pattern again. Finally we reached Hutag—in the middle of a storm!—but we saw no sign that you were there. We camped on the outskirts. First thing in the morning, some boys came to our camp, saying 'Canadian, Canada,' and beckoning for us to follow. We felt sure we'd finally hit the jackpot as we followed the boys through the village. Instead of leading us to you, though, they led us to the home of some Canadian missionaries."

I interrupted, flabbergasted. "What? There were Canadian missionaries in Hutag?"

Remy nodded and continued, "It was fantastic. They were

a married couple from Calgary, and they worked for the New Tribes Mission. They had all the comforts of the Western world in their home! When they invited us to stay, there was no way we could resist after all we'd been through. For three days we indulged in hot showers and delicious meals—we even had peaches and homemade brownies for dessert! They also loaned us some power tools they had brought from Canada so we could make a new set of oars.

"We still had no idea where you were. Then one of the missionaries told us they had heard from a shopkeeper that a desperate-looking white man been in her shop, trying to trade film for food. Not only had you been in town, but you must have found the film bag! We hoped the videocassettes would be okay, after all the time they had spent in the river. It seemed as if we had missed you by about twenty-four hours.

"Finally, after three days of luxury, we said good-bye to our new friends and hit the river again. The new oars worked beautifully, and we were finally able to make some really good progress. It only took four or five days to get from Hutag to Sühbaatar. On the tenth day after the capsize, Ben called his mother and learned that you were alive and well in Sühbaatar. A couple days later, we reached the Orhon confluence, got your warning note, and, voilà, here we are—one big, happy family again."

It was an amazing story—almost as wild and crazy as my own. While I was eating stinging nettles and raw eggs, Ben and Remy were showering in hot water and dining on brownies and peaches.

There remained only one unanswered question: The two different men who'd said they'd seen a boat—what was that all about? Had I misunderstood them? Were they telling stories? Or had there been other men on the river in rowboats? I would never know.

*Tuesday, June 12*

Now that we were reunited, we would use Sühbaatar as a base to regroup and prepare for the next part of the journey. While Ben and Remy remained there, I would return to Ulaanbaatar and pick up my new passport. Before departing, I reminded Remy to pay off my Internet debt at the library. I boarded the train and settled in for the night in a near-empty car, sipping tea as I watched the verdant, rugged country clatter by.

*Thursday, June 14*

I arrived in Ulaanbaatar late Wednesday afternoon—too late to get to the Canadian consulate or the DHL courier office. I went to Nassan's guest house, and was embraced as if I were family.

At 3:00 A.M. I got up to do an interview with a radio station back in Vancouver. I was using the satellite phone, but I had to go outside, since the concrete walls impeded the reception. While I waited to make the call, a group of teenage ruffians sauntered over. They held out their hands and chanted the only two English words they knew. "I'm hungry. I'm hungry. H-u-u-u-n-gry." I couldn't pay any attention to the boys because my interview was to begin in a couple of minutes. Annoyed, they began pushing closer.

Moments before I was to go on air, a couple of policeman came along and drove the gang away. The policemen didn't speak English, but they made it clear that it was dangerous to be walking the streets alone. They indicated the departing youth, pointed at me, and made violent punching gestures.

I nodded vigorously to show I'd understood.

They smiled, and one pointed up at the guest house and made the universal gesture for sleeping: hands clasped at the side of the head, head tilted, eyes closed.

I nodded again, said thanks in a couple of languages none of them recognized, and gave them a wave good night. I wish I had paid heed to their warnings.

They walked away and I returned to my mission. I was soon talking to a radio interviewer about our journeys. I was telling him about the adventures we'd encountered so far and my time alone in the Mongolian wilderness.

"I'm hungry!" a chorus of voices screamed in my ear. A grubby trio of teenagers had returned to continue harassing me. "Hungry, hungry!" they taunted.

I ignored the pesky threesome and concentrated on the interviewer's questions.

"Is everything all right there, Colin?"

"Yeah, just some kids."

One of the ruffians stuck his head up close to my face and yelled into the receiver, "I'm hungry!" I recognized another; I had given him 500 togrogs the day before. He saw the flicker of recognition and hammered me on the chest. They were smaller than I was, but nevertheless, I was nervous. I tried brushing them off, but they only became more aggressive—getting louder and crowding in on me.

"I'll have to talk to you later," I told the interviewer. I racked the phone and turned, just in time to dodge a lunge by the oldest-looking teenager, who was trying to bash in my skull with a small boulder.

Jesus! The rock was the size of a pumpkin. It would have crushed my skull like an eggshell.

Normally I like to settle things peacefully, but in the pre-dawn Mongolian darkness, with another human trying to take my life, something inside me snapped. I grabbed the off-balance adolescent and threw him as hard as I could against the wall. He crumpled like a rag onto the ground and I began kicking him. I was enraged, completely out of control. The other two kids picked up pieces of brick and rock and hurled them at me.

I stopped stomping the would-be assassin and fled back to the hotel, pulling shut the fortresslike steel door behind me. That was the last phone call I would make at night in Ulaanbaatar. I returned to bed, trembling from the violence.

A few hours later, Nassan's husband, Inca, and I went to the immigration office to renew my visa. I was told I had to pay a $200 fine because my visiting permit had already expired. I didn't have that much cash with me, and I had no way to lay my hands on it. The nearest ATMs were in Russia or China.

"If you have a police report to confirm the passport was stolen, the charge is less," the woman behind the glass-fronted counter told Inca.

I was pessimistic. I understood that the Canadian consulate had sent the police report to Beijing when I applied for a new passport. Returning to the consulate, I found Ariaana, the consular general's assistant, and asked her for help. She wrote me a letter that urged the Mongolian immigration office to waive the fine.

The consulate letterhead and official stamp apparently provided as much authority as a police report, because the letter worked. Not only did the Mongolian bureaucrats waive the fine, but they also cut the processing fee in half to $20. Inca and I left smiling.

I went to the train station and bought a return ticket to Sühbaatar for the 9:00 P.M. train.

I had several hours to kill, so I went to the Internet café and logged on to check my e-mail. There was an urgent message from Remy: "Stay put!" it said. "We have reassessed the finances and don't have enough to make it to Irkutsk. With the border-crossing fees, we will arrive in Russia with nothing! Ben and I are taking the train to Ulaanbaatar. We can't get money here."

Hell! I had been looking forward to hopping on that train, and the visa I had been granted was good for only four days.

Remy's credit card was maxed out, and so was Ben's. I had money in my account, but no way of accessing it in Mongolia. Headaches, headaches. The boys would arrive at 7:00 A.M. We would figure it out then.

### Friday, June 15

Ben and Remy stumbled into the hotel at 7:00 A.M. They had $15 left. What could we do? I had to figure out a way to get money from my account into Remy's so we could use his credit card.

I e-mailed Dan Audet, my friend manning the website, asking if he would lend us $800 by depositing it into Remy's account. Time was of the utmost importance because my exit visa expired in three days, I told him. I felt bad about asking him for money: he was a student, and his funds were limited. But I knew he would do whatever it took to get the cash—he had already dug into his own pocket to pay photo-processing costs for us.

I had another idea too. Before we left, I had given my mum five signed checks to pay the monthly installments on my Hudson's Bay Company bill. If she crossed out "Hudson's Bay Company" on the checks and wrote "Remy Quinter," she could deposit the money directly into his account. He could then access the money via his credit card.

*Saturday, June 16*

It worked! My mother verified that the money had been transferred into Remy's account. Unfortunately, we could not access it until Monday, when the banks opened. I called a relieved Dan to tell him he wouldn't need to raid his Ichiban Noodles and Kraft Dinners fund, after all.

*Monday, June 18*

Once we got the money from the bank, we went to the train station to purchase our tickets back to Sühbaatar. The earliest train left at 9:00 P.M. We were behind schedule because of the delay caused by our financial crisis, and we were anxious to get back on the river. As well, my visa expired at midnight, and we would not arrive at the Russian border until the next day. I hoped the border official would be in a good mood.

I feel asleep quickly as we *clickety-clack*ed, *clickety-clack*ed into the night.

PART THREE

# SIBERIA

Old man and wife chopping firewood in Siberia.

# 8

# CROSSING THE BORDER WITH SERIOUS BAGGAGE

*Tuesday, June 19*

The attendant flicked on the overhead fluorescent light at 5:00 A.M., awakening us. Outside I could see Sühbaatar in the dim gray dawn, which gave a funereal cast to the grain silos, factories, and slatternly apartment blocks. It was like looking on a city of shadows, a city of the dead.

The train would stop for about five hours before making its final sprint to the border. Although we had pleaded with the Mongolian authorities to allow us to cross the border in our raft, they flatly refused. Foreigners must enter Russia on the train. As our goal was to voyage the complete length of the river under our own power, we did not want a gap. While I was in Ulaanbaatar, Ben and Remy had made the ten-mile walk to the Russian border. Now it was my turn. I put on my sneakers, left Remy and Ben sorting our gear at the train station, and jogged a brisk fartlek to the border. After slapping the steel fence dividing the two countries, I hightailed it back to the train, arriving with an hour to spare. Once in Russia, we would stroll back and touch the other side of the fence to ensure continuity.

We retrieved our kayaks from storage and surprised the train porters as we returned carrying boats, raft, rowing frame, oars, and overstuffed dry bags. There was no baggage car on the train and we couldn't fit all the gear into our sleeper. Surprisingly, the plump cashier came to our rescue. If we agreed to buy another ticket for the equivalent of $6.40, they would get our gear aboard. We agreed to the deal. The rear of the train was opened and the railway staff loaded our kayaks. The raft and the remaining gear were crammed into our compartment, leaving standing room only. Still, the first hurdle had been cleared. The next was Mongolian immigration.

Unfortunately, Bolor was not working, because his mother had died. We could expect no special treatment. I waited apprehensively as an official with a face like a bulldog approached me. "Passport?" he demanded.

I handed him the document and he flipped rapidly through the pages until he found my exit permit. His eyes rested momentarily on "June 18."

I babbled an explanation, but he ignored me, pulling a greasy piece of paper from his back pocket on which he wrote "$100."

"Expense number one as we try to cross the Russian border," Ben said, as he pulled five crisp twenty-dollar bills from the kitty. The official nodded, tucked the money into his pocket, and left the train.

There was only one carriage going into Russia, and the car shuddered as it lurched toward the border. Some friendly New Zealanders invited us to sit with them. The two middle-aged couples lavished watermelon, sweets, and chocolate chip cookies on us. One couple worked for World Vision, a non-profit organization that does a lot of aid work in Mongolia. They were riding the tracks to London.

We entered the border town of Nowshki and waited nervously for the Russian border police.

"Check it out," said Ben. He pointed to a stunning blonde with supermodel looks leading a gaggle of officials toward the train. The kind of official James Bond usually encounters—from Russia with love.

Like a bunch of schoolboys ogling the attractive substitute teacher, we waited anxiously for the arrival of the customs goddess. It was extremely hot, and the window wouldn't open, but none of us seemed to notice the heat until an officious uniformed man with short-cropped hair arrived.

"Whose boats are these in the hall?" he demanded.

"They are ours," I said.

An older man joined his comrade at the door. He took one look at our mounds of gear and called out, "Olga."

A stout fifty-year-old wielding a large, menacing calculator arrived and examined our compartment. She weighed the mound of luggage with seasoned eyes, and her sausage fingers punched the keypad. Then her fingers stopped dancing and one of her eyebrows rose.

"How much does your baggage weigh?" the gray-haired Russian asked.

"About six hundred pounds," I said.

He said something rapidly to the woman and her chubby digits hopscotched across the keypad again.

"We must charge import duty on your baggage. We charge you by weight."

I held my breath. We had $250 to get us to Irkutsk. If the

fee exceeded this amount, we were stuck; there was no ATM nearby. I peered over Olga's shoulder and gulped. Staring back at me was a number in the thousands! And she wasn't finished—her fingers were still tapping away. She showed the final figure to her superior. He nodded, satisfied.

"It will cost you one hundred seventy-two American dollars."

I sighed with relief. We'd spent almost $300 so far, but that was it. We'd cleared the final hurdle and were in Russia with our gear.

We disembarked and looked around. Most of the buildings in Nowshki were made of wood, either clapboard or log construction. Plank fences divided the properties, and I could see numerous vegetable gardens boasting rows of sprouting potatoes, onions, and lettuce. The railway station, constructed of granite, was by far the most impressive building.

We carried our gear down to the Selenge River, which flowed behind the station. With the help of a couple of friendly Russians, we were finished after about two hours. It was hot—over ninety degrees—and nearly a dozen children ranging in age from about six to sixteen frolicked in the river, swimming, diving, and jumping from a decrepit steel bridge. It seemed strange to see so many blond, blue-eyed kids after weeks of nothing but Asian faces.

The kids helped us assemble the rowing frame and pump up the raft. Alex, a bright-looking fifteen-year-old with short hair, noticed there were three nuts missing from the frame. He ran off and returned ten minutes later with three nuts in his hand. He quickly screwed them on, tightening them with a spanner he pulled from his pocket.

"Now, these are helpful kids," said Remy. "How can a nation with people so bright be crashing so badly economically?"

I gave the kids one of the kayaks to play on while we finished packing. Once our gear was organized and ready to go, we walked back toward the border fence while Alex guarded the raft. Guards eyed us from their steel watchtowers but did nothing to halt our approach to the fence.

"Give ya a nickel if you climb the fence," Ben joked.

We strolled back slowly alongside the hot, dusty tracks, the air pungent with melting creosote and pine.

The kids all climbed on the raft when it came time to leave, and we pushed away from shore like a refugee boat from Cuba. One by one the kids dived off and swam for shore as we moved downstream.

Only Alex remained.

"*Do svedania.* Enjoy my country!" he said, and with a splash disappeared into the coffee-colored water.

We rowed for three hours before setting up camp close to the Trans-Mongolian Railway line, which ran parallel to the river through the valley.

*Wednesday, June 20*

Amid a haze of mosquitoes and blackflies, Ben struggled to make a breakfast of rice pudding. An outboard motor, humming like an enormous mosquito, resonated in the distance. It was the first boat motor we'd heard since the start of our journey. Soon three fishermen came into view heading upriver in a ten-foot steel dinghy. The grim-faced men glanced at our campsite, but motored on without a word.

They returned ten minutes later as Ben dished out bowls of steaming mushy rice (any wetter, actually, and it would have been congee). This time the weathered driver cut back on the throttle and turned the boat toward shore.

"*Dobre utra,*" said a short man wearing a Caterpillar cap.

The boat slid the last few yards onto the gravel bank. The men jumped ashore, each extending his hand.

"Andrei."

"Yuri."

"Alexander."

Remy chatted with them in Russian, and they opened up, full of curiosity about our adventure. They wanted our autographs. The burly, weathered men pulled out cigarette packets and asked each of us to sign the backs.

Before leaving, they handed Ben a large fish. "You will need lots of food. Rowing is hard work."

We thanked them and the men departed, waving until they disappeared upriver.

After breakfast we pushed off, and Ben rowed gently with the steady, flat current. The river now was about two hundred yards wide and very deep. As the hours passed, we wilted under the heat of the broiling sun and did little more than watch the terrain slip by.

The landscape was far more cultivated than the countryside of Mongolia. Fields of wheat and other grains formed a patchwork quilt across the steppe between swaths of scrub forest. We no longer saw *gers*. The local people lived in plank or log homes roofed with corrugated steel or wooden boards. Many were decorated with vividly painted shutters and sported elaborate carved trim around the windows, like nursery rhyme gingerbread houses.

We camped on a low, gravelly island. For dinner I steamed the fish over the fire in a large pot. Although bony, the translucent white flesh of the carplike fish was remarkably delicate in flavor.

*Thursday, June 21*

Shortly after breakfast we came upon a large church. It was an odd sight—a beautiful Byzantine building surrounded by nothing but fields of scrub grass. Ben guided the raft to shore.

As we neared the enormous building, we could see that it was abandoned and decrepit.

We entered the once-whitewashed brick building through a collapsed arch that was intended to be the main entrance. The floor was covered with half a yard or more of dried feces, probably from animals that had sheltered there during the harsh winter. Inside, a fifty-foot domed ceiling was painted—à la Sistine Chapel—with a Christian mural of creation. The air was filled with the amplified shrieks of hundreds of nesting birds and the whisper of their beating wings as they swooped among the rafters and in and out of the shattered windows.

Outside, we visited the small graveyard. Ben found three fallen tombstones bearing dates between 1820 and 1870. Where was the community the church had been established to serve? We couldn't figure it out. We pushed back out onto the river.

At five we reached a small village. It too had a church—a tiny weathered log building with a shiny, aluminum onion dome on the roof. We pulled the raft over, and Ben asked a woman walking along the road if there was a store anywhere nearby.

No," she said in Russian. "There is another village about five miles downriver. You can buy food there."

We thanked her, she wished us bon voyage, and we continued on. Another river had joined the Selenge, and the main channel was now nearly 350 yards wide. Unlike the upper Selenge, the river flowed in a relatively straight line and at a steady rate. The mountains lining the valley were different too—younger, I would guess, from their sharp, fractured peaks. Their slopes were forested and cloaked in hues of green.

It was broiling, and a brisk headwind slowed our progress.

We arrived at the second village at about eight and, again, after beaching the raft, found ourselves faced with a matronly woman in a red scarf. This woman had a brood of five kids scrambling around her feet. "Yes, there is a store, about a mile down the road," she said, eyeing our boat curiously. "If you need some milk, you can buy it from me. My house is the one straight across the road. I am Anna."

She left to milk three cows that were waiting patiently by the gate. About a dozen other cows dawdled along the road that led to the village.

"It doesn't look like it will be difficult finding fresh milk around here," Ben said as we strolled toward the store. Remy was staying with the boat to watch the gear.

There was no sign, and the shop looked no different from the other wooden homes, but we knew this was the local store because we could see racks of food through the open window. The door was locked. Ben knocked loudly.

"*Dobre vecher*—good evening," we chorused.

A grumpy-looking woman of about fifty, hair in curlers, answered. "*Da?*"

"Excuse me. Food. We want," said Ben in his broken Russian.

Begrudgingly, the woman stepped to the side, allowing us to enter. The first thing that caught my eye was a glass-fronted refrigerator packed full of unwrapped chicken pieces. The store didn't have much else: two cans of beef, a can of sardines, rice, mayonnaise, one can of tomato sauce, some home-canned vegetables, and a selection of small chocolate bars and sweets.

"It's too bad it's so hot out," said Ben. "I could do with a bit of chicken."

The woman's attitude changed as we struggled to answer her questions—no, we hadn't come on the train; no, we didn't have a motor on our boat. She couldn't believe we really planned to cross Siberia in a rowboat. Excitedly she called her daughter, Natasha.

Natasha was an athletic sixteen-year-old dressed in black-market faux Adidas. She hovered shyly in the corner while her mother asked the questions. Interview over, we bought two jars of canned veggies, the can of tomato sauce, a can of corned beef, a jar of mayonnaise, the lone loaf of bread on display, and six chocolate bars, all for about $2.40.

"I don't think the double standard for charging has begun yet," I said as we handed over the rubles.

Before returning to the boat, we stopped at Anna's to buy milk. She led us into her tidy one-room cabin and told us it would take a moment. In the center of the room was a wood-stove. A small bed, an electric stove, a large chest freezer, and a few other pieces of furniture were placed around the room's periphery. On the table sat a porcelain bowl filled with cottage cheese.

Anna returned with a gallon jar full of milk, two 1.5-liter plastic pop bottles, and a funnel. She filled the bottles.

"How much?" asked Ben.

"Fifteen rubles [about fifty cents] for the three liters," she said.

Ben pulled out two ten-ruble notes, the smallest denomination we had. "Here. Don't worry about the extra five."

She shook her head firmly. "That is too much. I can't accept it. I will get you more milk." Anna left and, after some mooing from Betsy, she returned, the jar half filled with milk. "I have no more containers, so you will have to drink this now," she said, pouring the milk into two mugs.

We drank it down. It was thick and warm—delicious.

We said good-bye and returned proudly to the boat with the first fresh milk we'd had in months. We set off for a little island we could see downstream. After reaching the substantial sandbar, we made camp, fired by thoughts of fresh milk, caffe lattes, and creamy milk sauces.

The remaining liter of milk turned into yogurt overnight.

I guess with unpasteurized milk, you don't need to stimulate the process. Still, it tasted great.

*Saturday, June 23*

The bugs were becoming worse every day. There were so many mosquitoes and blackflies that sometimes it felt like every bit of exposed flesh was being brushed with an itchy feather duster. We inhaled bugs; bugs clotted our eyes. We were being eaten alive.

The weather was hot and humid. Not quite the ninety-degree-plus weather we'd been experiencing, but close. We had a light rain in the morning, and I went for a swim. The river was warm. It sure didn't feel like the Siberia portrayed in popular culture: a barren, frozen wasteland, little more than a giant gulag archipelago.

At about 6:00 P.M., with Remy at the oars, we reached the beginning of the Selenge's enormous delta. We expected to reach the main body of Lake Baikal before dark, but three young fishermen roared up in a steel boat and disabused us of that notion. The friendly lads chatted with us for about fifteen minutes, gave us some fish, and left after telling us we had another twenty-five miles to go through the silty delta.

*Sunday, June 24*

We awoke to howling winds and rain lashing the tents. By noon the wind had abated enough that we could push off, but it was difficult to make any progress in the sluggish current and choppy conditions. We rowed until 10:00 P.M. without pause, and still we had not reached the lake. The expansive delta had become a labyrinth of channels, a watery maze that threatened to trap us. After our battles all day with violent rain and squalls, fog rolled in as night neared, and we were enveloped in pea soup.

Our slow progress was especially frustrating because we had arranged to meet Tim Cope, the Australian who would join us for the remainder of the journey, on the other side of Lake Baikal. We didn't want to keep him waiting too long.

With gale-force winds on our nose, it was dangerous and fruitless to continue—but where to spend the night? We were surrounded by thousands of acres of swamp, and I had visions of us trying to set the tents up in a knee-deep quagmire of mud and water. The rain hammered down, the wind moaned like a banshee, and Ben hummed the *Twilight Zone* theme as we drifted through the foggy nightmare.

I was shivering and feeling disoriented when a dark shape materialized out of the milky fog. An old boxcar! How did it get here, in the middle of the delta? I rowed up to the rusting railway car.

"This looks like a vehicle used to transport prisoners to gulags, if ever I've seen one," Ben said of the derelict hulk. The car could have been straight out of *Schindler's List*, only the setting was spookier than anything Hollywood could create.

It looked sinister, but inside someone had installed a woodstove and four wooden bunks. A small pile of damp firewood lay on the floor. It obviously wasn't occupied, and we didn't expect anyone to arrive this late in the evening.

"We're stylin' tonight," I said. "I thought we'd be setting up our tents in six inches of water and only dreaming about a fire."

I climbed onto the roof of our temporary home and surveyed our domain. The fog was clearing, revealing an extensive marshland. Streaks of mist slithered over the ground like ghouls searching for lost souls. I shivered and returned to the dank interior of the boxcar to start a fire. Ben and Remy went to get the bags, and I torched some damp newspaper with Russian matches. It took about a dozen before the paper sparked and the damp wood shavings began to ignite.

We called it a day at about 1:30 A.M.—just about the time it became completely dark. The wind was screeching. If it didn't subside, we'd have to hunker down there until it blew itself out.

## Monday, June 25

A persistent loud thumping noise roused us at 2:30 A.M. Remy tensely investigated—nothing.

"Must be the metal around the stovepipe contracting," I volunteered.

The sound was coming from above, in the ceiling. There was a space of little more than a yard between the board ceiling and the roof, and no visible entrance up into that cubby area. A slight irrational fear crept into my mind.

I was lying in the upper bunk, and the rusty metal springs could barely support my weight. My body was suspended mere inches above Ben on the bunk below, as though in a woven metal hammock. Earlier, when I had needed to go pee, it had taken five minutes to extricate myself. It felt as though the bed had arms that were trying to hold me, trying to smother me.

*Thump, thump, thump.*

I fell back into fitful sleep and dreamed of the misery of work-camp slavery.

I welcomed daylight as it seeped in through the open door, penetrating the black interior. The wind had died down and we could leave the railway car behind. I was both excited and nervous about the prospect of rowing our tiny raft out into the world's largest lake (by volume). The Selenge River flowed from the south into Lake Baikal and exited a hundred miles beyond on the northern shore. The lake could be considered an extreme widening and deepening of the river, since it is included when measuring the length of the Yenisey River.

Lake Baikal was produced when two major geological systems, the Siberian Platform and the Sayano-Baikalsky folded belt, separated. This created a jagged chasm four hundred miles long and some six and a half miles deep. It is by far the deepest cavity in the surface of the earth. In this unstable region, large earthquakes occur frequently—monitoring equipment registers up to two thousand tremors and quakes a year.

Over millions of years, silt deposits and landslides have filled in some of Baikal, but it remains over a mile deep—the deepest lake in the world. It would take all the rivers on the planet an entire year to fill that gaping abyss. And because of its depth, this ancient inland sea features unique, unusually evolved marine life that can be found nowhere else. Even now biologists are still finding new fish species that have adapted to the extreme pressure and darkness of Baikal's deepest waters.

The lake acts as a filtering system for the murky rivers emptying into it. The silt and mud settle slowly to the bottom and an army of snails and freshwater shrimp remove algae and other impurities. In the summer, visibility in the crystalline waters is an astounding 130 feet. In winter, the ice is so thick that roads are created on it. The Siberian Railway has even run short-term tracks across Lake Baikal, reducing the distance the trains had to travel. Perhaps that was how our haunted railcar ended up in the middle of the Selenge delta.

———

We emerged from the delta and into Lake Baikal late in the morning. The flat, marshy land opened up into an oceanlike expanse of steel-gray water. The brown silt of the Selenge vanished below us, and we were left floating as if on a pool of mercury, gently rocking.

The change in temperature was abrupt. We were accustomed to the eighty-five-plus temperatures of the Selenge, and the rapid plummet to forty-three degrees made me shiver. The great depths below us had effectively stored the frigid Siberian winter, releasing the cold slowly throughout the summer to chill even the hottest day.

I could barely see an indistinct blue line on the horizon—the strip of mountains and cliffs that formed the opposite shore, fifty-five miles to the northwest. The Russians we met along the Selenge had repeatedly expressed concern about our attempt to cross Baikal. It is one thing to splash along a river in a little rubber boat, but entirely another to try crossing a freezing inland sea. Baikal is renowned for its violent storms, especially in the summer, when the temperature contrast between the lake and the surrounding land produces a quicksilver microclimate. The maximum water temperature of thirty-nine degrees ensures hypothermia within minutes if you are unfortunate enough to fall in. Every year numerous fishermen perish in Baikal's waters when storms sink their large, diesel-powered ships.

The sheltered waters of the delta had been left astern, and I felt very alone and very exposed on that great lake. It was like venturing out on the ocean, complete with a slow, rolling swell. Only a few millimeters of rubber separated us from almost certain death.

"Okay, no playing with knives, anyone," I joked.

In the distance we saw a few big oceangoing-type vessels

with high bows. The crews shook their heads disapprovingly at us as they passed. They thought we were asking for it by using a rubber raft to cross a lake that was notorious as a hunting ground for killer storms.

We estimated it would take between twenty-four and forty hours to reach the far shore, depending on the weather. It was hard to be certain. We no longer had a current to assist us, and the slightest headwind would stop us dead in our tracks. If the winds were stronger than ten miles an hour, once the waves began building we would be pushed backward. On this lake the prevailing winds came from the north and were supposedly very frequent. I crossed my fingers as we continued to slice through the glassy waters. A persistent steady breeze could easily extend our crossing time to three or four days, or even longer—the perfect recipe to drive us to insanity.

Ten hours into our crossing, towering, angry anvil-head clouds appeared over the far mountains and moved with frightening speed toward us. I could see the water ahead being whipped into a swath of cat's paws and spray while we were still moving through oily calm. Moments later, an icy blast of wind hit our boat and the seas around us were whipped into chaos. I rowed as hard as I could, but our half-ton boat was moving slowly backward. The strain of pulling on the long oars was phenomenal. Within minutes my shoulders, back, and joints were aching.

"Next!" I yelled.

Ben slid onto the seat I had vacated and I huddled behind a dry bag for protection. We were bundled up like Michelin men, but the cold wind ensured that we were still freezing. I sat dejectedly and watched as Ben worked his hardest, yet we still lost progress. I had thought I was being too cautious earlier when I put fleece, sweaters, jackets, and neoprene close at hand. Now I was wearing it all and still trembling from the chill. Darkness was settling in, the storm was intensifying, and I felt very insignificant and cold.

Luckily, by the time daylight had all but vanished, the wind started to subside. It had only been a squall. We ate a cold dinner of rice and borscht prepared before leaving the security of shore. Remy ate his food slowly, the violent rocking of the boat having eroded his hunger. I washed my hands in the frigid water and discovered it was possible to get an ice cream headache in your hands. When darkness was near total, the wind abated and we continued on. The only sounds were splashing oars and heavy breathing as we intermittently fell into a restless doze.

*Tuesday, June 26*

The winds remained calm throughout the night. I was at the oars as the subtle transition of Siberian dawn revealed the progress we had made. We were now more than two-thirds of the way across, but I could see only the higher lands to the north. In every other direction the water seemed to stretch to infinity, merging indistinctly with a pewter sky.

The weather stayed pleasant, and it became possible to make out the opposite shore more distinctly. The forested slopes were surmounted by the jagged, snow-clad peaks of the Barguzin Mountains. At 9:00 A.M. we arrived on the north side of Lake Baikal. The landscape was completely different from that through which we had already traveled. A wall of mountains cloaked in larch and pine rose out of the water. There was no foreshore, only steep stone slopes and precipitous granite cliffs. Thousands of dickering seagulls darted hither and yon.

Occasionally we could see white-sand beaches no bigger than postage stamps at the base of towering cliffs. Add the sapphire lake dappled with golden sunshine, and we could have been looking at a Greek island. This beauty and warmth was certainly not my idea of Siberia.

We followed the rugged shoreline west until, rounding a headland, we came upon a Russian holiday resort, the probable source of lights we had seen during the night. People were lounging in beach chairs, sunbathing, and frolicking on the sand. I noticed that nobody was daring to swim in the icy water. A handful of rustic buildings overlooked the beach.

We pulled in, and the staff and guests stared as we disembarked. Remy spoke to a white-haired man in a wool sweater and flannel pants, asking if there was a restaurant or bar—we felt like celebrating our successful crossing. The man pointed to a large wooden building with a fancy veranda. We left our raft and gear in a highly visible location and stumbled over.

The studious-looking hostess acted as if we were expected. The dining area could seat a hundred people, but was empty save for a family in the far corner. We settled comfortably at a wooden table near the window, where we could watch the beach and our boat.

A youth of about eighteen with short-cropped hair, wearing a sleeveless shirt and an apron, approached with three cups and a steaming pot of strong tea. "The rest will be coming soon," he said.

While we waited for the food to arrive, I inspected the vivid mural that dominated the room. My first, quick glance at the bright colors and the almost childlike renderings of figures had fostered an impression that the scenes depicted would be benign, almost idyllic. The reality was quite different. The mural showed a series of unsettling vignettes—a ferocious bear stalking a group of happy campers; a large-fanged snake menacing an oblivious couple blithely picnicking; a shaggy, malnourished man languishing on a desert island; three fishermen wallowing helplessly in a foundering boat. Someone had a black sense of humor.

Our meals arrived—large bowls of buttered cream of wheat, croutons, and a basket of sliced baguette, plus more tea. We dug in hungrily. Afterward Remy asked the waiter how much we owed.

"Are you not staying at the resort?" he replied.

"No, we just rowed across the lake in our boat," Remy said, gesturing out the window at the raft.

The lad was confused. He pulled a meal ticket out of his pocket. "This is all you need."

"Where can we buy one?" Remy asked.

"You can't. Only resort guests receive them."

We looked at each other.

"Don't worry about it," he said, and waved us off.

We thanked him for our free breakfast and continued our journey. It was immensely reassuring to have a shoreline to follow—it offered a sanctuary if conditions got too feisty. As well, the cliffs and steep slopes created an effective wind block that sheltered us from the northern gales. In the afternoon, we could see waves forming farther out, while we remained in relative calm. Apart from the resort, which was serviced by boat, the region was pristine wilderness, and we frequently saw deer, otter, and small, unidentifiable beasts coming down to the water's edge to drink. Occasionally a high-prowed cargo or passenger boat would motor past, the captain saluting us with a cheery blast of the horn.

As dinnertime grew near, a hopeful line trailed the boat, with Ben attached to one end. We hoped that a fish would soon be affixed to the other. Not very likely! Our rod, which we had purchased in Ulaanbaatar, had caught two fish so far. The Russians say that eight-hundred-pound sturgeon live in Lake Baikal. Perhaps we would catch one on our two-pound test line. Maybe a sturgeon would catch Ben!

Unfortunately the caviar didn't materialize; instead we cooked sardines and rice on a small, sandy beach. Shortly after we pitched the tents, I retired for the evening, falling into a deep sleep to the lullaby of waves breaking on the shore.

*Wednesday, June 27*

It was only midmorning when we pulled into Bolshoya Delusnia, a lakeside village of log houses, dusty roads, and about six hundred people. Fishermen in oilskins and wool sweaters were mending nets, cigarettes dangling from the corners of their mouths.

An American girl we met on the train crossing the Russian border had told us that a friend of hers lived in the village and that we should look him up. Ben drew the short straw and stayed with the gear. Remy and I headed into the village to visit Hank, an American who had fallen in love with Russia and had lived here for thirteen years. We were very curious.

We walked through a cluster of nearly identical log homesteads. Each sported a weathered clapboard fence, a vegetable plot, and a barking mongrel. A scowling teenage girl in a miniskirt watched us stroll up the street. Her lipstick matched the geraniums flowering in the window behind her. She wore her disdain like a medal—the perpetual bored pout of adolescents everywhere.

"Do you know where we can find Hank, the American?" Remy asked in Russian.

She snapped her chewing gum. "Straight ahead, turn left at the school, and it's the house with the new fence." Then she went back to perfecting her look of glum indifference.

"*Spasiba,*" we thanked her.

*Snap!* went her gum.

We found Hank's just where she had said. It was a modest log home no different from the others. Within the confines of his seven-foot larch fence, potatoes, lettuces, and strawberries grew abundantly. Two sawhorses, some hand tools, and lengths of cut lumber indicated that renovations were under way.

"Hello," I called. The ubiquitous mangy dog barked and a sleepy-looking Russian woman emerged from the house.

"Hank?"

"One minute, please," she said in heavily accented English. "I will get him."

A few minutes later Hank appeared at the doorway. He was a lean, intelligent-looking man in his forties. He wore plain leather shoes, dark wool pants, and a gray wool shirt. His beard and hair matched the gray of his shirt, and he peered at us through silver-rimmed oval spectacles. "Hello," he said cautiously in English.

"I'm Colin. We met a friend of yours, Amy. She said we must visit you."

"Ah, yes, Amy. Where did you meet her? How's she doing?"

"In Mongolia. She was at the border of Russia and Mongolia on the train. She seemed quite happy."

Hank nodded. "Come on inside. Have you had breakfast yet?"

We shook our heads and followed him inside.

"This is one of the oldest houses in the village. It's more than a hundred years old."

I looked admiringly at the cozy, functional interior. A large brick woodstove dominated the small living area. There was no plumbing. Above the porcelain sink hung a galvanized water container with a spigot. The sink drained into a bucket.

Hank's Russian wife, a strong-looking middle-aged woman, busied herself in the kitchen while the rest of us sat at a small wood table. Shafts of sunlight pierced the cabin's twilight, lancing through mullioned windows.

Hank's four-year-old daughter leapt onto his lap and he murmured something in her ear.

"So what made you decide to leave the luxury of America and immigrate to a tiny village in Siberia?" Remy asked.

"Simply, simplicity," Hank said with a sigh. "Thirteen years ago I was involved with an American peacekeeping program. We came out to Russia to try to improve relations between our two suspicious nations during the Cold War. It was then that I fell in love with the country. Shortly after, I fell in love with something else."

He smiled at his wife, who placed some bread, salted fish, and cottage cheese in front of us.

"In their quest for material goods, people at home have completely lost sight of why they are on this planet. Here a professional makes ninety dollars per month and they don't complain. Four or five years of university education and they are making a quarter of someone on welfare back home. Yet the people on welfare in America claim they are not getting enough: 'A human cannot live in dignity on four hundred dollars a month.' The teachers want more, the garbagemen want more, the bus drivers want more, everyone at home wants more money. Here in Siberia there is no more money to have.

"Instead of digging for money out here, we dig for our roots. We dig our gardens, we help our neighbors, and we read books. Have you noticed what broad knowledge all Russians have?" He paused a moment, but didn't wait for either of us to answer.

"You can find a trapper living five hundred miles from the nearest city and he knows about the whole world. He knows about satellite telephones, he knows about the Internet, he knows about the United States and Canada. But he is content to spend each day tending to his traps and picking berries and mushrooms. That is why I am living in Russia."

I put some cottage cheese and fish on a slice of rye. Hank's wife put a kettle on the stove. "Where does your water come from?" I asked.

"We fetch it from the lake. The cleanest water in the world comes from Lake Baikal," Hank said proudly.

"It won't always be, though," he added quickly, "if they keep dumping pollution in it from the pulp mills. Since perestroika, too many businessmen have emerged with too few regulations. I used to work as a ranger for the national park just east of here. I wasn't corrupt, though. I was a servant of nature and not of the mafia, so soon I found myself without a job. That is the way Russia works now."

"So what are you doing now?" I asked.

"I sometimes work as a guide. Foreigners come and seek me out because I am a Westerner and know the local area. I don't think this is right, though. It should be the native inhabitants displaying their land. So I am creating an organization to teach guiding skills. More than half the local population are indigenous Buryats. They are losing touch with their roots."

The Buryats, Hank explained, were about 250,000 people of Mongolian ancestry who lived around Lake Baikal and in the surrounding area, on land long disputed among China, Russia, and, on occasion, Japan. The nomadic Buryats were the original inhabitants of this rugged land.

During the early days of the Russian Empire, the Cossacks migrated from western Russia, pillaging what they could of Siberia's riches. They treated the indigenous people of Siberia as serfs and expropriated prime land for their own uses. Local history recounted how they had terrorized the women and children and forced the men to provide as tribute (or at criminally low prices) furs that were then sold at an obscene markup to the well-heeled European market. The Buryats were also forced to stop practicing their traditional shamanism and were compelled to convert to Christianity. Several revolts took place, and the Buryats valiantly clung to their own culture.

The final blow to their dying pride was Stalin's iron-fisted policies, according to Hank. Stalin rounded up all the Buryat spiritual and social leaders and had them executed. The remaining population were absorbed into the Soviet machine, their culture all but lost.

Now, Hank told us, the Buryats were again trying to recapture their past. It was a difficult process; many, having lost their dignity, had resorted to alcohol and cared about nothing other than where the next bottle of vodka was coming from.

Hank said he was part of the movement to preserve and promote Buryat culture. "Sharing their culture with foreigners," he said, "will give them more cause to celebrate their history. The land and people in this region are intertwined to the point where they can't be separated. That is why I don't feel that I'm the one to show tourists around. I am as much a tourist as you are."

After breakfast Hank asked if we would like to stay the night and have a *banya*—a local type of sauna. There was nothing we would have liked better, but we didn't want to keep Tim Cope waiting. We had arranged to meet the Australian adventurer the next day in a village called Listvianka, at the entrance to the Angara River.

Hank walked with us down to the boat and Ben.

"Would you like to make a call home?" I asked, realizing there were no telephones for hundreds of miles.

Hank broke into a broad smile. "Much as I like the simple life, I do miss speaking to my mother. I haven't talked to her in years."

Ben handed Hank the Iridium handset and within minutes he was talking to his elderly mother in San Francisco. He seemed very touched when he rang off, and was quite emotional as he shook my hand good-bye.

"I wish I was coming with you. It's not often I'm discontent with my life here, but—" Hank hesitated. "There's just something magical about the thought of rowing twenty-five hundred miles from here to the Arctic Ocean. Maybe I will build my own wooden boat some day."

With a wave, he was gone.


*Thursday, June 28*

We rowed for almost twenty hours after leaving Hank, each taking a turn at the oars. We stopped once to cook a pot of rice, sardines, and tomato sauce. Around 1:00 A.M. it was fairly dark, but a swath of pale light along the southern horizon was always with us.

Around four, as dawn's mother-of-pearl fingers raked the horizon, we grounded the raft on a sandy beach at Listvianka. Straight ahead, Lake Baikal stretched off into the distance, its waves sparkling in the twilight. To our right, a mighty river flowed out of the lake—the Angara. Almost every guidebook and encyclopedia likes to point out that this is Baikal's only outflow, despite the numerous rivers and streams flowing in. I don't find this particularly amazing, since it is a geographical fact that every lake in the world will have only one outflow (and occasionally none at all). We would be following the Angara for 1,250 miles, until it joined with another major river. From there on, we would be on the Yenisey proper.

Listvianka, which had been a thriving lakeside center since the mid-1700s, was now a tourist mecca for Russians in the region. The main street faced the bay that drained into the Angara River. In the middle of the river, at its head, stood a precipitous rock cliff. This massif was protected by the government as a national site because of its place in local folklore. According to legend, old Chief Baikal wanted to marry his beautiful daughter Angara to a young warrior named Irkut (a tributary of the Angara). But Angara fell in love with another knight, Yenisey, and ran away to join him. Her furious father cast the huge Shaman Cliff after her.

We waited for Tim on the beach with anticipation. What would it be like having another member on board after so long with just the three of us? Sunlight dappled the waves and burnished the hulls of a smart-looking fleet of fishing boats and sparkling charter vessels. We took turns exploring the adjacent village. In front of the docks, tourists milled among tables laden with carved jade fish, postcards, polished rocks, wooden handicrafts, and smoked fish. Others lounged around plastic tables under huge umbrellas, sipping coffee or beer. The shipyard that was the town's main industry sat idle; partially finished ships lay in various stages of completion.

About 11:00 A.M. a shiny new Lada with the Russian Television AS Baikal logo on its side came roaring up. Five occupants spilled out, along with a big TV camera. A young man with shoulder-length sandy hair, who looked like a surfer, stepped jauntily ahead of the others. "Hi, I'm Tim," he said, as the cameras whirred away.

The Russian news team remained for about an hour while we got acquainted with Tim. He was fluent in Russian, and translated the news reporters' questions so we could answer. Compared with Remy's rough, halting version of the tongue, Tim sounded like a native.

After the camera crew left, we pushed the raft off the beach. The conversation became more relaxed as we got to know one another. Tim stands a lanky six feet tall and, although a little clumsy in appearance, he took to the oars quickly. He is a passionate man whose blue eyes fired with excitement as he spoke about his love of Siberia and the joy he felt at being back.

The most treasured item Tim brought with him was a

$6,000, three-chip video camera. It was a far better camera than what we had with us. Encouraged by the success of his previous expedition's documentary, Tim said his primary goal was to put his energy into recording this trip.

In some ways, it almost felt as if we were embarking on a new journey. As well as picking up a new team member, we also planned on purchasing a new boat—better suited to the flat water that lay ahead. Lake Baikal is renowned for its traditional fishing dories, and we felt this style of boat would be ideal for our purposes. With Tim on board we would begin the search for our new vessel.

A calm day on the Angara River.

# THE LITTLE DORY THAT COULD

*Thursday, June 28*

We stowed Tim's gear and set off down the Angara River to Irkutsk, the capital of east Siberia. The river was about five hundred yards wide and the current was brisk. I had never seen such a large river with water so clear. It felt as though we were flying rather than floating over the rocks and boulders of the riverbed two yards beneath us. After a few hours, though, the river widened, the water deepened, and the current slowed to a snail's pace. It was the first indication that the river was backing up behind the giant Irkutsk Dam, which stood downstream and would mark the end of one leg of our journey.

As we traveled, we scoured the riverbank for a suitable boat that we could buy for the next segment of the trip. Before leaving Canada, Ben and I had envisioned acquiring a clinker-built wooden dory. Our raft and kayaks were designed for whitewater, and our progress on the flat was now painfully slow. Because of the raft's bulbous proportions and flat bottom, even a light headwind would stop it dead in its tracks. For much of the river, because of the huge hydroelectric reservoirs, we would have no current assisting us. A wooden dory, on the other hand, would be better suited for cutting through the wind and waves. As well, its longer waterline length would allow us to row faster even in calmer conditions. Speed now was of utmost importance if we were to get to the end before freeze-up.

Back in Canada, we had presumed that there would be plenty of traditional fishing vessels around Lake Baikal, and we'd have no trouble acquiring a boat. Surprisingly, most were aluminum and too small to transport four adults and a load of equipment. The larger boats were generally steel-hulled fishing vessels with diesel engines. There was nothing really suitable.

We did come across a thirteen-foot aluminum skiff, tapered at the front and back, that was tempting, though not quite perfect. It was a little small for our purposes, but we were getting anxious. So far we had not seen a better boat in Siberia. The owners stood excitedly as we hemmed and hawed. "Fifteen dollars," they offered.

"We'll keep looking," Tim told them.

Tim bantered and joked with the locals. It was amazing seeing just how easily he communicated with the people along the way, an asset that would prove to be invaluable over the next few months.

*Friday, June 29*

After hours of scanning the banks, we spotted the perfect boat lying apparently abandoned beside the tiny community of Nikolai, a hamlet of perhaps ten or fifteen log homes.

"Hey, guys, how does that boat over there look?" Ben asked.

The boat was about eighteen feet long, wide and deep, and a lapstrake—constructed with overlapping planks—specimen of the finest craftsmanship. But it was old and decrepit, its blue paint almost completely buffed off by the weather. Many of the planks were rotted and cracked; big chinks yawned between the overlapping planks. The boat would sink within minutes if launched.

Two old men stumbled down from the dachas to see what we were doing. They told us that the owner of the boat had died three years before and it had sat there ever since.

"So who owns it now?" Tim asked in Russian.

One of the men rubbed his bushy eyebrows, sucked on his hand-rolled cigarette, and exhaled a stream of smoke. "No one."

"Didn't he have any relatives or friends?" Tim asked.

"Nah." The old man spat, a long string of brown spittle falling onto his bare chest like a piece of Spiderman's web. "He didn't have any friends here. We all reckon it was the mafia that finished him off. The police say it was an accident."

"If you want this boat, just take it," his withered sidekick interjected. "It's an eyesore and we plan on burning it pretty soon. You'll never get anywhere with it—it's a rotten piece of garbage!"

We returned to our raft satisfied and full of schemes. The plan was to continue on to Irkutsk, find a place to store our whitewater gear, and return by road to take this boat back to Irkutsk by truck. In Irkutsk we would spend two weeks making it seaworthy—and then on to the Arctic Ocean.

The two old men shook their heads as we rowed away.

We continued until the last rays of sun vanished before landing on a small beach surrounded by a mixture of stunted pine and birch trees. It looked like a little bit of paradise to me. What we didn't count on were the ticks—thousands of them.

Ticks in this part of Siberia carry the often-fatal disease encephalitis. If you are bitten by a tick, without swift medical intervention you have a one-in-ten chance of dying. Ben and Tim found five ticks on their bodies, but fortunately they had not been bitten. I found one with its head buried deep in my flesh.

It is important not to pull on the exposed tail end of the tick's body: usually that causes the head to come off under the skin, where it rots, causing later medical complications. So we tried a variety of techniques to extract the stubborn, crablike creatures.

Ticks breathe through their abdomens. When smeared with Vaseline, the tick should voluntarily withdraw its head to avoid suffocation—at least in theory. Unfortunately, it didn't work, and the tick continued to burrow deeper into my flesh. Ben recommended dumping DEET on it. Again, no luck. We tried a burning ember. The intense heat blistered my arm but did nothing to the tick. A Russian doctor had once told Tim to tie a thread around the tick's body, hold on to both ends of it, and twist and pull simultaneously. The boys tried this technique for what seemed like ages, pulling and twisting and twisting and pulling as I waited anxiously for the head to snap off. It didn't; the stubborn creature was finally extracted.

Twenty minutes later, we found a tick burrowing into

Tim's back and repeated the whole process. His was much smaller; when we got it out, we were unsure if the head was still under the skin.

"We'll go the hospital in Irkutsk and have our tick shots," I said.

Tim laughed at the thought of Russian medical care. "You know, on my last expedition," he said, "I went to the doctor's, limping through the door with a large gash in my leg. He eyed it and said, 'She's all right. Pour a bit of vodka on it each day for two weeks.' I said, 'You sure?' The doctor took a second look at the gaping wound and said, 'Make sure you drink a lot of the vodka too.'"

We all laughed heartily.

*Sunday, July 1*

"Check out that plane!" Ben exclaimed, looking into the sky.

We were back on the raft, with Tim rowing us steadily toward Irkutsk. I looked up to see a jetliner making a broad, sweeping turn as it approached the airport.

"Back at home they would never bank that close to the ground," Ben said incredulously.

I didn't take much notice of his comment, not being too concerned about the finer details of airplane handling. Two days later, though, right where Ben had been pointing, a jet plunged into the ground, killing all 143 people on board.

After a day of skating along at a fine speed, despite the lack of current, we came upon Irshee, a small community of gingerbread dachas on the outskirts of Irkutsk. We needed to find a place to overhaul our wooden dory, and this hamlet was a perfect location for the job.

"Which cottage shall we try first?" Tim asked, as he maneuvered the long oars.

"That brown one with the pagoda out front looks inviting," I said, directing his attention to three young women in string bikinis.

"I second that one," Ben said.

Tim guided the raft to shore. As we got closer, the young women, who didn't look older than sixteen, began chattering. Tim hailed them in Russian. They replied quietly, as though they wanted nothing to do with us.

But Russian hospitality prevailed. Within a few minutes, the veil was lifted, and the giggling teenage girls offered us cups of tea. A few minutes later, their scowling parents arrived to investigate the commotion. The father bore such a striking resemblance to Al Bundy from *Married with Children* that we immediately dubbed him Al. "Sure, you can leave your gear here and work on your new boat," he said, after hearing about our expedition. "If you need any tools, I have an assortment you can use."

The girls helped us store our gear within the fenced confines of the little cottage. The raft was deflated, the frame disassembled, and the kayaks carried up. The whitewater equipment was being retired; we would cover the remaining 2,500 miles in the wooden dory.

After we had stowed our equipment, one of the neighbors offered us a ride into the center of Irkutsk, about fifteen minutes away by road. We planned to stay with a friend of Tim's while we organized the retrieval and repair of the battered wooden boat.

*Monday, July 2*

We were excited to have made it to Irkutsk, an industrial hub of nearly a million people built below the massive dam. It is named after the Irkut River, a tributary that enters the

Angara nearby. The Trans-Siberian Railway passes through as well, making it very accessible. The city has a large student population, and it pulses with pubs and clubs. Earthquakes frequently rock the region and the fifty-year-old dam does not inspire confidence, but residents are unconcerned about living in its shadow. Although it is almost four hundred years old, the city was decimated in 1879 by a fire that raged for three days and nights—a blaze as apocalyptic as the inferno that consumed much of Chicago only eight years earlier. The wealthy merchants and landowners rebuilt Irkutsk in grand style, importing the best architects from Moscow and St. Petersburg. It was their vision that greeted us.

The millionaire brothers Vtorov had 1,500 employees and shops in western Europe, China, and Mongolia. Their whimsical brick house, designed in the Neo-Russian style, is still standing. Another millionaire ordered a residence resembling the design of the Louvre in Paris. And the great architect Qwarengi considered it an honor to build for the powerful merchant Sibyryakov; his White House was dubbed by contemporaries the "Oriental Palace" because of its blinding richness. In rebuilding, the inhabitants of Irkutsk also laid out a plethora of parks, all of which led to the city's being christened "the Paris of Siberia." That heritage was still evident.

Money remained conspicuous everywhere, but it was not in everyone's hands. Many of the people I saw were poor, peering from tiny apartments as trains laden with the region's riches regularly pulled away, destined for Asia and Europe.

I knew that most Siberian cities were proud of their wooden architecture, but in Irkutsk the handcrafted artistic wooden elements were nonpareil. For carpentry buffs, there were sights everywhere—Baroque bands decorated with sun rays and fans were spanned by graceful volutes and embellished with splendid bouquets; carved tulips hung over windows; slim irises covered house walls; figured carvings ran along the edges of roofs—every kind of icing and decoration adorned the houses. I knew only a little of the mystery of wooden lacework, but traveling through Irkutsk was a veritable education in Slavic culture and extraordinary craftsmanship.

In the center of the city, some of the log buildings stood two and three storys high. Between these charming structures, trams jam-packed with commuters clattered back and forth. It was as if the nineteenth and twentieth centuries continued to coexist. Some streets were lined with buildings featuring the latest concrete-and-glass architecture, complete with atriums, fountains, and parks. On others, babushkas lined up at drinking-water pumps to fill their household containers.

Despite the severe poverty, people were dressed stylishly. The women favored high heels and sexy, fashionable prêt-à-porter. But the boulevards were lined with unkempt shrubbery and trees. In the summer heat, the city had a wild, junglelike, fecund feeling to it.

Tim had arranged for us to stay with a friend of his named Ela, who lived on the west side of the river, about ten minutes from the city center. A petite twenty-two-year-old who worked for the tourist bureau, Ela occasionally supplemented her salary by taking boarders into her small one-bedroom flat. She refused to let us pay, saying it was her way of contributing to the expedition.

Her apartment was in a twelve-story concrete-block building of the type favored by Soviet planners. There was a forest of such high-rises around the city, and we'd seen similar construction techniques in Mongolia. A large steel door protected the front entrance, and Ela's apartment was behind two more heavy, bolt-equipped doors. Steel bars covered the outside windows. The building was a veritable fortress. Inside the tiny but cozy apartment, Ela had painted the wooden floors and decorated with some well-used but functional furniture and a broken computer.

Ela assured us that anything we needed—blocks of tar, plywood, a gas stove, screws, paint, Australian Stanley wine, imported German beer—could be found somewhere in the city's abundant stores and markets.

Our first task, though, was to find some gamma globulin—it would boost our immune systems and ward off our chances of getting encephalitis from the ticks. It turned out that so many people were in need of it, we had to go to five chemists before we could buy enough for each of us.

## Tuesday, July 3

The four of us hitchhiked to Nikolai, the dacha community where our decaying clinker-built dory lay. Catching a ride was easy in that country; as usual, we were picked up by the very first vehicle, a Lada. We crammed inside, and I was surprised at how fast our maniac driver (who was about thirty-five) was able to coax his small car into going. He passed everything on the road—blind corners were irrelevant. I felt closer to death in that little red Lada than I had while crossing Lake Baikal. The only time the speedometer dropped below a hundred miles an hour was when we encountered a chaotic jam of emergency vehicles tending to the jetliner crash of only hours earlier. Our destination was only two and a half miles distant.

The boat lay exactly as we had left it, and we still needed to find a truck to take it back to Irkutsk. It was so heavy the four of us couldn't budge it.

"Don't worry," Tim said, "things always work out here in Russia. Just watch."

I didn't share his confidence.

We retraced our steps to the main road, about half a mile away down a rutted track. We watched as a trickle of vehicles passed—mostly rusted Ladas. When a truck with a built-in crane rumbled toward us, Tim stuck out his hand and said, "This is us!"

The air brakes hissed and the large flatbed pulled to a stop beside us.

Tim asked the driver and his partner, a pair of local haulers returning from a construction job, if they were interested in another trip for $20.

"*Da,*" they said eagerly.

After giving them directions to the boat, we leapt on the flatbed. The truck rumbled and bucked down the pitted road back to Ben and Remy.

We attracted quite a crowd from the nearby dachas. Everyone was interested in seeing a half-ton dory swinging on the end of a cable. But the men knew their business, and they were able to hoist the boat aboard without incident, using the hydraulic crane on the back of the truck.

I felt quite nervous. Despite what the old men had told us, it still felt strange to come into a tiny village in the middle of Siberia and grab a boat with a big truck. What if they had been pulling our legs? I half-expected someone to emerge from the gathering crowd to ask what the hell we were doing with his boat. Or even worse, if it really was the mafia that had killed the owner, perhaps they might consider the boat their property.

Once the boat was loaded, the driver, Andrei, asked Tim for the bill of sale. Tim shook his head.

"There are many police roadblocks," Andrei said. "If we are stopped, the police will ask for proof of ownership."

"We don't have papers," Tim said. "Nobody owns the boat."

Andrei laughed, pulling out an official-looking book. "If you don't have papers, I make papers for you. No problem."

Two hours later the boat was at Al's cottage in Irshee.

*Wednesday, July 4*

We didn't want just to make the boat float; we also had elaborate plans to build a small cabin, a sliding rowing seat, long, efficient oars, and a system of incorporating oarlocks spaced out from the boat. These elements were essential if we were to cover the remaining distance rowing 24/7 under adverse conditions.

Back home, with access to a garage, a car, and tools, it would have been an ambitious undertaking. In Siberia, without proper tools, working on an expanse of grass miles from the city center, and dealing with a foreign language, the job was even more intimidating. Still, we were even planning to put little knobs on our cupboards!

Now that we had our boat and a place to work on it, we began to ponder the logistics of our intended creation. Boris, one of the local residents whom we called "Al," had offered to let us use an assortment of his hand tools. As well, he had given us the address for a large builder's supply that would have most of the hardware and materials we would need. The amount of work we planned on doing over the next two weeks was immense. It would need to be a streamlined, coordinated effort.

Since transportation was so difficult, it would have been easiest if we could have purchased all the paint, brushes, sandpaper, caulking, lumber, etc., in one go. Because it was such a complex project, however, we were unable to calculate the precise amounts we would need, and almost every day we created a new list of materials to be purchased. A shopping trip usually took the better part of a day, so generally a work-day consisted of two of us working on the boat while the other two bumbled around in crowded markets looking for materials.

Making the hull shipshape was the most important job, and it took nearly a week. First we scraped off the remaining paint and tar to expose the bare wood. We identified the rotten and cracked planks—a lot of the hull was rotten—and strengthened them with a layer of fiberglass and epoxy resin purchased from the builder's supply.

I was a little concerned about the quality of the Russian materials. Instead of becoming rock-hard, the resin dried to a flexible, leathery finish. It didn't seem to add much strength to the rotten planks, and the tightly woven glass cloth wouldn't conform to the curves of the wood very well. The result was far from satisfactory, but we didn't have time for alternatives.

Dmitri, a local TV reporter who had been following our story, suggested that a good way to seal the cracked planks would be to apply tar to the boat. He took us on a hunt for a block of tar. His father-in-law was in the road-building business and had a seventy-pound lump stored in the garage. "This is what the poor children chew on instead of gum," Dmitri told us.

His father-in-law refused to take any payment for the tar, saying he was happy to help our expedition.

We built a large fire near the boat and suspended a bucket of hard tar above the flames. Within an hour it was a bubbling cauldron of treacle, and we painted it liberally onto the boat. As it cooled, the tar hardened into a tough barrier. We hoped it would keep the hull watertight by sealing the myriad, infinitesimally small holes and hairline cracks in the wood. We painted over the tar with ocher enamel and let it dry in the hot sun. We were quite proud of our efforts.

*Tuesday, July 10*

As work progressed on the boat, we met many of the locals, some of whom were pretty eccentric and set in their ways. I met a man named Valery in the market and had a long chat with him. His English was excellent, but the thirty-four-year-old carpenter wouldn't stop talking. I was anxious to get on my way because the others were waiting for me back at the boat. Finally, in a polite bid to get away, I invited Valery to drop by the boat sometime and hastily departed.

The following day Valery was waiting at the boat when we arrived at 8:30 A.M. He was staring at the dory, sporting a heavy frown. "Many people stupidly try deceiving themselves," Valery said after scrutinizing the boat. "The work you are doing to the vessel is garbage—no good! I have seen boats in much better shape sink quickly."

Valery did not mince his words. Our method of patching the boat, he explained, was definitely not advisable. From his professional view, we should replace the rotten and cracked planks, pull the rusted screws, and re-form the cracked ribs. To do less was to invite disaster, he said.

"Yes," I replied. "I do realize that what we are doing is not the ideal way to fix the boat. We do not have time to restore this boat back to her original condition. Instead of two weeks, it would take six months. The river would be frozen over before we could start. The fiberglass and tar we are laying over the rotten planks will do."

Valery wouldn't listen; he predicted tragedy. "You cannot be serious. Slapping a coat of tar and a coat of paint on a bunch of rotten planks is asking for trouble."

I tried again to explain to him that while our methods were not ideal, I believed they would work. "Stupidity is trying to sail back to Canada in the thing," I said. "We're just trying to get down a river!"

He wouldn't listen. Worse, he insisted on arguing the point interminably.

"Look, we *want* to do a shoddy job!" I said. "We need to do the bare minimum to make this boat float. I think it will float. You think it won't. Unfortunately, you're not building this boat. So you may as well shut up!"

He did, although he continued to stand around shaking his head.

Others were equally opinionated, but none was quite so annoying. Boris, the man who had lent us his yard to build the boat on, came by each day and viewed our progress with interest. We came to value his routine handshake, his supportive tone, and the tools he often lent us. Although he too suggested the boat would never float, by the end he was confident that we would make it.

We were also more than grateful whenever a local babushka brought us a cold bottle of kvass, a drink made from fermented bread. Others would come by and invite us to their homes for vodka or barbecued meat. Unfortunately, time was always a pressing concern and more often than not we would have to politely decline the invitations.

When the boat was ready for launching, we recruited a few local men to help drag it to the water.

"She's a two-dollar hooker in a hundred-dollar dress if I've ever seen one," said Ben.

"As long as she floats, that's all that counts," said Tim.

A few minutes later we were whooping it up from the deck of the boat that Valery had insisted would sink like a stone. We slapped each other on the back. If she could float for half an hour, we'd consider her river-worthy.

Valery strolled to the water's edge, shaking his head. "It is foolish to think your boat will make it."

We paddled out into the lake, away from his doom and gloom.

*Wednesday, July 11*

During our hectic time in Irkutsk we occasionally made nocturnal visits to a few of the hundreds of pubs and clubs in the area. Except for the heavy security—complete with metal detectors and full-body searches—the nightlife wasn't much different from things back at home. The people were a little more sophisticated in their dress, and the music was invariably Russian electronic pop. Young and old alike enjoyed jiving to this new style of music.

At a jazz club we visited, Ben became acquainted with a young Russian woman who was an adventure-sports enthusiast. She had recently been a participant in the Camel Trophy Race, Russia's equivalent of the Eco-Challenge, sponsored by a tobacco company.

Olya was a tall, healthy-looking twenty-three-year-old who had been born in Irkutsk. Her proper name was Arkadyevna Olga Artemieva, but she called herself Olya. She jogged, rode a mountain bike, and swam to stay in great shape, and regularly competed in triathlon-type events. She was completing postgraduate work in psychology at Irkutsk State University. She spoke passable English in a high-pitched voice that bordered on falsetto. Like so many Mongolians and Russians we met who had a basic grasp of English, she was hungry for a chance to practice the language and learn about Western culture. Ben invited her to drop by the boat to see what we were up to.

After her first visit, Olya began arriving at the work site daily on her mountain bike to help us sand, paint, scrape—anything that was required. In Canada we had talked about inviting a native Russian on part of the journey as a kind of cultural exchange, and she seemed a suitable candidate. What better way to learn about another people than to be cooped up on an eighteen-foot boat for days on end?

So far, Russians still seemed a bit of a mystery. Their culture is so different from our own, and it is evident in their every action, every mannerism. On the streets and in their homes, we were proffered only brief glimpses into what made people tick. A week with a female Russian student of psychology, we hoped, would offer some insight into a culture that only a few years ago had been an ominous mystery to most.

We were pleased with Olya's reliability and bubbly personality, and ended up inviting her to join us for the ten-day, four-hundred-mile trip to Bratsk, the next major city downriver. She was enthusiastic, saying the trip would allow her to observe and document the interaction of four men in a tiny boat (which especially intrigued her as a psychology student), practice her English, and gain some insight into Western culture. We thought it was a fun idea.

As we got to know Olya, we learned that she was a born-again Christian with some rather rigid views about the world and personal conduct. Remy had been a born-again Christian for years and shared many of Olya's views on morals and spirituality. The two of them got along like a house on fire.

*Thursday, July 12–Saturday, July 14*

After we had finished the hull, the good weather broke and heavy rain and violent winds strafed Irkutsk for four days, flooding many surrounding communities. Our work came to a standstill, and I used the time to visit the local Internet café.

The woman on the computer next to me was having a great time in a chat room with some English-speaking friends. She leaned over, introduced herself as Elena, and asked if I could help her with her vocabulary.

Could I? Struck by her sculpted features and shining shoulder-length brown hair, I not only gave her all the help she needed, but also asked her for a date. The next day Elena and I sat in an outdoor bistro on an island in the river. Two bridges connected the island and the mainland, and it must have been an idyllic spot in the summer sun. In spite of the unsettled weather, people filled the red-and-white plastic chairs and tables of the bistro.

"I once had my own business selling flowers," twenty-two-year-old Elena said wistfully at one point. "I made more money then than I do now as a banker with a degree in economics."

"So why did you quit with the flowers?" I asked gamely.

"I am an honest person," Elena replied. "In Russia, honest businesspeople do not survive. The government takes ninety percent and the mafia takes the rest. I sold lots of flowers and felt guilty for only declaring half. After several months I was visited by a man in a suit. He told me I would have to share . . . or else."

"Or else what?" I asked, leaning forward.

"I don't know. That's when I stopped selling flowers."

A stocky waitress arrived at our table with two *shashlyks*—barbecued chicken—and black bread.

"The mafia are everywhere in Russia," Elena said, pushing the crispy chicken around with her fork. "The only wealthy businessmen are mafia. They are in the government, in the police, and in the army."

"So you're saying everyone I see driving around in a flashy car is corrupt?"

"Yes," she said bitterly. "The average wage in Siberia for professional workers is ninety dollars a month. Where you come from, the doctors and lawyers drive around in Mercedes. Here the doctors take the autobus or walk. Only businesspeople make money. Only mafia are businesspeople. So now I work as a banker and make eighty dollars a month."

Elena stared at her plate morosely. "Would you like the rest of my chicken?" she asked after a moment or two.

I nodded and eagerly dug into the tender meat.

"The only way for an honest Russian to make money is to leave Russia," she said.


*Sunday, July 15–Wednesday, July 18*

Finally the rains stopped, and we resumed work on the boat's cabin. We borrowed more hand tools from the generous Russians and continued purchasing hardware. Without Tim's fluent Russian, our hands would have been tied. As it was, we bought plywood, two-by-twos, screws, foam rubber, upholstery cloth, hinges, caulking, cupboard knobs, flooring, and more paint. We ferried the supplies to the work site by hitchhiking.

We worked from dawn till dusk, and it still took three full days to build the boat's superstructure. We drilled holes in the sides of the boat and attached the aluminum rowing frame from the raft. The heavy-duty oarlocks bolted onto the frame were just what we needed. The frame allowed us to position the oarlocks about a foot out from either side of the boat, providing a better mechanical advantage for rowing.

Remy had done some rowing while he was in university. Before embarking on the trip, he had asked a Canadian rowing coach to give him any old equipment that might help. Since the beginning of the journey we had been carrying with us an old rowing seat and the necessary parts to create a track it could slide along.

The only oars we could find in Irkutsk were too small. With such a large boat, and using the rowing seat, we needed oars about ten feet long. We ended up making them from tough larch wood, carving the blades into shape and attaching them to long two-by-twos.

At last the boat was ready!

We now had a seaworthy hull (well, relatively), a rowing system to propel our ship, and a Lilliputian cabin. We had cut open circular portholes into the sides of the cabin to allow light and fresh air into the claustrophobic interior. It had only one hatchlike entrance, which led aft into the open rowing area. We planned to keep moving around the clock, so the cabin's space—about two cubic yards—was designed to house four people. In a pinch, the small V-berth up front could take two people.

In the central area, we had created a tiny kitchen on the starboard side: propane stove, counter, cupboards, and an enamel bowl for cleaning. On the other side was a settee that sat two people during the day and doubled as a single bed at night. Somebody would always be outside at the oars, so this would help ease the cramped conditions slightly. Still, while Olya was on board, one person would be forced to sleep on the floor between the settee and the galley.

We were a bit behind schedule with no time to waste. The first thing we had to do was transport the boat to below the dam, so we rented a truck with a crane. While the boat was being moved, Tim, Olya, and I went shopping for hundreds of pounds of food. Ben went to buy a stove, propane supplies, and some other hardware. Remy busied himself at an Internet café, catching up on his e-mail and sending a report to the newspaper for which he was writing an account of the journey.

*Thursday, July 19*

During the day a crowd gathered and stared doubtfully as we loaded our gear and food into the boat. We were ready to set off across the Bratsk Sea—the reservoir of the largest dam in the world.

"The Bratsk Sea can get pretty big," one old man said, as he picked at a rotten plank with an index finger.

I nodded and continued to ram an endless stream of bags into the tiny cabin. The storage compartments we had constructed in the cockpit, under the beds, and in the cooking area were not large enough to hold everything. The boat was a disorganized mess of food and equipment—chaotic, but floating.

We pushed away from the industrial waterfront at 2:00 A.M. with Remy on the oars. We were swiftly enveloped by the river's darkness. Tim snuggled up on the bow outside while Ben, Olya, and I jammed into the cabin like sardines. After such a long day, I quickly fell into a fitful sleep, my head against a porthole, a lullaby of creaking wood and the squeaky rowing seat in my ears.

At four-thirty a crunching noise startled me out of a deep slumber. The boat tipped and an avalanche of bags buried me. As I struggled to free myself, I heard Remy and Tim shouting. I emerged, disoriented, from the cabin.

The boat was aground on a rocky shoal. The ripping current pressed her over at a 45-degree angle, pinning the hull against the rocks. Ben appeared beside me, rubbing his eyes. The port gunwale was two inches from going under. If that happened, the boat would swamp.

Tim, Ben, and I climbed into the icy water and began pushing the hull free. Poor Olya remained in the cabin, unsure what was going on. Remy pulled on the oars and slowly the boat inched through the roiling water of the shoal into a deeper channel. We leapt aboard before the current could sweep the boat downriver.

An old man's warning before we departed from Irkutsk echoed in my ears as we continued through the inky blackness: "Watch out for snags. Many fishermen drown every year by getting flipped by overhanging trees." I shivered. After our experience in Mongolia with the ill-fated flip, the danger of snags didn't escape me. Our wooden dory would capsize much more readily than the broad yellow raft. Its small wooden cabin would be a convenient coffin.

I strained my eyes in the darkness. Only shadows—real and imagined—could be seen. Tim was now at the oars, and I joined Olya and Ben, their faces eerily illuminated by a hurricane lantern.

"Is everything good?" Olya asked nervously. "Why was boat tipping over?"

"Remy was on the side pinching a loaf," Ben said with a sly grin, knowing the colloquialism would escape comprehension. "Nothing to worry about."

I lay restlessly, listening with every pore for the dull thud indicating we'd hit a snag. A few seconds after that, the boat would start to fill with water.

"Colin, it is your turn for row," Olya said, shaking my shoulder.

I looked at my watch. I had been asleep for half an hour. Through the round porthole, I could see that the sky was at its Michael Jackson stage—transforming from black to light.

"No snags?" I asked groggily.

"I don't think so. But if you want, I could cook up potatoes. You want potatoes for snack?"

I smiled and shook my head. I climbed into the cockpit and fondled the oar handles. This would be my first go, and I was eager to test the rowing seat.

Fully loaded, the streamlined vessel weighed about a ton and could normally be propelled through the water at about three miles an hour. Our lumbering yellow raft had moved at one and a half miles an hour at the best of times. With the swift current in this part of the river, we were clocking more than six miles an hour.

"I told you you'd love that sliding seat," Remy said as I pistoned back and forth. "By the end of the trip you'll have legs like an ugly elephant."

The sky was blushing. As the shore became illuminated, my morbid thoughts of snags turned to more cheerful, mouthwatering visions of breakfast. With twenty-six pounds of porridge in the galley, the only question was, what consistency?

Twelve hours after our launch below Irshee, the current began to slow as we entered the Bratsk Sea. We had reached the world's largest reservoir, created by the Bratsk hydro-electric dam. Three such dams lay along the Angara River; 690 miles of flat, currentless water is created by these concrete structures. We estimated it would take us ten days to row from one end to the other. Headwinds were my greatest concern, the huge waves that sometimes occur notwithstanding. I felt confident that the dory, with her high bow and many layers of paint, would ride out the worst of storms. But fully loaded she weighed more than a ton, so it wouldn't take much to stop her dead in her tracks—especially on such an expansive body of water with no current.

**(10)**

Remy, Sergio, Ben, Olya, and two other Russians on the Bratsk Sea.

# THE WELCOMING ARMS OF THE MAFIA

*Friday, July 20*

The Bratsk Sea widened until it was about six miles across. Industrial towns lined both shores, each sporting a stand of red-and-white smokestacks belching clouds of various hues. Occasionally the flatulent sound of a Lada with a leaky exhaust system reverberated across the water. The reservoir runs in a fairly straight line, so when we looked north or south, we saw only water and sky. Between the towns and villages on the eastern and western shores was a panorama of pine and birch forests, rolling green fields, and red ocher cliffs.

"Is that water okay?" Olya asked. She pointed to two inches of water sloshing around under the floorboards.

"Sure," I replied. "All wooden boats leak. If there was no water, then I'd be worried."

My answer didn't calm her much. Olya seemed to have lost a bit of her enthusiasm. The reality of five people living in a leaky rowboat was beginning to sink in, so to speak. It was cramped—no, worse than cramped. The cook made dinner on a single burner while fending off the encroaching mess of bags and bodies. Finding needed utensils or supplies was often impossible. For Olya, like all of us, going to the washroom was a degrading ritual that demanded sticking her no-longer-private parts over the side. This was not a cruise ship.

We had developed a system for taking care of the day's chores, and it was working well. Each day one of us took a turn as "boy"—the boat's Cinderella. A boy's duties included cooking breakfast, lunch, and dinner, washing the dishes, cleaning the boat, making coffee and tea, keeping the thermos filled, and filtering the water. One day out of every five you took a turn working like a dog. On the other four days, you were waited on and catered to.

I have heard people use the term "marriage" to describe the in-your-face relationships that develop among team members on an adventure such as ours. On this expedition, marriage didn't come close to describing our interaction. When you are married, you can escape each other. Partners have different jobs, often different circles of friends, and are usually free when frustrated to go for a long walk or enjoy a day alone. They are also not forced to make life-or-death decisions on a daily basis. In contrast, living twenty-four hours a day in a rowboat was far more intense—tempers flared, emotions simmered, small annoyances became major irritants.

Yet, in spite of the hardships, Olya seemed intent on toughing it out. I felt confident that she would become less withdrawn once she had adapted emotionally and physically to life on the river.

*Saturday, July 21*

We were making very little progress. The tailwind we had enjoyed the night before had switched around and was blowing on our nose. Around noon, the wind became too strong, and we pulled into a sheltered harbor to wait for the weather to abate.

Grassy slopes and birch forests stretched back from the shore. A rutted dirt track connected this area to some distant civilization.

Three Russian couples were camping not far from where we parked the boat. Within minutes, a short, balding man of about thirty approached. "I am Kolya," he said—the Russian equivalent of Colin.

"I am Colin too," I told him. As we shook hands I could see his right thumb had been cut off at the first joint.

"Would you like to join us for lunch?" he asked.

We readily accepted. We ambled up through the tall grass and Scotch thistles to join the other Russians around a campfire. Three attractive middle-aged women handed us panfried *omuul* (a local fish), wild strawberries, *salaa* (salted pig fat), and bread.

Sasha, a burly man at the table across from me, was also missing the thumb of his right hand. I wondered if this was some kind of punishment meted out by the Russian mafia— a local version of the Japanese yakuza's disciplinary code, in which minor mistakes were punished by chopping off a segment of the errant gangster's finger.

After lunch we returned to the boat and took to the water at about 3:00 P.M., making the same slow progress toward Bratsk.

*Sunday, July 22*

Just about suppertime, we passed a large steel motor cruiser nudging the shore, with about a dozen people on its deck enjoying a barbecue. Young women in bikinis accompanied by potbellied men waved to us, beckoning for us to join them. Soon we were on the beach shaking hands and joining the party.

The barbecue was fit for a king—marinated pork, salads, bread, cheeses, salami, sauces, vodka, beer, juice, sweets, coffee, tea, fruits, and cola. It was as though they had been expecting us and had spent the day preparing the sumptuous repast.

"Eat, eat," said Alexander, a bear of a man about fifty.

"Do you think they're mafia?" whispered Ben, referring to the wealth these people seemed to possess.

Who knew? The mafia thing was almost becoming a bit of a joke with us. If a Russian possessed more than a rusty Lada, the Godfather jokes would start errupting. We kept our plates and glasses filled, smiling at anything that was said.

After dinner, one of the men, Volodia, invited us aboard the seventy-foot cruiser. The engine thundered to life and the boat sprinted away. It was a rocket. One of the women took the helm, and soon 120 tons of steel was carving tight figure eights. Someone turned on some disco music, and amid the cacophony of thumping dance tunes and inebriated hooting and hollering, Volodia produced a handgun and staggered onto the roof of the pilothouse. He brandished the pistol and fired several shots into the air.

Perhaps forgetting he weighed close to three hundred pounds, Volodia jumped from the roof of the pilothouse and landed hard on the steel deck. He crumpled into a heap like a pile of rags. Sheepishly getting to his feet, he stuck the gun in his waistband and pulled out a cigarette.

"You'll soon realize that parties in Russia are unlike any other you'll ever experience," Tim said. "These people have character."

The boat rumbled back to the beach, where it loomed over our tiny vessel. It was time for us to go. The wind was calm, and we had to make the most of such rare moments.

*Monday, July 23*

Our vessel moved at a fast walking pace with one person at the oars and no wind. Any more than a heavy breeze and a small swell, though, and the quarter-horsepower generated by the rower was lost. Our feeble splashes might disturb the water and scare the fish, but the boat would remain stationary.

The wind was strong, so we again beached the boat to wait for it to die.

The five of us gazed dejectedly through the little portholes, waiting for calm. It was a miserable, claustrophobic experience. Rain dribbled through small cracks in the cabin, the water finding its way down our leather-tanned necks and seeping through our T-shirts. Space was tighter than ever without someone at the oars. But the incessant rain confined the five of us to a cell of a cabin eighty centimeters high and nine feet in tapered length. We tried to cheer ourselves up by drinking tea and writing in our journals, but we were five grumpy peas in a wooden pod.

*Wednesday, July 25*

We had been rowing for seven days and had spent a total of four hours on land. Our boat was a tiny commune. Everyone had different duties—rowing, cooking, communicating on the sat phones, etc. When each of us performed his or her chore efficiently, we slowly came closer to achieving our goal of reaching the Arctic Ocean. And we were doing well, having covered sixty-five miles in the past twenty-four hours.

As our perfect model of communism inched forward, around us we saw the remains of the less successful Soviet empire. Hulking cranes hung rusting and idle over the water. Rundown tugs plied the waters, their barges struggling to stay afloat.

We passed a wrecked barge—still loaded with gravel—sitting on the river bottom, half submerged. The only paint left on her russet hull was a proud hammer and sickle.

Hundreds of silver fish surfaced near the boat, leaping like miniature dolphins. Tim grabbed the rod and cast into the school. Within minutes he had two fat, glistening, troutlike fish. We hoped we would soon catch more, as our twenty-two-pound bag of rice had somehow gone missing and our food wasn't stretching the way it should have.

Twilight was a magic time: the warm, bronze light dappled the water and caused the forest-cloaked shore to glow golden in the dying sun as white birch and dark larch created their own primitive pattern. The air was calm; only the splashing oars broke the silence. At moments like this I found picking up the satellite phone to do a radio interview with someone half a world away most surreal: "The roads this morning, folks, are gridlocked. It'll be a long time before you get anywhere, so relax and prick up your ears—we've got a lot on the show. Coming up, a chat with Colin Angus on the Yenisey River, somewhere in central Asia. Are you out there, Colin?"

Yes, I'm out here. Call it the mind-shifting travails of a twenty-first-century Huck Finn.

*Thursday, July 26*

We were in the largest part of the Bratsk Sea, and the city of Bratsk lay about fifty miles away. The wind and swell began picking up. I felt a little apprehensive. This was an area, according to a captain we'd talked to, notorious for storms, and the waves would often reach sixteen feet. Tim, at the oars, made a beeline for the shore—we didn't want to join the numerous boats that had gone down here.

I was impressed at how quickly Olya had adapted to the river way of life. She seemed to trust the boat's seaworthiness now and worked hard on the oars propelling the vessel through the water. Remy and Olya's relationship continued to blossom, and they would spend hours talking about their religion and the righteous paths they strove to follow. Throughout the boat Olya had decorated the plywood surfaces with hearts and small inscriptions professing how much she loved Remy. She felt she had finally met Mr. Right. The complete lack of privacy on the boat meant the two lovebirds could do little more than whisper sweet nothings to each other as the oars creaked through the night.

Although Olya didn't offer much in the way of a psychological analysis of our group dynamics, her presence was definitely a welcome addition to our team. Her local knowledge of culture, customs, and even ecology was invaluable in our quest to learn as much as possible about the land through which we were traveling.

Cooking became much more challenging when the weather was choppy. The interior turned into a shaking, swaying roller-coaster ride. The big black pot perched precariously upon a flickering blue flame. Eyes glanced frequently, nervously at the steamy scene. So much bare skin, so much potential energy in that pot, so much rocking!

Outside, the swell was compounded by reflected waves coming off the shore. Waves meeting waves reared up like fighting stallions. The product of their anger was a plume of spray and a violently rocking boat. The black pot jiggled precariously. Hands came from all directions to stabilize it. Lunch was ready.

Soon the Bratsk Sea and its storms would be behind us. But we had one more expansive reservoir to cross before we escaped massive manmade alterations to the environment, seas created where before only rivers had flowed.

Nights were now a time of eternal light. It was late July and, if we remained stationary, the days would get shorter. However, our northward progress was increasing the length of our days. During the darkest part of the night, although not bright, the southern sky remained aglow. Perhaps in another week or two it might be light enough at night to see obstacles in our path clearly, thereby making nighttime voyaging much safer, especially in strong currents.

*Friday, July 27*

We rowed slowly into Bratsk Harbor, a chaotic collection of large ships rocking and groaning against log piles and half-submerged wooden floats. The air was redolent with the scent of tar, diesel fuel, and putrid fish—the acrid perfume of ports the world over.

Bewildered, we searched among the maze of vessels for a spot to pull ashore.

Tim stood on the bow as a scout. He had been to Bratsk two

years earlier during his cycling expedition and had encountered a couple of interesting characters. One was an influential mafia man and the other was a salty dog named Pasha who owned a large charter boat that plied the Bratsk Sea.

Although Tim had lost the phone numbers of his Bratsk friends, typical Russian luck was on our side. As we entered the small port through a conglomeration of steel boats, submerged hulls, and welding flashes, the first person we saw was Pasha. About forty, blond, and adorned with a tidy mustache, Pasha was standing at the bow of his boat, organizing ropes. Almost as though he were expecting Tim, Pasha nodded casually as we rowed up in our wooden contraption.

"Tie up alongside. You can stay here as long as you want," the soft-spoken sea dog said with a smile. "You must really like Siberia, Tim."

Soon we were luxuriating on the expansive back deck of Pasha's cruiser, drinking tea and observing the vibrant atmosphere of an inland Siberian port. Pasha phoned Vladimir, Tim's mafia friend, and told us that he would be at the boat within half an hour. Little did I know, as I sat enjoying the late summer heat, that we were about to embark on a weekend like no other.

A honking horn marked the arrival of Vladimir. We glanced toward the shore and saw a slight but energetic man stepping out of a brand-new Lexus. Vladimir skipped up the gangplank, saw Tim, and gave him a big hug. He then turned to the rest of us, grinning broadly, and shook our hands.

One of those men who seem to have harnessed the energy of the sun itself, Vladimir radiated a warmth that belied the killer instinct one expects of the mafia. About forty-five, he was immaculately dressed in white shoes, dress pants, and a crisp white tailored shirt. His black hair was close-cropped, accentuating his sharp, sculpted features.

On Tim's previous journey through Siberia, he and his

traveling companion, Chris, had stopped at a café, exhausted after weeks of cycling through the Siberian wilderness. Vladimir, a man who respects those who take destiny into their own hands, had spotted the laden bicycles at the curbside. He immediately wanted to meet the owners of the bikes, feeling that they would have free spirits like his own. Tim and Chris were pleasantly surprised when the well-dressed man marched into the café and took them under his wing.

Now it was our turn.

Like most people in this area, Vladimir spoke no English and our ensuing conversations took place with Tim translating. Noting our filthy state, Vladimir said the first thing we should do was luxuriate in his *banya* (bathhouse). First, though, he led us down the dock to a stunning fifteen-foot speedboat with a molded one-piece fiberglass body, an inboard jet engine, and a plush bed in the bow. We blasted across the calm waters. After executing a few tight turns and a dash in which he let her unwind to show her speed, Vladimir quickly bored of his toy and piloted it back to shore. "Come, let's get you cleaned up," he said.

We piled into the leather interior of the new silver Lexus. As we drove, every five minutes or so Vladimir's cell phone would ring. "*Da, da, da.*" He'd rack the phone. It would ring again. "*Da, da, da.*" It was a real *Sopranos* act.

Vladimir told us he had not been long out of jail for his suspicious business connections when Tim first met him. Then he was driving a beat-up Lada and working in the forest industry. He now owned four luxury cars and was running the city's giant aluminum plant. Still, his criminal record prevented him from leaving Siberia. He could travel only vicariously, by talking to people such as Tim who passed through.

"He looks no worse for wear considering the ten years he spent in jail," Ben whispered to me.

"While entertaining us, he's probably making another half million," Remy quipped.

Vladimir sped through the industrial city, where most of the buildings were constructed of Soviet-era concrete. The Lexus hummed, hurtling past everything on the road. Up ahead I could see a police roadblock. I braced myself as Vladimir accelerated. Anxious glances ricocheted around the car's interior, but Vladimir continued talking as if nothing were amiss. "This building we are passing here is the Judo Club," he said.

The car fired past the line of vehicles pulled over by the squad of uniformed police. The officers nodded at the Lexus as it raced by. Vladimir paid them no mind, continuing with his story: "The club is fully funded by our company, and we have twelve hundred children who are being trained in judo. We also have a summer camp for underprivileged kids. I will take you there tomorrow."

On the way to his home, Vladimir stopped twice to introduce us to people. One was a tough-looking Chinese businessman, the other a former judo champion—now a bodyguard for Vladimir—named Igor, who drove a specially built GMC Suburban and was the biggest man I have ever met. We arrived at Vladimir's home to find the sauna preheated and the beer on ice. After two hours of lounging in the sauna, drinking beer, and splashing in the Jacuzzi, I felt like a human being again.

"It is time to eat," said our host.

We dressed and were soon sinking back once more into the rich upholstery of the silver Lexus as it flew through the night. Back in the city, the car slowed at the security gate of a hotel complex. The gate swung open, and two armed guards saluted Vladimir. We parked at the entrance to a neon-lit nightclub called Louisa. Vladimir led us past guards, metal detectors, and a sign that said NO KNIVES, GUNS, RADIOS, OR BOOTS ALLOWED. We were led through a packed dance hall flickering with strobe lights and upstairs to an exquisite dining room.

We sat at a large table and beautiful women appeared, distributing juice, vodka, salted fish, breads, and cheeses. Men and women fluttered around Vladimir like moths around a flame. Everyone appeared intent on making sure that he and his guests were having a good time. The staff were sycophantic, but the 110 percent they were trying to give was hampered by nervousness; plates clinked loudly and drinks were spilled. Everybody who walked by gave Vladimir a little nod.

"I own this," he told us, gesturing with his arms to the room and everything in it. "It is the perfect place for conducting business." As he spoke, plates of baked salmon appeared in front of us. It was a fabulous meal—as good as any fine hotel kitchen would have produced, perhaps better.

After the meal, Vladimir led us to the dance floor. A waitress plucked a RESERVED sign off a banquette on the perimeter of the action. We sank into the soft couch and watched the gyrating dancers. Ice cream, espressos, and vodka arrived. Two beautiful women sat on either side of Vladimir. His arm slipped easily around the blonde one.

"He's got a wife and a kid too," Tim whispered. "The life of a mobster, eh?"

Pretty women flitted around us and asked us to dance. Ben and I knew only a few phrases of Russian, and after our halting utterances the women usually fell into an uncomfortable silence. Tim and Remy fared a little better as they could speak Russian, but the women were not really interested in us—only in Vladimir. Olya and Remy spent most of the evening dancing together on the floor—happy to finally have some open space together. Olya seemed to be reveling in the decadent lifestyle we were being treated to.

At 5:00 A.M. Vladimir drove us back to Pasha's boat—again at breakneck speeds topping hundred miles an hour. The Eagles' "Hotel California" blared from the radio, offering an ironic underscore to Vladimir's predicament: "You can check out any time you like, but you can never leave."

At the dock, the blonde on Vladimir's arm teetered on high heels as he pointed out our tiny dory. She shook her head in disbelief. "Four men in such a tiny craft!" She laughed. I left them joking about how we were traveling and, exhausted, crawled off to bed in Pasha's cruiser.

*Saturday, July 28*

"Wake up. Wake up!" It was Vladimir. I looked at my watch: 10:30 A.M.

"I have come to give you the tour." He looked as fresh as a daisy—shaved, nice crisp white shirt, eyes clear and bright. How did he do it? The rest of us looked like hell, hungover and still in bed.

"The press is here," he continued. "They will be coming along with us. Also Yuri, head of operations, will be coming with us too. He wants to meet you."

I splashed water on my face and stumbled outside to shake hands with a gaggle of well-heeled people on the foredeck. Formalities over, we were ushered to a convoy of vehicles in the parking lot.

Igor, the former judo champ, led us to his blue Suburban. The windows were bulletproof glass, the body was reinforced with armor plate, and the rear windows were curtained. Muscle-bound Igor squeezed into the driver's seat and out of habit hit the central locking button with a meaty paw. "Normally Yuri comes in this vehicle, but today he will be going with Vladimir," he said.

The convoy pulled away.

After a half-hour drive into the surrounding larch forest, not far from the river, the vehicles pulled into a compound of cabins and sports fields filled with children. Although we had come to a stop, Igor motioned us to remain in our seats. Ahead, two men in suits and sunglasses jumped out of a Lada and reconnoitered the area. One carried a heavy sports bag, the other a walkie-talkie. We heard an "okay" crackle over a speaker on the Suburban's dash, and we got out. As I walked past the man with the satchel, I noticed two black gun muzzles inside the partially zippered sack.

The kids, who had been playing happily, were directed over to us, and Tim was urged to explain the expedition. Soon we were signing autographs, posing for photographs, and answering questions for the TV cameras. When everyone was satisfied, we were herded back into the convoy, and off we went again.

When the cars stopped, Igor again motioned us to remain in the vehicle while the bodyguards in black went through their security ritual.

We were at the dam. Vladimir told us it was one of the world's largest hydroelectric dams. He loved to come here to swim. "I absorb the energy of the river itself," he boasted. At the base of the superstructure, he stripped and launched himself into the frigid thirty-eight-degree river. Watching him thrash through the water, it was hard not to agree that the river energized him.

After an hour of watching Vladimir swim and touring the dam site, we were off again. This time we arrived at a veritable fortress. This was Yuri's dacha, we were told, an armed, military-style compound behind a ten-foot wall and a thick steel gate. Yuri got out of his car, and the gate opened. A man in camouflage, holding a machine gun, emerged and shook his hand. They both grinned and waved us to come in, so we got out and followed.

There were more armed men behind the gate, with guard dogs. The snarling dogs were fettered as we were led to the rear of the building to see Yuri's bear cub. The three-month-old animal bounded across the grass toward us and immediately suckled our fingers. Although not much bigger than a dog, the bear was already very strong. When the dogs were let loose and bounded up to us, barking noisily, the cub sent them packing with a swat.

"In a few more months, those dogs are going to be sorry that they didn't make friends with the bear," Remy said.

"Perhaps they'll recruit it as one of their heavies," Ben mused. "I'm not so sure that Igor isn't a shaved bear himself."

"Now we will go to eat," Vladimir announced. "I'm sure you must be hungry after all this touring."

The convoy pulled up outside a restaurant and again we waited while precautions were observed. The coast was clear, and we were hustled from the Suburban into a private room. A fifteen-foot-long table groaned under a smorgasbord of skewered ribs, chicken, and pork. There were salads, cheeses, a spectrum of vegetables and fruits, soups, and bread. We were in heaven.

As we ate, Vladimir talked with his associates. Meanwhile we pondered among ourselves what we could do to show our appreciation for his hospitality.

"Perhaps the phone," said Tim.

"Yeah, the phone thing," I said. "He'll like that." So far, anyone we had met on our journey was overjoyed to be offered a chance to use our satellite telephone.

After dinner we returned to Pasha's yacht. "If you would like to make some long-distance calls on our phones, you're welcome to use them," Tim told Vladimir. "It doesn't cost us anything."

Vladimir clapped Tim on the back and chuckled. "Thank you, but I've actually got two satellite telephones, and the company pays for all the calls I make." His levity vanishing, he soberly looked at the floor and said, "What I would really like, you can't give me."

There was silence.

"I want to travel abroad, but I can't. Despite all my connections, I can't get out of this country with a criminal record. Your company is the only gift I need. You are my window to the outside world."

Like a summer squall, the seriousness of the moment vanished and he grinned. "Another toast, and tell me more about your adventures."

"I've got a tape of my Siberian cycling documentary, but we've got no TV," Tim said.

Vladimir gave him a who's-kidding-whom look, drew out his phone, and punched in a number. Tim translated his Russian for us: "I need a TV, a VCR, and food for seven people—now!" Twenty minutes later a burly man with short sandy hair came up the gangplank, struggling with a television and a VCR. Vladimir exchanged pleasantries with the man as he put the equipment on the table and left. He returned a few minutes later with two bags containing bread, salads, pickled tomatoes, *pilmenny* (pierogi-like meat dumplings), and cognac.

"I hear that where you come from, bread is nothing to you," Vladimir said, bringing out a knife. "In Russia, bread is like life, so we cut it close to our heart." He grabbed the heavy black loaf and held it against his chest with his left hand, carving thick slices by pulling the knife across the bread with his right hand.

"I am a happy man," he said. "Do you know why I am a happy man? Because I have friends. Because I have my friends and my family, and that's why I am happy. I love my city, and I am a patriot."

We watched Tim's video and ate more food on the back deck of Pasha's boat. I was beginning to think food was such an important element of the Russian sense of hospitality that when you were with them you had to eat twenty-four hours a day. It was close to two in the morning when we finished.

"Anyone like anything else?" Vladimir asked.

"How about some ice cream and chocolate?" Ben mused dreamily.

"*Marozhenae? Nyet* problem," said Vladimir, drawing out his phone again.

"I was just kidding," said Ben. "You don't need to go to all that bother just for some ice cream."

"It is no bother. How hard is it to make a phone call? We will eat ice cream!" He dialed a number and spoke rapidly. Within minutes the same man who had delivered the TV returned carrying blocks of Italian-style ice cream and rich dark-chocolate bars.

"You like it?" Vladimir asked, as we wolfed down the dessert. "I own the ice cream factory that makes this. Tomorrow, if you like, we can go on a tour, and you can eat some more."

We laughed.

*Tuesday, July 31*

Vladimir started the day by taking us to see his golden goose. He and "the Brothers," as he called them, owned the world's largest aluminum smelter. It was a massive factory that spewed great polluting plumes of smoke and industrial steam into the air.

Afterward we toured the ice cream factory, and then it was time to visit a special project Vlad was building—a memorial to his fallen comrades—all affiliated with the Brothers. It was a morbid tour. Vladimir strolled about the cemetery talking about his dead colleagues—the downside to participating in Russia's corrupt business world. More than twenty of his friends lay in the small graveyard, he said. Vladimir had constructed a memorial with four bronze angels maintaining a vigil over the graves of his colleagues. The tombstones were jet black and designed so that a shadowy ghost image of the dead peered out at the living. It was creepy. We stood in the pouring rain marveling at the kitschy sentiment.

Vladimir pointed to seven tombstones that bore the same date of death: Friday, 13 March, 1998—certainly not an auspicious day for those gentlemen. They had been between twenty-two and thirty-five years old, butchered by machine-gun fire as they sat in an apartment having a few beers. Some of them had nothing to do with "the business."

"Does it not worry you, Vlad?" Tim asked. "Knowing that a rap on your door could happen at any time and—*bang*—you're here?"

Vladimir shook his head. "Why be a businessman if you can't handle the pressure?" he asked with a wry smile. "I enjoy my life. I mourn the loss of my friends and the loss of my colleagues, but I won't mourn the end of my life before it happens."

Vladimir was soaked, his flattop haircut hanging limp over his forehead as we walked back to the Lexus. "You see," he emphasized, "this is the price of doing business in Russia."

*Wednesday, August 1*

Vladimir ordered his men to move our boat from where it was moored to the base of the dam, while he took us shopping for supplies. The first stop was his wife's business, an auto repair warehouse with an attached restaurant. We strolled through the warehouse, passing a new Mercedes, a BMW, and a 1400cc Suzuki Intruder motorbike. "My other toys," Vladimir said.

"Do you customize these yourselves?" Remy asked, pointing to the thick armored glass of another bulletproof Suburban.

"*Nyet,*" replied Vladimir. "They come from America like

this. GMC does it in the factory—two hundred seventy thousand dollars is what they cost, each."

"So what made your wife decide to get into the auto repair industry?" I asked. The shapely brunette hadn't struck me as mechanically inclined.

Vladimir shrugged.

At 7:00 P.M., with the grocery shopping finished, we went to the base of the dam to see if the boat had survived the trip. A crowd of well-dressed wise guys milled around the parking area. Olya came too, to say a final good-bye to us. She would take the train back to Irkutsk the following day. Tears welled as she and Remy had their final embrace.

"Come and visit me in Irkutsk before you leave."

"Sure," said Remy as he strolled back down to the boat.

The boat looked no worse for wear. As we were packing our supplies, the sky opened and rain bucketed down, chasing the farewell crowd back into their vehicles. Vladimir stayed outside with us and got soaked. We all looked like drowned rats, but Vlad just ripped off his shirt and gave us good-bye bear hugs. "*Shasliva*, and be careful," he said.

We wished him well and set off into the driving rain.

Child gathering firewood in Potopova.

# BANYAS AND DAM FISHING

*Thursday, August 2*

In Bratsk we had achieved only a fraction of what we had hoped; too much time had been spent enjoying the hospitality of the mafia. The boat's superstructure required repairs, sponsorship logos had to be painted on the hull, and we needed a new stove.

Since we hadn't made the necessary repairs, the cabin leaked like a sieve from the rain. The caulked seams in the roof had cracked from the wear and tear of the trip and from people walking on them. We spent a miserable, chilly night sleeping in damp sleeping bags between two-and-a-half-hour shifts on the oars.

The countryside reminded me of northern Alaska. The river was a little over half a mile wide and pristine boreal forest blanketed both banks. The trees were about 60 percent coniferous—pine, spruce, and larch—and the rest were birch and alder. During a brief hike I took when we stopped for breakfast, I saw a variety of mushrooms and an Eden of herbs and flowers beneath the forest canopy.

The rain had stopped, and we tried to dry everything out. Ben was cooking crumpets when we heard the roar of a speedboat. As the sleek fiberglass boat drew nearer, we identified the occupants as friends of Vladimir.

"Once in the family, you can't escape," Ben said. They had already been hunting and fishing and invited us to join them for breakfast. We followed their boat over to a sandy bank at the base of some chimneyed charcoal cliffs.

Ryeka, a well-muscled man of about thirty with cropped blond hair, stepped off the speedboat carrying a duck and a slew of fish. His sidekick, Valery, a thin man dressed in fatigues and a gray bandanna, built a fire.

"I used to be part of the Russian paratroop brigade," Ryeka said, surprising us with his English. "I worked for a while as a parachute firefighter. We were dropped into the middle of forest fires to put out the flames. Our team was hired by the United States for several months to fight fires in America. That is where I learned my English. Now I only parachute for recreation. In Bratsk, the Brothers have a parachuting club."

We ate a hearty meal washed down with vodka before bidding good-bye to our new friends.

*Friday, August 3*

"Have any of you guys managed to piss off the side without getting any on the boat?" Tim was standing on the back of the boat trying to urinate through a miscellany of oars, poles, and hardware lashed to the side.

"Not I," said Remy.

"There's a knack to it," said Ben. "You have to finish with a hard push of the bladder and a forward thrust of the hips— no shaking it."

"My technique is to stuff it back in my underpants before I'm completely finished," I said.

"Yeah, and then wear the same pair for a month," added Remy.

It was good to be on the water again and also to be a boat-load of guys again. We might have our differences of opinion, but we were united in a common purpose and we recognized that commitment in each other. Occasional spats couldn't erase the bonds of shared time, companionship, and physical hardship.

The current was once again diminishing. We were entering the reservoir created by the last of the three massive hydro-electric dams that constricted the Angara's flow.

*Saturday, August 4*

The sunshine and placid waters had us in mellow, cruise-ship mode. An elegant island broke the monotony of the silent green forest and the deep blue river/reservoir. No larger than an acre, the island presented a triangular cliff as its southern face. The white wall rose out of the water like the sixty-foot fang of a giant Siberian tiger. Behind the cliff, a gentle slope covered with pine trees and berry bushes rose from the water. We pulled in—this would be a good spot for more filming.

It was my turn as "boy," and I did my best to transform moldy black bread and mushy vegetables into something edible. Dessert was an all-you-can-eat buffet of berries, which were growing on the island. Afterward I climbed to the top of the cliff and fought back vertigo as I gazed at the clear blue waters below. Small fish with black stripes drifted in lazy schools as larger predators stalked behind.

When I was younger, I would have leapt into the deep water below with nary a second thought. The knot of fear, the intense desire to make the leap, those seconds of panicky free fall, and the impact of slamming into the water, like being hit by a slow-moving bus—I relished those sensations. So why wasn't I jumping now? Cowardice?

I pulled off my shoes and socks. Fear gripped my bowels. I was getting old and soft—not! I leapt before the yellow fever could rise from my belly, and hit the water hard, my legs jackknifing sideways. My rump took the impact as I slammed into a surface as unforgiving as concrete. I plummeted under—down, down, down—and thought for a moment I would hit bottom. But my descent slowed and stopped, and I began to shoot upward, exploding onto the surface. I bobbed in the water, my rump bruised and aching.

I swam to shore and hobbled across the rocks, moaning and groaning like an old man. But I felt good—I hadn't lost it yet!

I had the first rowing shift, which meant that seven and a half hours of uninterrupted sleep would follow. I would need it.

*Sunday, August 5*

I woke up about nine-thirty to Remy rummaging around the cooking area making breakfast. Our progress through the night had been minimal as strong headwinds and swells beat at the bow.

After breakfast the wind became so strong it pushed the boat backward. Remy fought to steer us into a protected bay. We tied the dory to the skeleton of an old pine tree bent over the water and huddled in the cabin, watching the weather. It was a beautiful, clear, blustery day. The sky was deep blue and the water various shades of navy, accented with tufts of white where the wind whipped at the waves. When the Siberian mistral died, we unhitched the boat and pushed off, Tim propelling it through the collapsing swells.

Two hours later Ben spotted a log house among the wind-blown trees. A tiny aluminum skiff puttered toward us, piloted by a weathered man of about fifty-five. He wore a fisherman's hat, a bushy mustache, and a smile. Ahead of him sat a heavyset man who sported a big goofy grin. "*Dobre dyen*," the mustachioed man said. "I am Nick."

"*Dobre dyen*," Tim replied.

They eyed our boat for a few seconds, asked where we had come from, and invited us for a sauna and dinner.

"Ooh, yeah!" said Ben. "There's nothing like unexpected Siberian hospitality."

The two men *putt-putt*ed back toward their cabin and Tim put his back into the oars. We tied up at a dock made from two logs nailed together. The riverbank was a slope of unkempt grass, nettles, and immature spruce trees that climbed up to the cabin.

In front of the rustic retreat was a homemade grill: a cast-iron grate set upon a metal box filled with embers. Eight troutlike fish were sizzling and a black kettle steamed away. Nick sat near the door of the one-room cabin; the fat man was nowhere to be seen.

Nick gestured to a nearby table about three yards long made with four roughly hewn two-by-six boards. "Sit, sit," he encouraged. "The sauna will be hot in about half an hour."

Inside the cabin I could see a woman moving about a large brick stove built in the middle of the room. Nick lifted the kettle off the grill and poured tea into chipped enamel mugs. He slapped six blackened fish on the table.

"They're not gutted, mate," Ben whispered.

"Are you supposed to eat the guts?" I asked him, sotto voce.

"I don't know," he replied.

I pulled the fish apart and separated the wormy entrails from the creamy white flesh. Nick glanced over at us. Rather than insult his hospitality, I scooped up a teaspoon of quivering offal and smacked my lips. He turned away and I discreetly dropped the heart, liver, and intestines to a dog under the table. The translucent flesh of the fish was excellent.

The fat man was still nowhere to be seen.

"My daughter Nastye," Nick said, introducing a stern-faced woman of about twenty-five who emerged from the cabin. He explained that his wife worked in Ust'Ilimsk, sixty-five miles away, and visited only occasionally. It didn't look like much of his wife's meager sixty-dollar-a-month salary had made it this far. Nick and his daughter were living off the land as homesteaders. There was no electricity or plumbing. Bear fat obtained on his winter hunting excursions was incinerated in a kerosene lantern to provide light. They survived on fish, game, and produce from the garden. Nick said they had a root cellar under the cabin that was accessed through a trapdoor.

The *banya*, a log structure with a corrugated roof, was nearby, nestled amid the birch trees. It had three rooms: a changing area, a washing area with two wooden barrels with large metal ladles, and a sauna room equipped with a round woodstove big enough to have powered a steam locomotive. A big bucket of rocks sat heating on the stove. Three bleacher-style benches sloped away from the roaring inferno.

On the wall hung bunches of dried birch branches still

bearing their leaves. The local tradition was for the sweating, naked supplicants to beat each other with the scratchy boughs. The massage was said to stimulate the circulation, help slough off dead skin cells, and relieve stress.

Nick spent his time smoking fish while Remy, Tim, Ben, and I sweated away our aches and cares. Afterward we ran down to the river and plunged into the frigid river. A full moon suspended above the Angara spilled peach-tinged quicksilver across the water.

"I didn't know they had piranhas here," Ben said.

I looked at him quizzically.

"It looks like they've taken a couple of inches off the end of your dick," he said with a grin.

Boys will be boys.

We bunked down at Nick's for the night.

*Monday, August 6–Friday, August 10*

After a breakfast of smoked fish and soup, we said good-bye to our hosts and began rowing toward Ust'Ilimsk. We made good time and covered the distance in two days.

Late on Tuesday afternoon, the last of the three great dams on the Yenisey River system rose before us. It was our welcome to Ust'Ilimsk, a city of 140,000 people next to the giant structure. At first the city had grown up primarily on the western shore of the Angara River, but it now sprawled across both banks. The newer neighborhoods were on the eastern side—swaths of gray, pink, and white apartment blocks, squat four- and six-story buildings. Like Bratsk and Irkutsk, the heart of the municipality was a cluster of red-and-white barber-pole smokestacks standing tall above heavy industries fueled by power from the dam.

Forty years ago, Ust'Ilimsk did not exist. The region was

nothing but untouched taiga forest stretching forever. In 1967, however, the Soviet government began building the dam and what was then called "the great northern artificial city." Although much of this region's wealth is still earned from the forest, we could see little from the river to indicate extensive resource exploitation.

We rowed up to a sagging pier that supported a mess of rusting vessels—it was the local yacht club. In Bratsk, Vladimir had told us that a friend of his was a member of the club and would ensure our stay was free. We moored and went to the clubhouse. The boats were decrepit, but the clubhouse was first rate. Built from finely crafted timber, it featured elaborate murals of the great explorers: Captain James Cook, Sir Francis Drake, Abel Tasman, and Marco Polo. Each was portrayed at the helm of his ship or manipulating a large brass sextant. The effort that had gone into giving the club a nautical ambience had been so successful, it was hard to believe that we were in the middle of the Siberian boreal forest with the nearest ocean some eighteen hundred miles to the north.

The yacht club was empty save for a receptionist, who was chatting on the phone in a small office. She was unfazed by the arrival of four strangers, as if she expected us—which she probably did, for a friend of Vladimir's quickly appeared on the scene. A black Mercedes whispered into the parking lot and a sharply dressed, muscular man sauntered down to our boat. He looked thirty-five and had short, dark brown hair and a stunning twenty-something model trailing in his wake.

"I am Sergio, a friend of Vladimir's," he said, extending a hand. "You will be my personal guests while in Ust'Ilimsk. I will help you get provisions, have your boat moved over the dam, and assist you with anything else you need. Treat the yacht club as your home. There is a kitchen, and you are welcome to sleep here too."

We thanked him profusely and he said he would stay in touch. With that, he was gone.

"Vladimir's certainly got long arms," I said.

First on our list of things to buy was a new stove. Propane was impossible to find as we traveled farther north, which made our current stove useless. We needed one that would burn kerosene. We also needed sundry other items: a fuse for the satellite-phone charger, plastic to cover the portholes, some warm clothes for the onset of winter, and a Canadian flag to hoist at the end of the journey.

We didn't expect to find the red Maple Leaf, but we hoped to find a seamstress or tailor who could sew one for us. Ben and I scoured the city until we found a tailor's shop. The walls were lined with dozens of traditional Russian fur hats with big earflaps. We showed the matronly woman there a miniature Canadian flag and asked if she could duplicate it for us. She chuckled. "How big?"

Ben pulled his Australian flag from his backpack. "Same size exactly," he said.

"No problem," she said in Russian. "Come back tomorrow."

We returned to the boat, and Ben, Remy, and Tim went into the city while I stayed to complete some chores. Sitting on the deck, I could see a nearby beach where the locals were swimming to escape the muggy heat. In the grass above the pebbly beach, wisps of smoke drifted from picnic fires and people lay soaking up the sunshine. A few looked as if they were performing tai chi—standing upright with their hands in the air, rotating their bodies in slow motion like ballerinas—but I think it was the Russian style of tanning. I suppose at these latitudes, with the extreme angle of the sun, you can catch more rays standing up.

Beyond the beach, a flotilla of small sailboats—Optimists and Russian Lasers—chased each other like seagulls in breeding season. The children piloting the little craft screamed with delight as they scudded this way and that, skimming over the water.

My main task was to paint the logos of some of our sponsors on the side of the boat. By the end of the afternoon I was feeling proud of my handiwork, accomplished with handmade stencils, small brushes, and some cans of oil paint. Although far from perfect, the logos looked good. As I was putting the paints away, a can of chrome yellow spilled into the bilge. I spent the next two hours mopping up the sunshine-colored sludge using salvaged rags and newspapers. Without turpentine, it was impossible to completely clean up the mess, but I was able to make it appear as if someone had painted the bilge a rather yucky shade of saffron. After a bit of time it would dry, I hoped.

As I worked, some of the kids ventured over to ask for my autograph. I thought their enthusiasm was related to our expedition, but it wasn't. They hadn't seen a Westerner before! Their only link with the West was through TV. I was as exotic as Mel Gibson or Mick Jagger.

The lads returned with similar tales of adults and children alike stopping them to ask for autographs. Talk and laughter in the buses had faded to a hushed silence when people heard their voices. Shopkeepers plied them with so many questions it took more than half an hour to buy an ice cream.

At eight o'clock we went up to the club for a *banya*, as recommended by Sergio.

"This is a sauna, not a swimming pool!" said the woman in charge. "Take your underpants off. Take your watches off! A sauna isn't a sauna unless you're naked."

We quickly complied. Sweat dribbled off the end of my nose as Tim poured more water over the hot stones. The rocks hissed and the room filled with lung-searing steam.

"It's the Russian way," he said, settling his naked body on the highest bench.

The door opened and a group of Russians filed in—all wearing swimsuits.

"If it's the Russian way, it doesn't seem too popular around here," I said, self-consciously pulling on my underwear.

After we emerged from the sauna, I could tell from the glint in her eyes that the attendant had enjoyed her joke. We had tea and *shashlyks* before calling it a night.

The following day Ben and I returned to the tailor's shop. I was overjoyed—the seamstress had sewn us a beautiful Maple Leaf standard from red and white satin. It was perfect. I uttered profuse thanks and we left to continue our shopping.

Our next stop was a grocery store, where both Ben and I tried desperately to communicate with the saleswoman. She laughed at our broken Russian and hand gestures. Two twelve-year-old girls stood in the corner watching the comedy. It took us ages to explain what we wanted, but eventually the shopkeeper finished piling the onions, coffee, bologna, bread, and yogurt onto the counter beside the till.

A man of about sixty-five with gray floppy hair and an intellectual face arrived. He gave us the once-over and looked at our supplies. "American?" he asked, in heavily accented English.

"No. I Canadian and he Australian," I said.

The sprightly older man nodded and turned to the woman behind the counter. "*Adin vodka, pazhalst.*" She placed a 750-milliliter bottle in front of him.

"My name is Antonio," he said, turning back to me. "Will you come to my place for some vodka?"

"Too much work to do on our boat," I said. "And our friends are waiting for us."

"I will come and look at your boat, then," he said. "Please, drink with me."

He would not take no for an answer; he was a lonely man. As we walked back toward the yacht club, he told us that his wife had died three years before. "It was very hard when she died. It was only then that I realized how tough it is living alone. She was a great woman."

Antonio grew melancholy and we walked in silence. Although sixty-five and a heavy smoker, he handled the steep hill to the upper reservoir more easily than I could. His mood grew lighter as we passed near the dam wall. "I was the chief engineer in the construction of this dam," he said. "Thirteen long years it took—the finest hydroelectric facility in the world."

"So who actually designed the dam?" Ben asked.

"In Moscow they have a special hydroelectric institute where this dam was designed." Antonio winked. "Sometimes I'd make changes here and there if I didn't like their ideas."

We gave him a grin and nodded. "Of course."

At the boat, Antonio arranged two discarded radiators on the pier to create a makeshift table. He placed his bottle of vodka on the rusted metal. "Now we will drink!" he said. And we did. Nowhere in the world have I encountered heavier drinkers than in Russia. We were beginning to find it easier to join in the cheer than to resist the constant urging, "Drink, drink. You must drink." It was the catchphrase of this empty land.

Russia and vodka have always gone hand in hand. Adam Olearius, a traveler in Russia and the Ukraine in the 1630s, noted, "The vice of drunkenness is prevalent among this people of all classes, both secular and ecclesiastical, high and low, men and women, young and old. To see them lying here and there in the streets wallowing in filth is so common that no notice is taken of it . . . none of them anywhere, any time or under any circumstances lets pass an opportunity to have a draught or drinking bout."

### Saturday, August 11

Once again our boat sat at the base of a dam, thanks to the Brothers. As we busied ourselves packing, the wise guys who had come to see us off slipped away in their fleet of big Mercedes-Benzes and BMWs. We pushed off as the light began to fade.

I had the first shift on the oars and pulled hard to guide the provision-laden boat into the current. It was the first extended section of flowing river we'd been on for more than 750 miles, and we were excited. At last, nothing but moving water lay between the Arctic Ocean and us. The gray concrete wall of Ust'Ilimsk Dam was borne away into the past with each sweep of the oars. Deep, dark, primordial forest replaced the squat apartment blocks and factories.

As I rowed into the immense wilderness, the color evaporated and was replaced by a gray shadow-land under a black-velvet sky scattered with diamonds. I was awed by how little visible damage man had done. That did not speak to a lack of rapaciousness, only to how huge Siberia is—bigger than the forty-eight contiguous United States. As much exploitation as there is, it is masked by the enormous breadth of the country.

Tim interrupted my thoughts by handing me a blue enamel mug. I stopped rowing to peer at the inch of clear fluid sloshing at the bottom. "Drink up, mate," he said. "It's time to celebrate passing the last goddamned dam!"

Tim, Remy, Ben, and I raised our cups in unison and clinked a toast. We could also celebrate that we were almost halfway to our destination, the Arctic Ocean.

We had a few more shots, and I took up the oars again. When we came upon a small work camp, I pulled the boat over to the muddy shore. In the twilight we could see some buildings set back from the river. There was a loading dock, a crane, and a watchman's hut, but no one was about.

We were leery of continuing downriver in complete darkness because we had been warned of a fairly large waterfall downstream. There was no point in taking any chances, so we tied up to a log overhanging the bank.

*Sunday, August 12*

Just after dawn I climbed out of the boat, intending to push us into the current and begin my rowing shift. I was staggered. The boat was aground on a mudflat and the river a good fifteen feet distant. It was as if the tide had gone out—but there was no tide.

Then I realized that the dam behind us controlled the water level. The flow must fluctuate depending on electricity demand, which determined how much water was allowed through the floodgates. At night, demand would fall, so less water would spill through the dam from the reservoir. It was Sunday. Here was a problem. Would demand be low all day? How long would we be beached?

When Ben, Remy, and Tim got up, they were equally perplexed. We tried to lever the boat across the mud to the river, but it was too heavy. We gave up, exhausted.

Two fishermen wearing traditional fur hats with earflaps came along the river in an aluminum boat. We waved to them and Tim yelled in Russian. They hollered back.

"The water level will be back up in three hours," Tim translated.

We waved our thanks as they motored away. I climbed back into the tipped boat and rested my aching head against my sleeping bag. There was nothing to do but wait. Sure enough, the river rose a few hours later, and we were on our way.

But by suppertime we had run into another problem. The river was flowing fast and wide—too wide to provide enough depth. We were in constant fear of running aground. Still, the water was crystal clear; we could watch silver fish dart among the weeds and polished rocks that passed so dangerously close to our keel.

*Bang!* The boat shuddered and slipped sideways off whatever submerged boulder it had hit. *Scrape . . . scrape.* The sounds were terrifying. It was like being in a submarine waiting for a depth charge to explode on top of you. We didn't know when the boat would strike another rock and its wooden hull shatter.

*Scrape.* A boulder could capsize us. We grew paranoid.

"Mates, if we do capsize or sink, are we ready for it?" Ben asked. "Are our valuables—film, cassettes, and passports—in waterproof containers and easily accessible? And the sat phones—" He pointed to the handsets hanging against the port rail. "It wouldn't take much to end the life of those babies."

We pulled into an eddy near a large, mosquito-plagued meadow, stowed the gear, and tied everything down more securely. So far we had used the dory mostly in flat, unmoving waters. We had not anticipated how unstable it might be in a fast-flowing river. *Scrape.* It was more than a bit harrowing. "It's like flying," I said, watching the bottom of the river rush beneath us. "And now it looks like we're going to land."

The keel scuffed against the bottom, clipped a small ridge, and gently twisted in the current. Ben leapt over the bow into the water, shoved the dory backward, and climbed back on board. From then on, in an attempt to lessen the collisions with rocks, we began taking turns on watch, sitting on the bow and barking orders to the rower.

*Monday, August 13*

The river narrowed again and grew deeper as it did. Soon it was running fast and deep and we made very good progress, coursing along confidently, prepared for the worst. The forest, in more shades of green than I could imagine, sped by.

We came upon a small village, and a few obviously bored locals puttered out to investigate. Grinning like children, they approached in two leaky aluminum boats whose engines appeared to be held together with baling wire and duct tape.

"*Dobre dyen,*" Tim said.

They were full of questions, which they fired in rapid Russian: "Where have you come from? Would you like a tow?"

The men had difficulty controlling their boats out in the river, and the larger of the two craft, loaded with urns filled with fresh milk, banged into us so hard I was afraid it had ruptured the hull. Two robust women with short blond hair sat at the front, giggling as the inept driver manhandled the exposed outboard and struggled to steer the boat. He tossed a thick hemp rope to Tim at the oars.

"Tie it to the front and we will tow you," a curly-haired man said in a heavy Russian dialect.

"Tow us where?" Tim asked.

"Where are you going?" The man looked confused.

"The Arctic Ocean," Tim answered.

There was a long silence before one of the women finally replied, "Would you like to come to our cabin for a *banya*?"

We declined. It would have been wonderful, but small delays can add up, and I feared the northern portion of the river would be frozen before we could finish our voyage. We thanked them and continued on.

*Tuesday, August 14*

According to our map, we were about 1,700 miles from the Yenisey River's source in Mongolia. We were almost exactly halfway to the Arctic Ocean, four months after starting, and we had just over a month before the river would begin to freeze. We would have to move fast! At the moment, though, the river was running almost due west. In a few days we would reach the point where the Little Yenisey tributary joined the Angara. Their combined flow create the Yenisey proper.

*Thursday, August 16*

We were cruising through virgin wilderness. I was sure that millennia ago the area had looked exactly as it did today. Suddenly the silence of the forest was shattered by a scream-ing outboard. Two warmly bundled-up men roared up the river toward us. They identified themselves as the local con-stabulary.

"Some convicts have escaped from the prison and are be-lieved to be heading downriver by rowboat too," Tim trans-lated for us.

"Be on the lookout, and be wary of strangers," the burly fair-haired officer added. "If you see anything unusual, give us a call on your *telephonaya sputnik*." The men wished us luck and sped off. Moments later the tranquillity of the wilderness was restored.

"They didn't give us a phone number," Tim said after a few minutes.

We laughed and continued to slide downriver.

Later in the afternoon, we heard a rumble. The sound was so indistinct that initially we thought it might be the hum of another town. The river was almost a mile wide, so I didn't immediately think of rapids. But soon I could see an unbroken line of dancing waves far ahead, tiny rainbows appearing and disappearing in the iridescent mist and froth that stretched from one side of the river to the other.

Our boat wasn't designed for whitewater, and the rot in her hull made us all nervous. One rock could send us rapidly to the bottom. Tim was on the oars as we drifted closer to the maelstrom. He steered the boat into a green chevron-shaped current—usually an indication of the deepest and least disturbed channel. But it vanished in the white mass of churning rapids. Tim pulled this way and that on the oars.

"Aim more upstream!" shouted Ben.

"Aim more downstream!" Remy yelled.

"Angle it!" I added. "Angle it! Row harder! Pull, pull, pull!"

Tim was confused. He straightened her out and the boat picked up speed, slipped down the oily tongue of a small waterfall, and crashed through a series of standing waves.

"YE-E-E-HA-A-A!" Remy yelled.

It was like riding a roller-coaster. The boat crashed through the rapids and made it out the other side like a veritable white-river champion. We were fairly sluicing along.

"Another day passes without us sinking," Ben said.

"Yeah, but we've still got those convicts to worry about," Tim replied. "And remember *Deliverance*? Who's got the prettiest lips around here? Sooey! Sooey!"

I looked up to see a boat bearing two disheveled men. One wore a black toque perched at an angle on his head, his right ear protruding like an elf's. The older one waved at Tim, and they began talking intently in Russian.

"This is it," Ben whispered to me. "These are the convicts. Prepare to be shot dead."

The wizened man with black eyes like two bullet holes stopped talking and barked at his companion. With a nod, the lanky fellow reached under the seat.

"He's grabbing for a gun," Ben said.

The man brought out a bowl of blueberries and three fat fish. I looked at Ben and shook my head with a grin. We tried to return their generosity, but typical of proud Russians, they would take nothing. Finally Tim persuaded them to accept a pack of cigarettes.

"Watch out for the convicts," they warned as they left, their motor's two-stroke tatto echoing off the trees and lingering long after the boat had disappeared from view.

*Saturday, August 18*

Another dam! We had heard rumors of its existence upstream, but only the sketchiest of details were available. The ten-story superstructure was only half built, but it already towered over and spanned the river, channeling the current through a sluice under the dam. In time it would stretch from one side of the valley to the other, and most of the lowland we had just come through would be inundated by its reservoir.

We pulled the dory up onto a muddy beach to figure out how we could get the boat around the enormous obstruction. Straws were drawn and I was left with the boat while the others went into the wooden town beside the megaproject, which was called Boguchany. I watched hundreds of workers scurry over the face of the huge structure like insects—

trucks coming and going, cranes picking up and lowering loads, rebar bent in every direction. It was an incredibly well-orchestrated, animated Meccano set. But I had work of my own to do. I gave up watching the dam building and busied myself cleaning the boat.

The boys returned with a bag of food and some interesting news. A lock lay parallel to the main flow of the river and could take us safely through the center of the dam.

We rowed across the river and into the tiny gap that led to a placid, manmade channel. This in turn led to an enormous steel door at the base of the dam. Behind the door was the lock, situated in a tunnel that went straight through the dam itself.

"We just have to go and tell the lockkeeper we're ready to go through," said Tim.

We pulled up on the shore near the lock gate, and Tim and I strolled up over dusty mounds of gravel to the face of the dam. The huge, 160-foot structure dwarfed us as we ascended some roughly welded steel stairs into the inner workings of the dam.

"Just think, many years down the road, this will all be under twenty fathoms of water," said Tim.

It was an eerie thought.

A suspended metal walkway went right down the lock tunnel and we strolled through alone, looking at the massive pieces of machinery that operated the lock system. In typical Soviet style, everything was built for strength and simplicity. The two lock gates moved straight up and down, running on what looked like vertical railway tracks and steel wheels.

I was looking at the machinery in awe and singing at the top of my lungs in falsetto—taking advantage of the acoustics—when the lockkeeper appeared. She was a smiling lady who looked like any middle-aged mum. Unperturbed that we were wandering around an "authorized personnel only" area, she began telling us the procedure for going through the lock.

"The currents are strong when the water is draining out. There is a special spot you can tie up to. It drops at the same rate as the decreasing water level," the lockkeeper said, pointing to a tying ring on the far side of the tunnel. "Whatever you do, don't tie up to the ladder—otherwise your boat will be swinging in the air."

Tim stayed on the walkway to film while I went back to the boat. Machinery hummed as the gigantic door began to rise like the cargo door of a sci-fi spacecraft. It was intimidating to row our eighteen-foot boat into the seven-hundred-by-seventy-foot lock. When the door slowly began to drop, I felt as though we'd climbed inside the mouth of a giant whale. As the gap narrowed, it cut out most of the sunlight, leaving us sloshing about in an eerie twilight. I rowed the boat to a tie ring, and the moment it was secure, the water around us shifted into motion. It was as though we were in a giant toilet cistern and somebody had pulled the plug. Currents yanked and pulled on the boat, and we rapidly dropped down the face of the concrete wall as water drained from the lock.

It took about three minutes for over five thousand tons of water to be displaced and our rowboat to be lowered ten feet. The second steel wall, at the far end of the tunnel, then began to rise, and a flood of sunshine promised us freedom.

As we passed beneath the door, Ben noticed the lockkeeper above us collecting buckets of fish. A clever engineer had created a grating system so that when the water drained from the lock, any fish swept through would be caught in the mesh.

Tim had heard the complete history of the dam from the lockkeeper. The project had begun in 1973 as what was expected to be a thirty-year undertaking. A decade ago, when the Soviet Union collapsed, the money stopped and so did work on the dam. Eventually the workers returned because there was nothing else to do, and for five years men and women had toiled on the dam without wages. They grew their own vegetables, tended cattle, foraged berries and mushrooms, hunted—and kept working. If the half-completed dam couldn't provide electricity, at least it caught fish!

The Russian economy was picking up, and workers were now collecting meager wages from the government. No one knew when the dam would be finished. The lockkeeper wouldn't even hazard a rough guess. "Maybe twenty-five years, maybe a hundred," she had said with a shrug.

Before we pushed off, the lockkeeper brought us a half-bucket of fish. "Good luck, and don't give up," she said, waving.

If anybody knew about not giving up, it was the people of Boguchany.

River traffic was increasing continually. Between Ust'Ilimsk and the dam there had been no large boats at all, despite the fact that the river was apparently navigable. Now we encountered a boat about once an hour. Tugs could be seen pulling log booms downstream and then returning upriver unburdened. We also saw tugs pulling big steel barges, and the occasional working boat whose purpose we couldn't determine.

We were treated to a display of nautical ballet at its best. A tug was towing a long, slender log boom about 1,500 feet long and only 100 feet wide. Three attendant tugs farted around, seemingly with no purpose. We watched the fleet for a while, since the log boom's speed was only slightly slower than our rowing pace.

When the fleet entered the rapids, we learned what the

auxiliary tugs were for. The three little boats belched black smoke as they pushed and prodded the long train of logs in strategic spots to make it slither like a snake through the restricted passage. For a while the current clawed at it so violently we thought it was going to run up on the rocks. In the end, the little tugs and the boom emerged triumphant.

We followed them, our boat riding the rapids a little less gracefully, but just as successfully.

## Monday, August 20

A sleepy lumber town fronted by log booms rolled into view in the morning. The river was so large and wide by now, and the disturbance created by the current so subtle, that it felt like we were in the middle of a humongous placid lake. Our little boat seemed to be standing still while the land rolled by.

Most of the homes in the town were one- and two-story dwellings made from the wood that grew so plentifully in the region. Unlike settlements we'd encountered in Mongolia or farther upstream, most of the buildings were painted, either white or in light pastels. A hum emanated from the town, perhaps from the sawmill or maybe an electrical generator, and a couple of smokestacks lazily burped billows of white effluent into the cerulean sky.

We wanted to stop and explore the community, but time would not allow it. We had only one more month to complete the remaining 1,500 miles.

## Tuesday, August 21

The sweaty, humid weather of the past few days had broken. In its place was a high, thin veil of overcast and a crisp breeze.

Birch and poplar trees dominated the southern riverbank, while the northern bank was cloaked in the darker hues of evergreens. It was impossible to put ashore because of the mauve and gray cliffs that sliced into the water. There was no foreshore to speak of—it was as if we were boating down a fjord.

The breeze turned into a full-fledged gale and the clouds grew thick and dirty gray, like so many soiled sheets. It began to rain—heavily. Ben, Tim, and I retreated to the cabin, which resembled a smelly, chaotic clubhouse filled with a disarray of blankets, sleeping bags, dirty socks, and other debris. In his pea-green Helly Hansen rain gear, Remy worked the oars.

Ben and Tim sat on the little settee, which was so low that their knees came up to their chests. At least the foul weather had eliminated the bugs that were plaguing us.

*Thursday, August 23*

The river split into a hundred turbulent serpentine channels coursing between bedrock that had been sculpted and polished smooth by the current. It reminded me of the coastal reef-strewn channels flowing between the islands of British Columbia. We had come to the confluence of the Angara and Little Yenisey rivers. The Little Yenisey, about a quarter of the size of the Angara, entered from the left. Emerging from the churning current, we entered the newborn Yenisey River.

## 12

Yuri, captain of the mail ship, in Yeniseysk.

# VODKA AND OLD SALTS

*Friday, August 24*

Just before lunch we rowed into Lesosibirsk, about twenty-five miles downstream from the confluence. Although the population is only about thirty thousand, the heavy industry lining the waterfront gives the impression of a much larger city. I couldn't see the town for a gaggle of cranes and a Maginot Line of factories. A constant flow of barges and log booms seemed to be docking and unloading timber, coal, oil, and other resource materials from upstream. The cargo was hoisted from the water and loaded into railway boxcars by the giant cranes. From there, the world was the customer.

We had difficulty finding a place to dock amid all the industrial activity. But we found a strip of muddy beach and moored the dory. Tim drew the short straw, so Ben, Remy, and I headed into town to reprovision, fix the battery charger, and buy stove fuel.

As we strolled along the clean, tidy streets, it was apparent that something was not quite right. The older people looked normal, but numerous children bore misshapen limbs, withered arms, close-set eyes, cauliflower ears, and the physiological marks of Down syndrome.

I had read previously that radiation levels in this section of the Yenisey and the surrounding countryside were through the roof because of three decades of discharges of radioactive particles. During the Cold War, the former Soviet Union operated a nuclear facility near here: the Mining and Chemical Combine at Krasnoyarsk-26. Since the disintegration of the USSR, studies have shown that the Yenisey is severely contaminated in places downstream.

The contamination insinuated itself into the sands of the riverbed, the islands, the floodplains, and the food chain. In downstream villages, experts have found a disturbing statistical pattern of illnesses—increased numbers of children with leukemia and cases of breast cancer among women—as well as genetic aberrations and a higher-than-normal death rate. All signposts of radiation exposure, yet no cleanup was under way. The local authorities insisted there was no serious health threat.

I couldn't imagine what it would be like to live in such an environment. How could anyone even contemplate having a child, with the risk of genetic damage and mutation so prevalent?

*Saturday, August 25*

We moored beside the large commercial fleet in the town of Yeniseysk. Neatly painted gray, white, and red tugs, hundred-foot river freighters, and an assortment of rusty smaller boats dwarfed our dory. We pulled up on a gravel beach.

Yeniseysk was quite different from the other cities and towns we'd encountered. Most had been built fairly recently under the Soviet regime, their clapboard and log houses erected quickly to shelter industrial workers sent to the region to strip its natural resources. In contrast, Yeniseysk was founded in 1619 by the Cossacks as they pushed west. They built a fortress there and used it as a base for the exploration of Siberia. The city, steeped in history, played an important role in the development of the surrounding wilderness, as it stood at the crossroads of diplomatic and trading paths. That is why it is also called "the father of Siberian towns."

Many of the buildings were elaborately designed and constructed from brick and stone. Even the log homes had a sense of permanence, their weathered wood adorned with brightly painted window shutters. I was struck by the city's charm, grace, and green spaces. Parks were ubiquitous. Two old churches—one Roman Catholic, the other Russian Orthodox—overlooked the residential neighborhoods as they vied for supremacy.

But the city also had a darker side. The Cossack fortress was used as a prison for more than three centuries. It is said that Tsar Ivan imprisoned one of his wives there, and Stalin exiled numerous "enemies of the people" to Siberia and Yeniseysk.

We wanted to explore further, but the looming winter weather made it impossible to tarry. Ben, Remy, and I shopped as quickly as we could and staggered back toward the boat, our backpacks stuffed with cheese, salami, and bread. As we walked back through town, it was obviously Saturday night.

Five well-dressed young couples fell into step behind us. "Hello," one of the women called in English.

"Hello," we chorused.

The group behind us erupted with English phrases: "How are you?" "My name is Olga." "Good-bye." "What is your name?" "I am fine, thank you." It was a scene from *Saturday Night Live*: ten twenty-something Russians muttering English nonsense and three scruffy adventurers with backpacks bantering with them. We kept up the repartee as best we could while we strolled. At an intersection, the young Russians indicated they were turning the corner and heading for an open waterfront bar. They gestured for us to join them for drinks.

"*Peeva?*" a miniskirted girl inquired, as her boyfriend tugged impatiently on her arm.

What the heck, we decided. A couple of hours drinking wouldn't hurt anyone. A blond girl grabbed my hand while holding her easygoing boyfriend's with the other. Remy and Ben too were beset by attractive girls with equally unperturbed mates.

We were herded into the nearby bar, an establishment that felt more like a Brazilian beach than 60 degrees north in the middle of Siberia. Red plastic chairs and tables were adorned with advertisements for Russian beer. More beer companies were advertised on cards fluttering in the wind, like Christmas cards strung over the mantelpiece. The bar was situated at the top of a concrete wall fronting the river, giving us a 180-degree panorama of the busy waterway. Young Russians in various states of intoxication occupied most of the tables. Others gyrated to the loud technomusic thumping through the bar and across the river.

"Sit, sit," said Igor, wrapping his burly arm around my

shoulder. His short hair and long nose made him look like a muscular version of Tom Cruise. "You will drink Russian vodka."

Four bottles of vodka materialized along with thirteen shot glasses. Igor's girlfriend, Olga, a brunette with shoulder-length hair and a black dress ending halfway down her thighs, rubbed her breasts gently against me as she handed me a brimming shot glass. I glanced uncomfortably at Igor, but he was smiling.

As the vodka flowed, Olga's attentions became more and more pronounced. Her left hand was sliding up my thigh. I noticed that the same fate was befalling Ben and Remy with other girls. I began to wonder—perhaps the sense of owner-ship we have in Western relationships was a foreign concept in this remote Siberian town. It was now obvious that the girls were making moves on us, and their beaus seemed to be endorsing it.

"We are celebrating wedding," Olga told me, gesturing to a couple across the table. "Sergei and Olya get married yes-terday."

At least the married couple seemed to be faithful, as they gazed at each other with lovey-dovey eyes. Olga's hand slipped off my thigh, and she tugged on my hand. "Dance?"

The whole table rose to their feet and we joined the al-ready large crowd bouncing, bobbing, and staggering in the cleared area in front of the bar. My head was swimming; while I indulged in foggy thoughts of sympathy for Tim back guarding the boat, Olga nibbled on my bottom lip. I noticed Igor playing tonsil hockey with the girl who had been sitting on the other side of him. Glancing my way, he smiled en-couragingly. A hard pull on my left arm brought me back to my senses. A plump girl with a pleasant face stood there smiling.

"My name is Leana," the girl said in the first coherent

English I'd heard in Yeniseysk. "I am student of English in University of Krasnoyarsk. My friend here, Marina, want to dance with you but she not know how to ask. You want?"

I looked at the petite blonde standing beside Leana.

"I am in the middle of dancing right now. I will dance with Marina next dance," I said.

"No," Leana said. She and Marina pulled simultaneously on both my arms. Olga shrugged her shoulders resignedly as Marina slipped her arms around me, squeezing me in a vise-like bear hug that belied her tiny size.

"Have you ever experienced anything like this before?" a beaming Remy asked as he spun in front of me, a dark-haired girl kissing him on the neck.

"Holy shit, I've been kissed by three different girls." Ben's voice came from behind me. "I couldn't stop them if I tried."

It became apparent that the novelty factor of having three Westerners in town was the reason for the immense attention being lavished on us. Even the guys in the group seemed pleased to have such different company. A group on the other side of the bar decided our new friends were monopolizing our time and tried getting us to join them, almost causing a fight. Finally, in the wee hours of the morning, we staggered back to the boat with the groceries.

*Sunday, August 26*

A voice bellowing in Russian awoke me: "Come and eat and drink with us!"

I peered through the porthole. On the bow of the rusted cargo ship beside us, an old sailor in a blue toque was leaning over the rail peering at our boat. The sea had etched his face with sharp, deep strokes. His shirt was unbuttoned to his waist, exposing a barrel chest covered with a thick mat of curly salt-and-pepper hair. His shoulder was tattooed with the image of a maiden having sex with a dolphin.

I was alone in the boat; the others had gone into town. I climbed out of the cramped cabin. "I must write," I said in halting Russian to the old sailor. "I come visit in two hours."

The man shook his grizzled head. "I am the captain—Yuri!" he shouted. "Write later. Drink now!"

A handful of sailors appeared on the deck behind him. When it comes to drinking, no is not a word that exists in a Russian sailor's vocabulary—especially if the captain offers. I climbed back inside the little cabin and began writing. I had composed two sentences when a heavy knock sounded on the roof. It was Yuri, holding out a shot glass. "It is bad luck to leave a glass untouched," he said with a sly smile.

I relented. For the sake of completing the expedition successfully, I downed the homemade liquid, which tasted like turpentine. "Food is waiting in the galley," Yuri said. "Come."

Three sailors stood in the galley, their eyes rheumy, their pasty alcoholic faces flushed with a road map of broken blood vessels. Over glasses of what might well have been paint thinner, I learned I was on a mail ship. Mostly it lay idle, moored against the riverbank. In Soviet times, she had been a proud vessel. There wasn't nearly as much time for drinking, Yuri said nostalgically.

"Is there another mail ship servicing this region?" I asked.

Yuri noticed he had a full glass. He downed it and tore off a chunk of stale bread. "*Nyet.*"

"And the last time you picked up mail was six weeks ago?"

"*Da.*"

I guessed Christmas cards weren't popular in this part of the world.

The boys returned with a stocky, bearded Russian named Piotr. He was a friend of Sergei, a local rock musician we had met in the bar who shared Ben's love of AC/DC. Piotr, a local professor of anthropology, had joined the boys while they shopped for fresh vegetables and had invited us to his house for a *banya*. He was also offering to help us with our chores in his old Lada Niva.

*Tuesday, August 28–Saturday, September 1*

We were ready to leave Yeniseysk, the boat loaded with food and radioactivity-free water. Piotr arrived with his family to say farewell. On our tour of the city, Piotr had said he was fascinated by other cultures, especially the indigenous people of Siberia and their belief in shamanism. But I wasn't quite prepared when he emerged from his beat-up Lada in full shaman regalia. He wore a feathered headdress similar to those worn by North American Indians. His was draped in a leather shawl that was a flail of ribbons, fur, feathers, metal ornaments, and twigs. "I am going to say good-bye and good luck in shamanist style," he said, pulling a homemade skin drum from the trunk.

Yuri surveyed the scene from the towering bow of the mail ship and shouted, "I'm going to say good-bye the Russian way," and let fly a string of obscenities. Then he laughed uproariously.

Piotr, looking a little uncomfortable, swayed and beat his cowhide drum with a drumstick wrapped in fox fur. He pulled a piece of bread from his pocket and tossed chunks into the water to appease the river gods.

Yuri's voice boomed out again: "Where are the damn ducks he's feeding?"

We pushed off into the current, leaving the surreal scene still unfolding.

———

We rowed nonstop after Yeniseysk. The current was brisk, and we covered nearly a hundred miles a day. The biggest hazard was shipping. On average, two boats an hour passed us—tugs pushing and pulling laden barges, small river freighters, hydrofoils, and local tinnies skimming hither and yon on what seemed like an aquatic autobahn.

At night it was truly dangerous. We put the hurricane lantern on the cabin roof, hoping to make our tiny vessel more visible to the passing behemoths. We didn't know if we would even show up on radar. And the frequent fog aggravated the situation exponentially.

Even at night we could normally have seen the lights of an approaching vessel a long way off and taken evasive measures. But the insidious fog left us blind both day and night. Boats roared out of the darkness mere yards from us—looming dark giants that threatened to run us over. There was an incredible risk that we would be plowed under. Sometimes, when the sound of an approaching boat was extremely close, we would hold up metal pots and pans to increase the chance of radar detection. The flat metal surfaces would stand a much better chance of reflecting the radar and creating a signal than could our low wooden hull.

Although the river looked clean, we were afraid it was poisoned by radioactivity and industrial pollution. We had seen almost no homes along the riverbank. As a precaution, we were drinking only water obtained from tributaries that flowed into the Yenisey. There was no shortage of them.

The Yenisey drains the great Siberian basin, and the largest marsh in the world stretches away to the west. To the east is the Siberian Plateau, a shieldlike slab of ancient rock that continues to the Arctic Ocean. The Yenisey runs along the edge of the plateau, giving a spectacular view of the hills, cliffs, and small mountains that demarcate the border between geological structures.

In 1908 the largest asteroid in recorded history streaked

across the Siberian sky and exploded above the ground in a ball of flame, flattening thousands of acres of forest. The epicenter was only about sixty-five miles from the confluence of the Yenisey and the Tunguska rivers.

We decided to camp near that spot rather than run the risk of traveling on the river in darkness. Yuri had warned us of rapids in this area. Coincidentally, in the semitwilight, the largest meteorite that any of us had ever witnessed scorched its way across the sky. A fiery green ball about a third of the size of the moon blazed toward the horizon, split in two, and fell beyond our gaze. Wow!

*Sunday, September 2*

I started rowing at 6:30 A.M. in spite of the fog and the hazard it presented. Steering the boat by map and compass, I rowed for about three hours without running aground. The menacing rumble of boat engines sounded a little louder than normal, which scared the hell out of me, but I persevered until the sun burned off the cloying mist and left me rowing through another sparkling fall day. Our latitude was just above 63 degrees.

Evidence of the spring flooding remained on the riverbank. Ten yards or so above the current water level, a tangle of logs, tree branches, debris, and flotsam marked the highwater mark—a kind of natural bathtub ring. Many of the trees along the forest frontage were scarred from being scraped and battered by ice and debris washed along by the floodwaters.

We stopped by the tiny village of Alsinove to fetch potable water from the nearby stream. About six or seven men and women gathered atop the high riverbank to watch. The women wore headscarves and long skirts, the men collared shirts, dark pants, and beards. Curiosity getting the better of them, two young men and a boy scrambled down for a closer look.

Remy was at streamside vigorously tugging at the water pump, which had been working flawlessly since it had been given a major overhaul in Mongolia.

One of the men smiled, exposing a row of polished steel teeth amid a bushy nest of red beard. "Why are you getting water from this stream?" the man asked. "Why not just take it from the river?"

"It is polluted," said Tim.

"*Nyet*, it is fine," the man replied.

He said they were Doukhobors, a Quaker-like, Christian sect persecuted under the tsars for refusing military service because of their pacifist beliefs. Many had immigrated to Canada at the end of the nineteenth century. During the Soviet era their religion was also forbidden, but since the collapse of communism, some Doukhobors had returned to Russia, and those who never left could live openly. This group of twenty-two had lived here for thirteen years.

*Monday, September 3*

The farther north we went, the more autumnal our surroundings. The deciduous trees were a palette of color—scarlet, orange, and yellow. The conifers had vastly diminished in number and the pines had disappeared completely. The weather was gloomy and gray.

A strong headwind was beating on the nose of our boat and threatened to keep us stalled. Yuri and others had told us that river traffic usually dried up by October 5 and that ice would start forming well before that. With the days shortening and the first blasts of winter hitting us, urgency was the order of the day. I could see rafts of ducks racing south. Smart men should have been following, but instead we kept heading north.

## Tuesday, September 4

"Colin, are you awake?"

I groggily lifted my head from the pile of soiled clothes I used as a pillow. It must be my turn to row. I shook my head, trying to clear my brain. Chill, damp air licked at my shoulders as I withdrew slightly from my sleeping bag. The stench of mildew greeted my nose. At that moment, I would have sold my soul to slink back into my warm bedding and go back to sleep. My brain and body were exhausted.

Hang on! Suddenly I remembered that I'd had the last shift—Tim was supposed to rouse Remy. Relief washed through my body.

"Uh, Tim—" I began.

He cut me off, his voice sounding slightly nervous in the darkness. "What side of the ship is the red navigation light on?"

Tim was referring to the lighting system, required by international shipping laws, that allows ships to orientate themselves to one another at night. A display of three colored lights, shining out at specific angles, allows passing vessels to determine the other boats' approximate bearing.

"Left," I said.

I could feel a deep bass rumble in the water beneath the hull—the telltale throb of a powerful diesel engine nearby. The engine was getting louder, very quickly. Too quickly.

"Uh, Colin, mate, would you mind coming out here for a moment?" Tim asked.

In my underwear I climbed out of the cabin into a windy black void. A barrage of lights hit me in the retinas. Tim tore at the water. When you can see both red (left) and green (right) navigation lights, a vessel is coming straight at you. The fact that we could see only a red navigation light meant that the vessel should be passing *beside* us, yet it seemed to be coming directly at us: there were lights everywhere, and the engine was getting louder. Perhaps the green light had burned out! Amid the white lights, a ruby-red eye stared at us. Like a moving city, the mountain of light and chiaroscuro shadow slid toward us at frightening speed.

"Row hard! Row like hell!" I yelled, gesturing in the direction Tim should be taking us.

Tim's superhuman efforts were beginning to pay off, and we were picking up speed, moving at a 90-degree angle to the assumed line of travel of the rumbling ship.

"FASTER! FASTER!" I shrieked, venting the terror that was pulsing through my body. The prospect of being mowed down by a ship with a huge churning propeller and tossed into freezing waters in the inky darkness looked imminent. Then for a moment my panicked mind became lucid, and I realized that something was wrong with the situation: Something was *very* wrong. We were going the wrong way! Somehow, in my sleep-addled state, I had mentally reversed the situation. I had pointed Tim in the wrong direction to escape the ship's path of travel. Hundreds of tons of steel were bearing down on us and we were moving toward its line of transit. The diesel was a thundering roar.

I screamed to be heard: "TURN AROUND!"

"WHAT?" Tim shouted in disbelief.

"WE'RE GOING THE WRONG WAY! TURN AROUND, TURN AROUND!"

"ARE YOU SURE!"

It's not easy turning a fast-moving, full-keeled, half-ton boat. But Tim had the fear of death spurring him on. He put all his weight into the starboard oar, its broad blade thrashing through the black water. In slow motion our wooden tub began to pivot in a great, broad circle.

I stared at the lights, now certain I could make out the shadowy shape of the hull gliding toward us. And then I saw it: a bright green light emerging from its hiding place. Red and green and a thundering diesel—every sailor's worst nightmare! There was no doubt now; we were on a collision course. It had been a mistake to turn around. Although our previous direction was taking us straight into the path of the ship, our speed would have carried us across in front of its bow and over to the other side. Now we were practically motionless, directly in the path of the ship and within seconds of being broadsided.

A spotlight of several million candlepower turned night into day, blinding me. I couldn't see a thing. We were bathed in incandescence and frozen in space.

"WHERE ARE WE GOING?" Tim yelled.

I had no idea. The world was nothing but burning white light. It was completely disorienting.

Then the light went out and the ship's horn blew a deafening warning.

Ben and Remy bolted upright in their sleeping bags.

I couldn't see properly; the white nova burned into my retinas. I could barely make out the hulking steel wall bearing down on us.

"ROW, ROW, ROW!" I screamed.

We were going to be rammed. In a few seconds we would all be in that freezing water and dragged under the ship. The great vacuum created by the whirling propeller would suck us into the giant blades. We would be shredded into hamburger. Ben and Remy were frantically clawing and struggling, trying to extricate themselves from the interior.

The engine changed pitch and thundered. I figured the captain must be throwing it into full reverse, but he would never be able to stop in time. Our boat was moving slowly in spite of Tim's efforts. The great moving wall, complete with a cresting wave, bore down—closer, closer, closer.

Time seemed to slow. We were going to hit—and then we made it! The ship's bow slipped past, three feet from our stern. A huge wave flicked our boat momentarily onto its side. Pots, pans, equipment, and bodies could be heard thumping and clattering across the boat. I grabbed onto the cabin frame just in time to avoid going overboard. We had been spared!

The tug continued to roar by, its length seemingly endless. Tim kept up his steady rowing, knowing that a laden barge would be following. At least we were moving in the right direction now.

Ten minutes later, we were left in silence. The tug was a splash of shimmering lights twinkling in the distance.

"Well, another boat passes us in the night without mowing us down," Tim said, with forced cheerfulness.

I began to shiver.

"Good night," I said, and crawled back in my sleeping bag.

At the best of times it was nerve-racking being inside the V-berth up front. Space was so tight that it was impossible to lie on your side or roll over. It took several minutes to wriggle your body through the mounds of gear and food to get into sleeping position. And it took just as long to get out. The trunk of a small Japanese car would be a luxury compared with the confined space of the forward cabin. At night, when everything was pitch black, that V-berth was twice as terrifying—being wedged into the deepest crevice of a rotten derelict boat was too suggestive of sleeping in a coffin.

On top of that, we were in the middle of a shipping lane, where our small boat was but an insignificant piece of flotsam. The encounter with the tug had highlighted just how vulnerable we were out on the river at night or in fog. Yet we had no choice. The end was so near, but we were behind schedule. If we stopped every time visibility was poor, there was no chance we would make it. Still, I wouldn't be able to lie down anymore without thinking I might be awakened by the prow of a ship splintering the hull.

With these thoughts playing through my mind, I lay listening intently for that deep, telltale rumble of an approaching diesel. All I heard was the rhythmic oars. I fell into a fitful sleep and dreamed of churning propellers, mutilation, death, and a watery grave.

**13**

Tim, Remy, Ben, and Colin at 70° north latitude on the Yenisey River.

# ABOVE THE TREELINE AND INTO THE TUNDRA

*Thursday, September 6*

The Arctic Circle is one of those imaginary lines around the globe, like the equator and the tropics of Cancer and Capricorn, and it circles the top of the planet at precisely 66 degrees, 33 minutes north. It marks the northernmost point at which the sun is visible at the northern winter solstice and the southernmost point at which the midnight sun can be seen at the northern summer solstice. In ordinary terms, above the Arctic Circle in the winter, the sun barely rises above the horizon. In summer there are days of twenty-four-hour sunshine and "nights" that never get completely dark and last only a few hours.

Crossing the Arctic Circle was an incredibly important psychological event for us—a milestone we had been talking about for months.

We actually crossed it three times, as the river took a snakelike meander at that latitude, a great aquatic serpent slithering toward the ocean. We stopped at a small trickle of a creek spilling down a steep rock-and-clay bank. Ben collected the tea-colored water while Tim and I ventured into the forest above. The trees were straggly, stunted, and scarred by the harsh weather they endured.

The spruce and pine weren't much higher than thirty feet and they were spaced far apart, which gave a light, airy feeling to the forest. The ground was carpeted with a thick sphagnumlike moss that formed abstract verdigris patterns between splashes of livid lichen. We were looking for the perfect spot to build a sweat lodge to celebrate crossing the circle, but this wasn't it. We returned to the boat and continued downriver.

*Friday, September 7*

"She looks pretty good here," Tim said. "I don't think I've seen a more perfect spot for a sweat lodge."

A small, clear stream burbled into the Yenisey from a bed of rounded granite and limestone. The land on both sides was marshy swamp grass that ran back three hundred feet or so and disappeared into the forest. Remy guided the boat hard onto the rocky shore, in true Russian fashion. It groaned as its keel grated on a couple of football-sized rocks and tilted lazily to port, skidding to a halt on the foreshore.

Ben and Tim began building an enormous bonfire, piling the plentiful driftwood between layers of large round river rocks. When they had a five-foot pyre, Tim set it ablaze. Meanwhile, Remy and I were building the sauna. We cut alder saplings into ten-foot lengths and wove them into a dome-shaped shelter, securing the branches in place with twine and weighting them down with boulders. We covered the cupola frame with a tent fly and blankets.

At 11:30 P.M., as the last of the northern twilight leaked from the sky, we sat naked on logs around a pile of hot stones. We streamed with sweat. Tim poured water over the stones, sending up clouds of billowing steam. Inside the tiny hovel I could see little but the retinal scar of that searchlight from the tug that nearly finished us.

"Cheers to coming a long way without sinking, and making it to the Arctic Circle," Ben said, raising a celebratory mug of beer.

We all held up the beers we had hoarded for three weeks for just this moment. "Cheers!" we said in unison. We sat there sweating, each of us in quiet contemplation, sipping the sweetest-tasting brew I'd had in a long time.

"Tradition says we should go for a dip in the Yenisey," Tim said.

"I'm in," Remy chirped.

"Count me out," I said. "I like the idea of sitting here and enjoying the last of this heat. We might not get any for a long time."

"Me, too," Ben said.

I closed my eyes, rested my chin on my sweaty chest, and enjoyed the last moments of the sauna.

*Saturday, September 8*

"The cover of the water filter is on too tight," Ben said, strolling back from the stream with three water containers. "I couldn't open it up to clean the cartridge."

Two of the containers were full and the other was three-quarters full. "I couldn't fill up the last bit because the filter was completely clogged," he added.

It wasn't a huge concern. The water that we were collecting off the Siberian Plateau was the cleanest water we had encountered yet. From then on we began drinking the water straight, with no ill effects.

We pushed the boat back into the river. Large plum-colored clouds clotted the winter sky and a cold wind blew from the north. We had little time to lose.

*Monday, September 10*

We were stuck on a tiny, barren, windswept island. The sky was a cloudless cobalt blue and the icy north wind was shrieking. The dark, navy river stretched one mile from either side of the island; it felt more like a vast sea than a river. Six-foot swells crashed onto an endless sandy beach. Huge, bare dunes extended back from the water until couch grass began to stabilize the sand. Seagulls screamed overhead.

And there we sat. Until the thirty-five mile per hour headwinds abated, we couldn't make any progress. We'd run out of kerosene, the car battery was flat, and we were almost out of food. How long the winds would last was anyone's guess. If that was the predominant weather, we were pretty much screwed, because the boat wouldn't move forward an inch up the choppy river.

Tempers were flaring and stomachs were growling.

We came across a small cabin occupied by three teddy-bear Russian men, all dressed in black-striped long underwear. They were from Krasnoyarsk on a fishing holiday, a kind of Siberian *City Slickers* event. They were surprised to see us, but jovially invited us in for fish, cookies, bread, and, of course, vodka.

Nicolai had a neck like a bulldog, a bit of a potbelly, curly hair, and mischievous blue eyes. He was an airline pilot who flew a 150-seat jet with Air Krasnoyarsk. He and his friends had flown to the cabin in a helicopter.

"My wife, she tells me every year, 'Let's take a vacation at the Black Sea. It's warmer there.' " Nicolai chuckled, imitating her voice. "But every year I come up here to the coldest, remotest part of the world. I love it. And the fish are huge."

His two companions prepared a couple of large fish as we sat on the wooden stools surrounding a small table. The fillets sizzled and popped in a sea of oil as they fried in a cast-iron skillet on the woodstove. A plate of salted fish, along with caviar and bread, was offered. As I munched on the delicate, if oily, char, Nicolai noticed me staring at the water stains streaking the walls. "This spring during the floods," he said, "the river was seventy feet higher than it is now. This house was completely submerged. Not even the roof was above the floodwaters."

I thought back to my time living off the land in Mongolia. That would have been when this little home was submerged under deep, swirling brown water.

*Wednesday, September 12*

Through the night, even though we had it moored on the sheltered side of the island, the boat was thumped and pounded on the rocky shore. We put the plastic folders we'd purchased in Ust'Ilimsk over the windows to help keep out the icy winds. The boat was rocking violently, but Ben and I decided to sleep on board, anyway. Tim and Remy opted to sleep in the cabin with the Russians.

The wind died just before dawn, and we pushed off at first light after a spectacular display of the aurora borealis—scarlet, emerald, and ivory bands flickering and dancing across the sky like a Pink Floyd light show. We had been holed up for some thirty-six hours and our anxieties were running rampant. Would the winds get worse as we neared the Arctic? In a few weeks the river would be frozen and our expedition would be over, whether we were finished or not. And the current was barely noticeable, so we had nothing to rely on but our own arm strength. We were not optimistic.

The phones had about forty-five minutes of power remaining, and we could not recharge them until we got to the next city or town. Remy called his girlfriend in Canada—or "secretary," as he usually referred to her—to tell her he couldn't dictate his story for the newspaper because there wasn't enough juice.

"Hi, it's me," he said.

Although it was Wednesday, September 12, on top of the world in Siberia, at home in North America it was 10:30 A.M. Eastern Standard Time, on Tuesday, September 11.

"What? . . . Hello?" he said. "The phone cut out." He had a strange look on his face. "That was the oddest thing. All she said was 'Four jets have been hijacked by kamikaze pilots.' "

"Who and where?" Ben asked.

"I'm not sure," said Remy. "I didn't get a chance to find out."

No one was too perturbed, just befuddled. I imagined four jets sitting on the tarmac somewhere, the hijackers demanding cash and the release of prisoners. It was strange that she had used the term "kamikaze pilots," though.

We had fifteen minutes left on the battery for the other phone. We had intended to save it for emergency purposes, but curiosity got the better of us. "Use the other phone."

Remy called her back. "Hi, it's me again. We don't have much juice. What's going on? . . . You're kidding . . . what—" He ended the call, his face ashen.

Remy relayed the news of the terrible attacks and we were stunned. The four of us ate sturgeon soup in silence as the frosted banks drifted by. The dry, wheat-colored leaves rustled in the wind and the forest glowed in the morning sunlight like some golden sacristy. We were in shock. The mouth of the river was near, but now our achievement paled and felt drained of relevance. We rowed through the forest, each of us contemplating the tragedy. It was beyond comprehension.

We arrived in the village of Potopova around 9:00 P.M. With seven hundred people, this was the regional hub. It was a frontier town of decrepit two- and three-story wooden buildings and small, faded homes in need of fresh paint. The streets were rutted tracks, black with coal dust. Piles of coal stood heaped in front of every building. The breeze carried the sounds of dogs barking, axes splitting wood, and children laughing.

The boat's keel carved a trench into the gravel beach and we disembarked.

About half the people in town were Nenets, one of the indigenous peoples of the Arctic. In my research for the expedition, I was especially interested in these people. They number about forty thousand and comprise about half the population of the Samoyed peoples of Siberia. The Nenets survived in Siberia's harsh wilderness by living in reindeer-skin tepees and hunting and fishing.

There is a theory that the aboriginal peoples who first populated North America may have been the descendants of these northern Siberians. Their appearance is different from the Buryats farther south, and the striking similarity between the Nenets and the Inuits is immediately evident. They share the same stocky features and flat faces—ideal for coping with freezing temperatures. Like the word *Inuit*, *Nenet* also means "the people," or "man."

In Russia the indigenous people have faced the same problems as their North American counterparts, and they are also being assimilated by the all-encompassing European culture. Stalin's period at the helm was an especially devastating blow to the Nenet culture—their medicine men and tribal leaders were taken away and slaughtered. The remaining population were mostly put into box homes and forced to be educated the white way. Their freedom and pride stolen from them, many resorted to the bottle and, to this day, live lives of eternal misery.

Potopova is a community of these lost Arctic souls. Long, bleak winters combined with idle lifestyles have led to extraordinarily high death and suicide rates. The life expectancy of Nenets is forty-five years, and fewer than half have paid employment, mostly unskilled labor. The wages of the natives are considerably lower than those of recent settlers. What they call the "glass ruble"—a bottle of strong alcohol—functions as the hard currency of the tundra.

Although some Nenets maintain a traditional lifestyle, in Potopova there was no sign of their culture. The village had a strong contingent of blond, blue-eyed Germans and handfuls of Ukrainian, Chechen, and Finnish settlers. There was only one genuine western Russian living in the whole village.

We stayed for two days, and the mayor let us sleep on the floor of his office. The balding, middle-aged mayor was from Krasnoyarsk, and had lived in Potopova for eight years. He dressed like any Western businessman—white shirt, tie, and gray slacks—and he seemed to be the only person in the village not living in a perpetual vodka-induced haze. As we walked through town with him, he said that for years he had tried to give some dignity to the people. Most of them were dressed in rags, their faces masks of depression.

The mayor's office was in a large log building. A Russian flag draped one wall, and two heavy wooden desks sat on opposite sides of the room. Next to the door, a small table held a kettle, tea bags, and sugar.

"I'd put you up in the hospital, but there are no beds there, either," he told Tim. "We have too many sick people in this town. It is the vodka!"

With that, he opened a cupboard and asked if we wanted a vodka nightcap.

*Saturday, September 15–Monday, September 17*

There were a few trees in Potopova—fairly scraggly, for sure, but trees nevertheless. Thirty miles after leaving the village, we entered the treeless landscape of the High Arctic. We had reached the end of the great Siberian boreal forest. Nothing but tundra lay between the Arctic Ocean and us.

The water was choppy and the air was cold when we arrived at Dudinka at two in the morning, a major shipping port of some fifty thousand people. Dudinka's harbor was awash in light. We headed toward a black patch between the lights and bumped heavily against a bouldery shore.

At dawn we found ourselves in a scene from a Mad Max movie. A factory outfall spewed warm water like a huge fountain into the river, sending an unmistakably chemical stench billowing across the harbor. A man and two children fished beside the pipe. Nearby, a huddle of children surrounded a small bonfire.

Huge amounts of nickel, cobalt, copper, and aluminum are shipped through Dudinka. Giant nuclear-powered icebreakers are used in winter to bull through the frozen river and the pack ice. Smelters and processing plants are everywhere. In the neighboring mining city of Norilsk, the pollution is so thick you can barely see a block down the street.

Remy, Ben, and I went into town while Tim guarded the boat. This was the first time I had seen Russian city folk dressed for winter. They wore the stereotypical fur hat with earflaps, thick wool coats, gloves, and boots.

In Dudinka the concrete buildings were raised on stilts to keep them from sinking into the permafrost. They were painted in various pastel colors, a desperate attempt to add cheer to an otherwise wretched environment. In a few months, there would be no daylight.

Supplied by ships from Eastern Europe, the local shops featured abundant exotic fruit and luxury items. There was a lot of money in the north, and high costs as well. We paid almost twice as much for supplies as we had earlier, but we had no choice. We spent half a day looking for kerosene, but there was none. Would the stove burn diesel? We had no choice but to buy liters of the yellow fuel. If it didn't work, the next few days would be extremely miserable.

We were ready for the final 150-mile haul.

*Tuesday, September 18*

"Just think, soon we'll be the first people to have voyaged the length of the world's largest river," Ben said.

"What? The Amazon's the largest," I responded.

"Not necessarily," Ben said. "What are they measuring when they say the world's largest river? Is it the amount of water flowing, or the volume of water actually in the river?"

"I don't know," I replied.

"If it's total water volume, the Yenisey is the biggest. Lake Baikal is included when measuring the Yenisey's length; therefore its water must also be included when measuring the Yenisey's volume. The Amazon is said to contain twenty percent of the planet's fresh groundwater—exactly the same amount that Baikal alone contains. So the Yenisey is bigger."

It was an interesting point—perhaps grabbing at straws, but definitely something to ponder.

The landscape was as lonely as the moon, the world transformed into abstract fields of desolate, dun-colored tundra, a low, dark pewter sky. The river was broad and wide, perhaps four miles across. Gusts of wind whipped it into a writhing beast with huge swells that slowed us to a near dead stop.

The diesel worked in the stove, but barely. Big yellow flames were blackening the pots, and the fumes were lethal. Earlier we had hoped to use the stove to keep the interior warm. No such luck! Instead we used it as little as possible to avoid the choking, stinging fumes. It was as though bus exhaust were being directed into our living space. Tears streamed from my eyes, and we all suffered from headaches.

Although we were lucky to be having unseasonably warm weather—averaging about thirty-two degrees—the north winds were making life a misery. We were struggling to make headway, especially since there was no current worth mentioning. The boat bucked and groaned on the swells as the designated rower sat lonely and cold, an icy wind in his face and his hands stinging. The others huddled in the cabin, seasick, lethargic, and cold, both day and night.

*Wednesday, September 19*

As the hardships increased, our stress levels became very high. We were all running out of reserves, physically and emotionally. It had now been well over four months since we had begun our journey at the source, and two months since we had started rowing around the clock. My entire body ached from the repetitive movement of the oars. It had been eons since I'd had a proper night's sleep. My knees were throbbing, I had severe tendinitis in my right elbow, my derrière was covered in boils, and my muscles were eternally stiff from the cold and overuse.

On top of the physical discomfort, our hygiene was abysmal, and there was nothing we could do about it. For the past three weeks the weather had been too cold to swim and clean ourselves. As well, washing clothes was impossible because of the frequent rain and limited space on the boat for drying. Once a garment got wet, a few days later it was invariably reduced to a stinking rag shoved in a corner somewhere. The leaky cabin and portholes allowed the rain and waves crashing over the boat to seep into everything. The sleeping bags were wet, food stashed in the deepest corners would become damp, and the clothes we wore often became soggy—until our body heat succeeded in drying them. In the boat we were desensitized to the smell, but whenever we went ashore to collect food or water, the rancid odor would be all too apparent on our return.

Our cramped lifestyle, bad hygiene, pain, and frustratingly slow progress led to frayed tempers and frequent arguments. We had been cooped up for too long, and constant foul weather dimmed the light shining at the end of the tunnel. We were gripped by cabin fever and by anxiety that, if we continued to be plagued by Arctic storms, we might never make it.

Remy tried making a pot of porridge for breakfast. A large wave hit the boat and the bubbling gruel went spilling across the cabin. Luckily nobody was seriously burned, but the mess was not cleaned up properly, and our stomachs were left growling. There was no more food until lunch.

*Thursday, September 20*

During the night the winds eased slightly and we made it to the village of Karaul, a scrum of tilting wooden homes surrounded by a litter of oil drums and stacks of coal. It was a bleak, lonely setting, like some interplanetary mining outpost. Tim, Ben, and I walked down the coal-dusted streets and entered the last store on the Yenisey. Its floor sloped at an incredible angle because the foundation had sunk into the permafrost. We left with cans of beef and sardines, bread, tomato sauce, and a lone chocolate bar. We were almost out of rubles.

Cinnamon tundra stretched in every direction, and thick clouds and a steeply angled sun gave the river a leaden look. I shivered. Karaul stayed in our wake for hours as we fought our way into a severe chop. We stayed as close to the shore as possible, since it provided a little more shelter than the rest of the river. The land around us now was low and flat as a pancake. The stunted vegetation of sphagnum, lichen, grasses, and dwarf willow was uniformly brown, ready for the approach of another long winter. Summer is brief in this frozen land, and animals and plants have quick life cycles to take advantage of the short period of relative warmth.

About seven hours after leaving Karaul, when it seemed we were the only people in a flat world, two men in a rowboat materialized from a stand of reeds near the shore. The two middle-aged bushmen wore wool pants and plaid wool shirts and had shotguns slung over their shoulders. Their faces were blank as they approached and exchanged pleas-antries with Tim. One of the men reached down and picked up a large white arctic hare. He grinned from ear to ear, ex-posing bloody gums and a row of teeth thick with plaque. Then he handed the still-warm carcass to us, and they left as quickly as they had appeared. We were pretty excited to have some decent meat once again, and planned to eat it the next day.

### Friday, September 21

Sitting on the foredeck, I skinned and gutted the hare for lunch. My fingers were numb with cold by the time I finished tossing the pluck overboard. The arctic hare now looked a quarter of its size. Still, it was a substantial chunk of meat, and would make a great lunch in a stew with potatoes, cab-bage, beets, and carrots.

As the rabbit simmered, the rain started, and a thirty-knot wind rose out of the west and pounded us. It pushed us far-ther and farther out into the river, and the waves grew big-ger and bigger with the increasing fetch between the boat and the shore. The scalding stew was splashing everywhere; I se-cured the pot on the stove and turned off the heat.

The situation looked dangerous. We were several miles from either shore, and the waves threatened to swamp the boat. Tim was exhausted at the oars and Ben hurriedly traded places with him. If the boat took one of the waves broadside, it would capsize. Even with the boat's nose into the wind, the motion was incredible. The bow rode up into the sky as it climbed the face of five-foot waves. The boat would crest the waves and then crash down the other side, plunging deep into the freezing green water. The river washed over the cabin, sending ice-cold water pouring into the interior, soaking us.

Ben was frozen and was spent within minutes. "Quick, someone switch with me!" he hollered.

I jumped out of the cabin and made the switch, which wasn't easy, since we had to keep the boat facing the wind. I climbed behind Ben and grabbed the oars, and he jumped over my arms and clambered into the cabin. For the first few strokes, I hauled without the aid of the rowing seat. It took me a few moments to work my feet into the straps and my butt into the hard, narrow seat.

I pulled with all my might, digging into the viscous emerald water and shoving with my legs. There was nothing I could do. The boat was being beaten back, and it took every ounce of strength just to keep it from turning sideways and rolling over. If that happened, we'd be dead within minutes from hypothermia.

My biggest worry, though, was what was once the far shore. We had been battered so badly by the gale that we had been pushed across the river and now were in danger of being shipwrecked. I could see a line of breaking waves four hundred yards from shore—a sure sign of a sandbar, a submerged shoal, or some kind of reef—and we were headed straight for it. The hull of the boat would be ripped apart or we'd flip. We'd drown before we could make it to the bank.

It was hard to get an even purchase on the oars. Most of the time I was hauling on just the left or the right oar, keeping the bow to the waves. The distance to the shoal was closing rapidly, and I pulled in a truly panicked frenzy. After five minutes, I was spent. "Relief!" I shouted.

Remy emerged and spelled me. The wind was gusting and the duration of each lull was growing, so he was able to make some headway. But he no sooner gained a bit of distance than the wind drove the boat backward. The wind would die, Remy would make some progress, and then it would blow again. It was three strokes forward, two strokes back; five strokes forward, four strokes back.

The tug-of-war went on for hours until all of us were exhausted. By 5:00 P.M. we were trembling wrecks, famished from a day of extreme exercise and no food (it was impossible to eat any of the stew I had made; it would have spilled all over us and the boat before we'd be able to get it into our mouths).

The wind abated later in the evening, and we were able to steer the boat across the river and into the lee shelter provided by the high western riverbank. Our nerves were jangled, but the boat was quiet. I lit the stove and put the stew back on simmer.

It was dark, and I feared we might face the same blustery nemesis in the night. It would have been safer to tie up, but we were worried that the river would freeze and we would be trapped in the ice.

In the middle of the night, when Ben woke me for my shift, the boat was aglow. Snow was falling heavily in large, wet flakes. But it was calm. I grabbed the icy oars and sat down. I pulled back—everything ached. I pulled again. *O-o-o-o-oh*, every muscle groaned. And it was cold—so very, very cold. I pulled and pulled and pulled. My teeth chattered; in my damp clothes, no matter how hard I rowed, I couldn't warm myself.

My shift lasted an eternity. When I climbed back into my damp, stinking sleeping bag I could think of only one word— *bliss*.

*Saturday, September 22*

"Tepees!"

I climbed out of the cabin into the falling snow and followed Remy's extended finger. In the flat, dim early-morning overcast, I could just discern two triangular structures. It was hard to distinguish for certain whether they were tepees, so Remy angled the boat toward shore. The wind was rising, and I prayed they were a habitation. All my clothes were damp and I couldn't stop shivering. It had been two days since we had last seen any other human beings. We were in the middle of the Yenisey's enormous delta, lost in a maze of channels and flat islands. We had resigned ourselves to being alone in this desolate land for the remainder of the journey. Now, possibly, we would be encountering the true inhabitants of the north.

They *were* tepees (in Russia they were called *chuums*), tents constructed from long poles bound together at the top and covered with hides.

The boat crunched into the snowy riverbank, and we disembarked. The wind was beginning to howl again, and big flakes of snow flew horizontally.

Around the two conical structures were wooden sleds loaded with furs, leghold traps, racks of drying meat and fish, stored fishing nets, and a pile of reindeer skulls.

We couldn't tell if anyone was actually inside the tepees. There was no sound, just the incessant whine of the wind. We explored the area for some time, unsure how to politely disturb the occupants, as there was no door to knock on.

Finally a man with Inuit features emerged, wearing nothing but his underwear and a vest. He saw us and stopped, bewildered. Where the hell had we come from? His broad face broke into a grin and he offered a hand.

"Ootla," he said, pointing to himself, and beckoned for us to come inside his home.

Compared with our leaky, smelly, damp, cold, and cramped boat, I felt I'd entered a domain of decadence. I was amazed at how large the tepee seemed inside. In the middle, a woodstove radiated intense heat, and my shivering body relished the saunalike atmosphere. A long stovepipe extended through the opening at the top of the structure. The walls were made of reindeer hide, and other skins were piled on the floor. Three beds were placed around the perimeter, each a combination of stacked skins and wool blankets. Three mongrels lay on one of the beds, curled up into tight balls. A small wooden table of Western design supported a stack of clean china plates and a few chipped enamel mugs.

A woman of about twenty-five, with long black hair and piercing black eyes, and a young boy appeared to have just crawled out of bed. Ootla introduced them as his wife, Laurissa, and his seven-year-old son, Andrei. Although Ootla and Laurissa spoke Russian fairly well, their son was more comfortable speaking his indigenous tongue.

Tim explained what we were up to, and Ootla nodded. As far as he was concerned, all white people were crazy, "up to strange things." As long as we weren't doing anybody any harm, his attitude was live and let live. His wife made breakfast, and Ootla invited us to stay and eat.

Ootla told us we were lucky to have encountered their tepees. There were few people in this huge expanse of myriad channels. On this island were only two others. The neighboring tepee housed a sixty-five-year-old woman and her thirty-year-old son. Apparently there used to be thirty Nenets living on this island, but they had left one by one, drawn to the bright lights of the towns to the south.

The woodstove crackled and steam hissed from my drying jacket and boots.

Ootla said that the Gulf of Yenisey was about fifteen miles

distant. If the storm raging outside died by morning, we could make a dash for it the next day. Another, much larger storm was brewing, he told us. It would hit in a few days and would probably freeze the river. He could tell by looking at the flight patterns of the migrating birds.

After our breakfast of raw, salted sturgeon and dry bread, Ootla's only neighbors arrived. The old lady looked much older than her sixty-five years, and she muttered incessantly—sometimes to people, other times to no one we could see. Both she and her son wore reindeer hides. The skins had been sewn into a tight-fitting coat with the fur facing inward. Mitts were affixed to the ends of the sleeves and the hood was so snug it was more like a balaclava. They wore thick hide pants.

The man's name was Nicolai, and it was obvious that he and Ootla were close friends. They chatted in their own tongue for a few minutes, chucking and glancing our way intermittently.

Nicolai left and returned ten minutes later with an armload of antiquated firearms.

"We will go duck hunting," Ootla told us. "Most of the ducks have gone south, but there are still a few stragglers."

We were each handed a firearm. Mine was a double-barreled shotgun. I opened it and tried sliding the hand-packed shells into the chambers. One slid in easily, but the other jammed halfway in. Ootla saw me struggling. He picked up a chunk of firewood and hammered on the shell. I winced. It was soon rammed into place.

Ootla handed the gun to me with a grin: "You pansy!"

We slipped out under the flap of reindeer skin that covered the door. The weather was lifting. The snow had stopped, and the wind was lighter than it had been. We walked toward the center of the flat, marshy island. Our feet sank deep into peat moss and squelched through the water that lay just under the surface. Stunted shrubs, no more than a yard high, grew wherever the ground rose slightly from the quagmire.

A frenzied, high-pitched barking filled the air, and a blur of white flashed in front of me. Seconds later, Ootla's white-and-gray mutt raced by as well. Ootla grabbed Tim's gun and fired two shots. The dog was close behind an arctic hare, and I was sure it would be hit by the buckshot too. But neither the dog nor the hare dropped, and both disappeared.

We walked until we reached a large pond. Ootla held up his hand for us to stop. The frenzied barking had resumed. This time it was on the far side of the pond, where the dog was trying to flush ducks. There were none. Winter was coming quickly; the only birds left were seagulls.

"Come, I have something to show you," Ootla said, beckoning for us to follow.

We continued our hike across the island, skirting ponds and sinking through the mud. Eventually we emerged on the eastern shore. The flooding river had deposited silt there, and a raised bank stood like a dike between the water and us. We stood on top of the mound. Below us a brown, sandy beach was stretched wide by the tide that pushed upriver. The river reflected the sullen gray of the sky, and the wind continued to howl in a sorrowful monotone. As far as I could see, there wasn't the slightest rise in the land, just alternating water and brown tundra, utterly flat.

On that empty tabletop plain, the wooden cross was visible for miles and miles. It rose ten feet out of the lichen. Shivering from the damp cold insinuating itself into my jacket, I nodded to the cross and asked Ootla what it represented.

"That is what I have brought you to see," he said, as Tim translated. "Our beautiful island was once a place of fear, death, and evil. This is the main reason why so many of my people have left. Although the bright lights of Dudinka offer nothing more than depression, alcohol, and suicide, for some people it is better than staying here and facing the demons. Two thousand people were murdered on this island by Stalin. You can still see their bones everywhere."

Ootla gestured across the sand. I realized that what I had thought were white shells were actually bones—human bones. Femurs, jawbones, clavicles, vertebrae were scattered as far as the eye could see.

"Stalin was the cause of all this," Ootla spat. "They weren't our people—our people were taken elsewhere to be slaughtered. No, the people killed here were Russians of German ancestry. They'd immigrated to western Russia hundreds of years ago, and Stalin in his paranoia felt they would side with the Nazis during an invasion. Rather than take a chance, he had them rounded up—men, women, and children—and shipped here to die. They didn't stand a chance. They were dumped off the boat at this very same time of year. Ill dressed, with no food, no shelter, and no equipment, there was no hope for the poor prisoners. Stalin's men were so confident that death was assured, they didn't even bother posting guards.

"There were a few Nenets here at the time; they were struggling themselves because Stalin had removed their leaders. Nonetheless, they did their best to help some of the German Russians, building tepees and sharing their own meager food supplies. There were just too many of the prisoners, though, and they slowly perished from starvation and cold. As winter dug its fingers into the land, the endless nights became a living nightmare of wailing and screaming. Eventually our people had to start fighting off desperate prisoners begging for food and shelter. Dying children lay beside lifeless parents. Eight weeks after they landed, all two thousand people were dead."

Ootla paused. He looked as though he were about to cry. I noticed just a few feet away from him a tiny shoe on the ground. The leather was rotted; only a few tattered pieces still clung to the rubber sole. I felt like throwing up.

"Some of our people still claim to see the prisoners wandering around the island in the wintertime. I have never seen any myself, but it haunts me."

Ootla looked at the sky. "Winter is not far off, and soon another storm will be here. If you don't make it to the end in another few days, you will have no choice but to spend the winter with us."

I was worried. What he said was true. Once the river began freezing, we would be stopped wherever we were. Much as the Nenet culture fascinated me, the prospect of living on this desolate island—at 71 degrees latitude, in eternal night, with two thousand ghouls—for seven months until the spring thaw was too much. We had left Canada more than five months before, and I was ready to go home.

Ootla's dog caught sight of an enormous leg bone and ran over to gnaw on it. He ran back, tail wagging, with the bone between his teeth.

We returned to the tepee, where Laurissa had a grand dinner waiting—chunky, melt-in-your-mouth reindeer stew and fish soup. We gorged ourselves, basking in the heat of the stove. It was the most comfortable moment I'd experienced in weeks, and it didn't take long before I was fast asleep.

*Sunday, September 23*

We were up at five-thirty. It was calm, and Ootla said we must take advantage of such a rare moment. I stepped out of the tepee to urinate and was immediately struck by freezing air. In the darkness, the northern lights flashed above in the most brilliant display I'd seen yet. Quickly I withdrew back into the warmth and we discussed how to coordinate this final day.

I was first on the oars and was hoping that the outgoing

tide would assist us. No such luck. Instead, there was a rising breeze on the bow. Daylight revealed a monochromatic world of winter. The temperature was about fourteen degrees, and a skin of ice was beginning to form on the river. Flurries of snow dusted us. The weather made for slow progress. My muscles screamed in agony but no longer bothered me—we were almost at the end of our journey. Within a few hours the pain would be nothing but a memory.

It was a bittersweet feeling. I knew this river intimately and felt as though I would be leaving an old friend. No one outside of our team knew this river as well as we did. No one else had experienced its entirety. I had glimpsed its soul, and to leave it tugged at my heart.

The boat too had become a part of our lives. It had been our home for so long, and it had proved the naysayers wrong. Our proud little boat had carried us for thousands of miles through storms, rapids, and collisions with rocks. Somehow it had become The Little Dory That Could.

By noon we emerged from the maze of the delta and found ourselves in a huge body of water. We had reached the Kara Sea, an arm of the Arctic, and the end of the Yenisey River. No land could be seen on the horizon. The boat rocked in a lazy, rolling swell.

We steered toward a nameless flat, low island on our left. This had been our goal for five months—the island of the Yenisey's delta that protruded the farthest into the sea. Some 3,500 miles from where the first trickle of snowmelt began, the mighty Yenisey—Russia's most powerful river by volume—emptied into the Kara Sea. The river was ending its journey just as we were ending ours.

Ben was the last to man the oars. His long, lanky body moved slowly as he savored the last few minutes of our expedition. The sandy, driftwood-strewn beach inched closer and closer. Then the hull slammed into the brown sand. A lone seal popped its head out of the water and stared. Gray clouds scuttled across the sky.

I thought back over the journey. I thought of the people and the land, the beauty and the dangers. And I thought about how fragile this watershed was—this watershed that contained more than a fifth of the world's fresh water. We jumped out of the boat and splashed our faces with the brackish water. We had reached the mouth of the river.

We slipped the oars from their locks and carried them to shore. The Canadian and Australian flags were affixed to the long shafts, and we planted them victoriously in the sand. I looked around at the others' faces—the bearded, sunken cheeks; the red, bleary eyes; the dank, lank hair. I surveyed the freezing, bleak landscape around me and basked in the thought that we had voyaged the complete length of the mighty Yenisey. Tim rooted around in a dry bag for the celebratory bottle of vodka. We lifted enamel mugs, the *clink* lost in a sudden gust of icy wind.

"Viva Yenisey!"

## EPILOGUE

The most common question I am asked about the expedition is, how did we get back? Sure, we had completed our expedition goal, but we were still at 71 degrees latitude, at the very top of Siberia. Well, I answer that question in my next book, titled *Rowing Back up the Yenisey*.

Of course I'm kidding, but the journey back did end up being an adventure in itself. The biggest problem, and a great contributor to our stress, was the fact that we had extremely limited time in which to make our way back home. Several months before, we had booked two theaters in which to do a group presentation about our trip. The bookings had been made impulsively while we were drifting through the thickest Siberian wilderness. Civilization seemed so distant that we didn't need a lot of courage to pick up the satellite phones and book the two 1,100-seat halls. We had anticipated finishing the expedition a little sooner, so the theaters had been reserved for November 6 and 7.

True to the theme of our entire journey, we simply didn't have the money to pay for the halls. It was a gamble we had made on a sunny Siberian day, when money and people seemed a fuzzy, far-off concept. If we didn't pack the halls, we'd be financially ruined. With the expedition over, the upcoming presentations became a very real and intimidating prospect. It was time to leave our fantasyland of endless tundra and head back to the real world.

Ootla and Nicolai came out to join us at the end in a small aluminum boat fitted with an outboard. They towed us back to their island, where we spent a second night and offered our dory and a load of gear to our gracious hosts. It seemed fitting that our boat had been given to us by Russians and now we had a chance to give it back. Ootla and Nicolai kindly gave us a ride in their tinny through the delta to where we could flag down a rusted tug pulling a barge laden with gravel, coal, and two houses. It turned out that the tug was going only ten miles up the river, but the captain took pity on us and made a twenty-two-hour detour. The following day, we were dropped off on the sunken barge that acts as a pier for Karaul. The captain refused to accept a ruble from us.

We waited in Karaul for two days for the last supply ship of the season to come down from Dudinka. The ex-mayor, a retired fellow of about sixty-five, invited us to stay in his home.

The supply ship arrived and tied up at the wharf for the night. The captain allowed us to sleep in the hold before the two-day trip back upriver to Dudinka. First thing in the morning, Tim and Ben made a quick dash to the store. But during their absence, the ship slipped her lines and began chugging south. Remy and I were asleep, oblivious to the fact that the lads had missed the last ship of the season.

Ben and Tim stood on the pier in disbelief, watching the rusty ship that carried Remy and me disappear around the corner, and howling at the prospect of waiting seven months for the next boat. Frantically they ran through the village asking if any fisherman with a fast boat would try to intercept the supply ship. A couple of grizzled salts sauntered down to the shore and told Ben and Tim to hop in their boat. The smoky forty-horse roared to life, and the chase began.

Half an hour later they caught up, but the captain wouldn't stop. The aluminum dinghy pulled alongside, matching the ship's speed. Ben and Tim had seconds to grab a tire hanging over the freezing water. With the boys still suspended in the air, the dinghy pulled away to avoid being swamped by the larger ship. Ben and Tim climbed up the rope and over the rail to safety.

Remy and I slept through the whole ordeal.

We arrived in Dudinka on September 30, one week after celebrating on the Arctic Ocean. We had a month before our presentations, and a long way to go with very limited money. All of us had flights departing from Beijing, but we needed Chinese visas to return to China. The nearest embassies were in Moscow and Ulaanbaatar. We opted for Ulaanbaatar since it was en route, while Moscow was three thousand miles in the wrong direction.

In Dudinka we split up. It was essential that Remy and I get back to Canada quickly to prepare for the presentations. We would fly out to Krasnoyarsk, while Tim and Ben would make the weeklong trip on the last riverboat. Tim wasn't part of the presentations, so time wasn't as important to him. Ben planned to take care of our gear in Irkutsk, so that Remy and I could splurge on plane fare and get a head start on the first eighteen hundred miles.

From Krasnoyarsk Remy and I took the two-day train to Irkutsk, where we had to wait several days for a Mongolian visa. Another two-day train took us to Ulaanbaatar, where we applied for Chinese visas.

Unfortunately, because of 9/11 and a conference in Beijing that U.S. President George W. Bush was attending, the Mongolian Chinese embassy had stopped issuing tourist visas. As

Remy didn't have his air ticket with him (his brother-in-law had sent it to a hotel in Beijing), the stern-faced official refused him a visa of any sort. Even with proof of my airline ticket, I had a fight getting a three-day transit visa from the Chinese.

Time was running out—our presentations were only three weeks away. We had to get home, edit the documentary, and promote the event. The halls alone would cost more than $8,000, which was $8,000 more than we had. The exhilaration of finishing the expedition was rapidly wearing off.

With no other choice, Remy maxed out his credit card and purchased a one-way ticket from Ulaanbaatar to Canada for $1,500. That was a blow to all of us, since we were splitting all the expenses.

I was frantic to get on my way to Beijing. With only $300 cash left, I tried buying a rail ticket, but all trains to China for the next two days were fully booked. I tried to purchase a $200 flight to Beijing, but again, all the tickets were sold out. I went to the airport to try flying standby, joining a crowd of desperate people waving money and passports in the air. No luck.

On Sunday afternoon, with my visa about to expire in twelve hours, I was so overcome by stress that I couldn't stop shaking. There wasn't a hope in hell I would get another Chinese visa. And if I didn't get into China, I couldn't afford to purchase a new ticket to Canada from Ulaabaatar. With ten hours to go, Inca, the co-owner of the guest house I had been staying at, kindly offered to help and, with his assistance, we bribed a conductor to let me on the train. Finally I was on my way to Beijing.

It was 3:00 A.M. when the train crossed the Chinese border, but the immigration official let me through anyway.

On October 20 I arrived exhausted in Vancouver and immediately went to work promoting our presentation. Ben arrived a week later, and the three of us went into overdrive as we coordinated promotion and ticket sales.

Although the timing was tight, we drew more than 1,500 people over the two nights. And the documentary turned out beautifully! In Victoria, as we looked across a sea of people giving us a standing ovation, we clapped each other on the backs. For me, that was when our journey truly ended.

It was time for a beer.

# ACKNOWLEDGMENTS

Aside from memories, the greatest treasures I brought home from both the Yenisey and the Amazon journeys are a stack of video cassettes that have forever immortalized some of the most dramatic and beautiful moments of these expeditions. It was the same reliable Sony video camera that I used on both these trips; a gift from my Scottish sister, Betty Angus. Without Betty's help, there would be no documentaries. Thank you, Betty.

The rest of my family has also been supportive in many ways. My mother took care of the various chores that need to be tended to when someone disappears overseas for many months without complaining (well, not a whole lot). Dan Audet, my old sailing buddy, contributed more to the expedition than anyone could ever ask of a friend. He built and maintained the website, was the PR man, and basically took on every expedition-related task that needed to be done while we were gone. My friend Catheryn Fife also deserves a big thanks for storing my belongings during and after my absence.

I would also like to thank the companies that had faith in us and helped us make our dream come true. Without the support of Gore-Tex or Iridium, I would probably never have experienced the beauty of the northern lights reflecting off the Yenisey River. Other companies and businesses that helped us on our way were: AIRE Rafts, Riot Kayaks, Whites Dry Gear, Aquabound Paddles, the *Globe and Mail*, the *Vancouver Sun*, Ocean River Sports, Prism Photos, and the University of Victoria.

While on the trans-Mongolian railway coming home, I met a vacationing Canadian flight attendant. Jennifer Jones is now my girlfriend, and has helped keep me sane through the whole book-writing process.

**COLIN ANGUS** began his adventuring career at nineteen with a five-year, mostly solo, offshore sailing odyssey. He has coproduced two documentaries including *Yenisey: River of Extremes* (runner-up for the "People's Choice" award at the Banff Mountain Film Festival) for *National Geographic*. When not in the field, Colin shares his adventures with the public through presentations and articles. He has written for *Cruising World*, the *Globe and Mail*, and *Explore*, among others. Based out of Vancouver, B.C., he is currently preparing for his next adventure. For more information on Colin's adventures, please visit www.colinangus.com.